AFRICAN AMERICAN
CRIMINOLOGICAL THOUGHT

AFRICAN AMERICAN CRIMINOLOGICAL THOUGHT

*Helen Taylor Greene
and Shaun L. Gabbidon*

*with a foreword by
Julius Debro*

State University of New York Press

Published by
State University of New York Press, Albany

© *2000 State University of New York*

All rights reserved

Printed in the United States of America

For information, address State University of New York Press
90 State Street, Suite 700
Albany, New York 12207

Production by Dana Foote
Marketing by Dana E. Yanulavich

Library of Congress Cataloging-in-Publication Data

Greene, Helen Taylor, 1949–
African American criminological thought / Helen Taylor Greene
and Shaun L. Gabbidon ; with a foreword by Julius Debro.
p. cm.
Includes bibliographical references and indexes.
ISBN 0-7914-4695-6 (alk. paper) — ISBN 0-7914-4696-4 (pbk. : alk. paper)
1. African-American criminologists—Biography. 2. Criminology—United
States—History. I. Gabbidon, Shaun L., 1967– II. Title.

HV6023 .G74 2000
364′.089′96073—dc21
00-032930

10 9 8 7 6 5 4 3 2 1

This book is dedicated to my sons, Tamaa, Hasan, and Amir, who have endured and sacrificed during the completion of this project, and to my extended family for their unwavering assistance, encouragement, and support.
—H. T. G.

To my parents, Daphne and Patrick Gabbidon, my bro-ski, Ian Gabbidon, my wife, Monica, and our two children, Jini and Jalen, who all, at some point along the way, provided the inspiration, support, and encouragement required to complete this project.
—S. L. G.

CONTENTS

LIST OF TABLES AND FIGURES

Tables

Figures

FOREWORD

In our teaching of criminology and criminal justice, we have neglected the works of African American writers who have contributed to our understanding of crime and delinquency in our communities. We have not utilized the scholarly works of writers such as W. E. B. Du Bois, Monroe Work, and E. Franklin Frazier in our discussions of crime in the African American community. Our classes are generally taught without multicultural writers, and we only apologetically teach African American crime as a response to their overrepresentation in the criminal justice system.

Helen Taylor Greene and Shaun Gabbidon have given us a book that we can now use in our classes to expand our knowledge of crime and criminology in African American communities. This is a book about African Americans who have made substantial contributions to our knowledge of African American crime, and the joy is that it is written by African Americans for a wider audience. Helen Taylor Greene (1979) compiled *A Comprehensive Bibliography of Criminology and Criminal Justice Literature by Black Authors from 1895 to 1978* (1979) and has continued to study African American contributions for over twenty years. Over the past few years, Shaun Gabbidon has also published works highlighting the contributions of African Americans. Most notably, Shaun's work on W. E. B. Du Bois's contributions to American criminology has resulted in the creation of the Western Society of Criminology's W. E. B. Du Bois Award, which is given annually to outstanding scholars in the area of race/ethnicity and crime. Together, Helen and Shaun have endeavored to pass along to students their knowledge gained through many years of research on African American authors.

The importance of this book is that it brings together in one text authors who devoted much of their lives to writing about black crime during the nineteenth and twentieth centuries. Not only will this book enlighten the majority community, but it will also serve as a valuable resource for all scholars who do not know of the many contributions of the profiled writers. Most young scholars have never read the works of Ida B. Wells-Barnett, Monroe Work, E. Franklin Frazier, Daniel Georges-Abeyie, Vernetta Young, Coramae Richey Mann, Lee Brown, or Darnell Hawkins, all of whom, as duly noted by the authors, have been notable contributors to the field.

This book should be required reading for every student of criminology-criminal justice especially if "Race Matters" in our studies. The book gives the reader a view of early criminal behavior when segregation was the norm in the United States as well as a view of contemporary America after segregation. The challenge for us all is to understand that there is very little difference in the causes of criminal behavior then and now.

I applaud both Helen and Shaun for their contribution to criminology-criminal justice. I highly recommend this book to students, teachers, legislators, community activists, and all others who would like to know what past and present African American scholars have said, and continue to say, regarding African Americans and crime.

—Julius Debro

ACKNOWLEDGMENTS

As with most endeavors, nothing is accomplished without the aid of someone. This is also the case with this work. First we would like to thank Christine Worden, Zina Lawrence, and Nancy Ellegate, our editors at the State University of New York Press for their assistance in the completion of this work. We also appreciate the comments from reviewers of both the book prospectus and the manuscript. Many students assisted us in our research, including Shawna Scott at Coppin State College in Baltimore, Maryland, Kathleen O'Shea at Penn State at Harrisburg, and Vladimir Handy and Lekeisha Washington at Old Dominion University in Norfolk, Virginia.

Several institutions made available resources to assist us in the completion of our work. During the summer of 1997 Dr. Gabbidon served as a Fellow at Harvard University's Du Bois Institute where he conducted research that was pivotal in completing this project. Coppin State College partially funded his visit to the institute. Dr. Taylor Greene was awarded a Faculty Grant in 1997 at Old Dominion University to assist with her research. We are especially grateful for other resources made available to us at Old Dominion University and Pennsylvania State University, Capital College.

We thank the contemporary scholars for agreeing to be a part of this endeavor, without their cooperation the project would not have been possible. We also thank several other colleagues who in numerous ways were instrumental in our completion of this project: Dr. Julius Debro, Dr. Ronald Jackson, Dr. Charles Jones, Dr. Sue Kent, Dr. Everette Penn, and Dr. Jeffery Senese. We both thank the past and present African Americans who have contributed to our understanding of crime.

Finally, these acknowledgments would be incomplete without Dr. Taylor Greene thanking Hasan and Amir for accompanying her on several trips to Washington, D.C., to conduct library research and for allowing her to be an absentee mother on numerous occasions over the course of several years.

INTRODUCTION

This volume originated out of a meeting between the authors at the Academy of Criminal Justice Sciences annual meeting held in Chicago, Illinois, in 1994. During their conversation, both authors expressed an interest in collaborating to write a book that would highlight the contributions of African Americans to criminology and criminal justice (C/CJ). As graduate students, both authors were intrigued by the absence of African American scholarship from their courses. Each, at different times, and for different reasons, embarked upon research that would lead them to discover a number of publications that were ignored by mainstream criminologists. Yet there was no book on African American contributions to criminology. After several correspondences, we developed a prospectus, received a contract, and a year later began our work.

We primarily had two purposes in mind when we decided to embark on this project. First, to provide a volume that presented an overview of the writings of African American scholars who, we believed, had or continue to make noteworthy contributions to the study of crime and justice. Second, we wanted to expose students and scholars to another body of literature that has, for the most part, been excluded from the discourse within the discipline (see, for examples, Caldwell & Greene, 1980; Ross, 1998; Taylor Greene, 1979; Taylor Greene, 1994a; Taylor Greene, 1994b; Taylor Greene, 1997; Young & Taylor Greene, 1995).

Essentially, we view this volume as a resource for both students and faculty. We hope those who are exposed to writings presented here are stimulated by some of the central issues and considerations set forth in the chapters. We also hope others will be inspired, as we were, to examine the original works of these scholars. At the very least, we hope the myth that African Americans were minimal contributors to the development of American criminology is dispelled.

It was not our aim to suggest whether or not the writings of the profiled scholars were either less than, equal to, or superior to those of mainstream authors. While some may be preoccupied with this question, we felt it unimportant. Clearly, we are enthusiastic about the scholars and their works profiled here. Some are "pioneers," while others have been less influential. We agree with Martin, Mutchnick, and Austin who noted:

> It has become evident that many criminological thinkers who were quite instrumental in the growth of the discipline have not perhaps produced work of sufficient merit to earn the label Pioneer. Designing a volume on often overlooked, but influential or minor writers . . . may . . . be appro-

priate for further understanding of the discipline of criminology. (1990, p. 409)

It is also important to remember the interdisciplinary nature of the study of crime and to acknowledge that several pioneers and influential scholars were not criminologists.

Initially, we proposed scholars that would be included based solely upon their contributions to the study of criminology. For the historical scholars there are only a few that have focused specifically on crime and/or the administration of criminal justice in their research. The works of W. E. B. Du Bois, Monroe N. Work, and E. Franklin Frazier are unquestionably the most important. We decided to include Ida B. Wells-Barnett's contributions to the study and solution of the problem of lynching for two reasons. First, her study of lynching predates that of the National Association for the Advancement of Colored People (NAACP) and others, including Monroe N. Work. Second, most criminologists are unaware of her pioneering studies of the crime of lynching.

Our selection of the contemporary scholars is more complex. Initially we proposed to include those African American scholars who had made significant contributions to the criminological body of knowledge. Based upon our personal knowledge and a review of the literature, we identified a number of individuals to be included. The reviewers of our prospectus suggested that we include several other persons as well. After considering their recommendations, and our initial list, we decided to include Coramae Richey Mann, William Julius Wilson, Lee P. Brown, Darnell F. Hawkins, Daniel Georges-Abeyie, and Vernetta D. Young. Our final decision to include an individual was not based on the number of his or her publications, but rather on both the quality and impact of their research on the discipline when we commenced our writing. We also decided to cover only their research appearing prior to 1997.

While our volume is titled *African American Criminological Thought,* we use the term *criminological* in a broad historical sense. Thus, both theoretical contributions and those to the study of criminal justice are presented. Finally, throughout the text we use the terms *Negro(es), Black(s),* and *African American(s)* interchangeably.

References

Caldwell, L. & Taylor Greene, H. (1980). Implementing a black perspective in criminal justice. In A. Cohn & B. Ward (Eds.), *Improving management in criminal justice* (pp. 143–56). Beverly Hills: Sage Publications.

Martin, R., Mutchnick, R. & Austin, T. (1990). *Criminological thought: Pioneers past and present.* New York: Macmillan.

Ross, L. (1998). *African-American criminologists, 1970–1996.* Westport, CT: Greenwood Press.

Taylor Greene, H. (1979). *A comprehensive bibliography of criminology and criminal justice literature by black authors from 1895–1978.* Hyattsville, MD: Ummah Publications. Inc.

———. (1994a). Black female delinquency. In A. Sulton (Ed.), *African-American perspectives on: Crime causation, criminal justice administration and crime prevention* (pp. 109–121). Englewood, CO: Sulton Books.

———. (1994b). Black perspectives on police brutality. In A. Sulton (Ed.), *African-American perspectives on: Crime causation, criminal justice administration and crime prevention* (pp. 139–48). Englewood, CO: Sulton Books.

———. (1997). Teaching delinquency: Using research by black scholars in undergraduate courses. *Teaching Sociology, 25,* 57–64.

Young, V. & Taylor Greene, H. (1995). Pedagogical reconstruction: Incorporating African-American perspectives into the curriculum. *Journal of Criminal Justice Education, 6,* 85–104.

PART I
HISTORICAL SCHOLARS

Overview

One hundred years ago, African Americans were struggling with adverse social, economic, and political conditions.

Following Reconstruction, they experienced severe oppression that included Jim Crow laws, lynchings, and disenfranchisement. More often than not, they were viewed as both inferior and criminal. When the University of Chicago established the first department of sociology in the country in 1892, studying and ameliorating social problems were major concerns. By the late 1890s, the department, commonly known as the Chicago School, emerged as an important contributor to the so-called golden age in the sociology of blacks in America (Bracey, Meier & Rudwick, 1971). From its beginning, the study of African Americans was plagued by racism and belief in the superiority of the white race. Although the discipline of criminology and criminal justice as we know it today did not exist in the late 1890s, the social problem of crime was important in sociological research.

While the Chicago School was a center for social research, historically black colleges and universities (HBCUs) were also involved in the study of Negroes. This was due, at least in part, to segregation in higher education. Pioneer African American scholars who were educated at predominantly white institutions were not hired to teach at these schools. Thus, upon leaving their graduate programs, most taught and conducted research at HBCUs. They paved the way for future generations of researchers and laid the foundation for the black studies movement that would emerge many years later.

Since the late 1800s, HBCUs, guided by these African American intellectuals, sponsored conferences, published their proceedings, established journals, and provided a training ground for students. While most African American sociological research was done at Atlanta University, Fisk University, and Howard University (Smith, 1976), Hampton University also sponsored conferences to study Negro problems, and Tuskegee Institute was a clearinghouse for information on Negroes during the early 1900s. Other HBCUs would also play an important part in preparing a cadre of African American scholars. Unfortunately, yet understandably, these early scholars were often frustrated with the precarious position they held in the African American community and amongst whites who never viewed them as either scholars or peers.

Part 1 presents the contributions of Ida B. Wells-Barnett, W. E. B. Du Bois, E. Franklin Frazier, and Monroe N. Work. Ida B. Wells-Barnett was a well-known antilynching crusader who challenged both citizens and the American government to recognize the implications of tolerance for lynchings on both law and order. W. E. B.

Du Bois, another well-known scholar and activist, was one of the first African Americans to focus on the causes, consequences, and potential solutions to crime among Negroes. Monroe N. Work, the first African American to receive a master's degree from the Department of Sociology at the University of Chicago in 1903, was a pioneer in the study of Negro crime after the Civil War. E. Franklin Frazier received his Ph.D. in sociology from the University of Chicago in 1931. His research on race relations and the family provides an important contextual framework for understanding crime.

All four scholars presented in Part 1 have several commonalities. First, their contributions to criminological thought challenged mainstream theories and research. Since the late 1800s, sociological theorists, with few exceptions, viewed Negroes as inferior and focused on their pathologies. Wells-Barnett, Du Bois, Frazier, and Work provided a sociohistorical context for understanding crime and Negroes that included the effect of segregation, discrimination, and second-class citizenship.

Second, each scholar had both national and international reputations. Wells-Barnett traveled to Britain during the early 1890s to speak against lynching. Du Bois studied at the University of Berlin, Germany, from 1892 through 1894. E. Franklin Frazier was a research fellow of the American Scandinavian Foundation in the 1920s, lectured in England in 1953, worked for the United Nations in France from 1951 through 1953, and conducted research in Brazil. Although Work did not travel abroad as extensively as the others, he was well known throughout Europe and Africa for his bibliographies on the Negro.

Third, in addition to their contributions to understanding crime, especially among Negroes, each was active in other aspects of Negro life. Barnett was a leader in the Negro Women's Club movement, Du Bois was a founding member of the National Association for the Advancement of Colored People, Work was involved in the interracial movement and Negro health movement, and Frazier was active in sociological associations. Unlike the others, Frazier made a conscious decision not to involve himself in various civil rights and other causes so that he could focus entirely on research.

Fourth, with the exception of Wells-Barnett, each taught at HBCUs throughout their careers. Between 1897 and 1910, Du Bois taught at Atlanta University where he was also instrumental in organizing conferences and preparing publications (Young & Taylor Greene, 1995). Monroe Work was a faculty member at Georgia State Industrial School (Savannah State University) before taking a research position at Tuskegee Institute in 1908. Frazier taught at several HBCUs including Atlanta University, Fisk University, and Howard University, where he spent most of his career.

While each scholar in Part 1 made important contributions to understanding crime, there are many others who have been omitted. These early scholars and the focus of their research are discussed elsewhere (Blackwell & Janowitz, 1974; Smith, 1976; Taylor Greene, 1979; Taylor Greene, 1994; Taylor Greene, 1997; Young & Sulton, 1991; Young & Taylor Greene, 1995). Table 1 presents a list of these scholars and a brief summary of their research.

Table 1 African American Scholarship on Crime and Justice, 1914–1959

SCHOLAR	DATE	RESEARCH TOPIC
Miller, K.	1914	Negro Crime
Grimke, A.	1915	White Crime
Johnson, C. S.	1922	Chicago Race Riot
Reid, I. de A.	1925	Negro Prisoners
Reid, I. de A.	1931	Negro's Relation to Work and Law
Reid, I. de A.	1932	Negro Prisoners
Washington, F. B.	1932–1933	Care of the Negro Delinquent
Moses, E. R.	1933	Delinquency in the Negro Community
Washington, F. B.	1933	Negro Delinquent in Nashville, TN
Moses, E. R.	1936	Community Factors and Juvenile Delinquency
Diggs, M.	1940	Negro Juvenile Delinquency
Watts, F. P.	1941	Comparative Study of Delinquent and Nondelinquent Boys
Cox, O.	1945	Lynching
Blue, J. T.	1948	Juvenile Delinquency, Race, and Economic Status
Grann, L. R.	1950	Delinquency
Mitchell, L.	1957	Aspiration Levels of Delinquent, Dependent, and Public Schools Boys
Reid, I. de A.	1957	Race and Crime
Blue, J. T.	1959	Concepts and Methodology
Clark, K. B.	1959	Color, Class, Personality, and Juvenile Delinquency
Douglass, J. H.	1959	Juvenile Delinquency
Hills, M.	1959	Metropolis and Delinquency
Hypps, I.	1959	Schools and Delinquency Prevention
Lewis, H.	1959	Juvenile Delinquency

References

Blackwell, J. E. & Janowitz, M. (1974). *Black Sociologists: Historical and Contemporary perspectives.* Chicago: Univ. of Chicago Press.

Blue, J. T. (1959). Concepts and methodology in the field of juvenile delinquency. *Journal of Human Relations, 17,* 473–82.

———. (1948). The relationship of juvenile delinquency, race and economic status. *Journal of Negro Education, 17,* 469–77.

Bracey, J. H., Meier, A. & Rudwick, E. (Eds.). (1971). *The black sociologists: The first half century.* Belmont, CA: Wadsworth.

Clark, K. B. (1915). Color, class, personality & juvenile delinquency. *Journal of Negro Education, 28,* 240–59.

Cox, O. (1940). Lynching and the status quo. *Journal of Negro Education, 14,* (4), 576–88.

Diggs, M. H. (1940). Problems and needs of Negro youth as revealed by delinquency and crime statistics. *Journal of Negro Education, 9,* 311–20.

Douglass, J. H. (1959). The extent and characteristics of juvenile delinquency among Negroes in the United States. *Journal of Negro Education, 28,* 214–29.

Grimke, A. (1915). *The ultimate criminal.* Washington, DC: The American Negro Academy.

Hill, M. (1959). The metropolis and juvenile delinquency among Negroes. *Journal of Negro Education, 28,* 277–85.

Hypps, I. (1959). The role of school in juvenile delinquency prevention. *Journal of Negro Education, 28,* 318–28.

Johnson, C. S. (1922) *The Negro in Chicago: A Study of Race Relations and a Race Riot in 1919.* Chicago: University of Chicago Press.

Lewis, H. (1959). Juvenile delinquency among Negroes: A critical summary. *Journal of Negro Education, 28,* 286–99.

Lloyd, R. G. (1950). Juvenile delinquency in a period of tension. *Negro Educational Review, 1,* 10–16.

Miller, K. (1914/1971). Crime among Negroes. In *Out of the house of bondage.* New York: Shocken Publishing Company.

Mitchell, L. E. (1957). Aspiration levels of Negro delinquent dependent and public school boys. *Journal of Negro Education, 26,* 80–85.

Moses, E. R. (1936). Community factors in Negro delinquency. *Journal of Negro Education, 5,* 220–27.

Reid, I. D. (1925). A study of 200 Negroes in the Western Penitentiary of Pennsylvania. *Opportunity, 3,* 168–69.

———. (1931). Notes on the Negroes relation to work and law observation. Report on the Causes of Crime. National Commission Law Observance and Enforcement. Volume 13. Washington, DC: US Government Printing Office.

———. (1932). The Negro goes to Sing Sing. *Opportunity, 19,* 215–17.

———. (1957). Race and Crime. *Friends Journal, 3,* 772–74.

Smith, S. H. (1976). Sociological research and Fisk University: A case study. In J. E. Blackwell & M. Janowitz (Eds.), *Black sociologists: Historical and contemporary perspectives.* Chicago: University of Chicago Press.

Taylor Greene, H. (1979). *A comprehensive bibliography of criminology and criminal justice literature by black authors from 1895 to 1978.* College Park, MD: Ummah.

———. (1994). Black female delinquency. In A. T. Sulton (Ed.), *African American perspectives on: Crime causation, criminal justice administration and crime prevention.* Englewood, CO: Sulton Books.

———. (1997). Teaching delinquency: Using research by black scholars in undergraduate courses. *Teaching Sociology, 25,* 57–64.

Washington, F. B. (1932–1933). Care of the Negro delinquent. In *National Probation Association Yearbook.*

Watts, F. P. (1941). A comparative clinical study of delinquent and nondelinquent boys. *Journal of Negro Education, 10,* 190–207.

Young, V. & Taylor Greene, H. (1995). Pedagogical reconstruction: Incorporating African-American perspectives into the curriculum. *Journal of Criminal Justice Education, 6,* 85–104.

Young, V. & A. T. Sulton. 1991. Excluded: The current status of African American scholars in the field of criminology & criminal justice. *Journal of Research in Crime and Delinquency, 28,* 101–16.

Ida B. Wells-Barnett
Courtesy of The University of Chicago Library

ONE

IDA B. WELLS-BARNETT
(1862–1931)

There is scarcely any reason why this woman, young in years and old in experience,
shall not be found in the forefront of the great intellectual fight in which the race is
now engaged for absolute right and justice under the Constitution.
—T. Thomas Fortune, 1893 (Thompson, 1990, p. 1)

INTRODUCTION

Ida B. Wells-Barnett was an antilynching and civil rights activist at the end of the nineteenth and beginning of the twentieth centuries. In spite of her national and international reputation and membership in the Negro elite of Chicago, her contributions have been sorely neglected until very recently. This was due, at least in part, to the masculinity of the civil rights movement. Furthermore, unlike many African Americans at the turn of the century who were silent on the issues of lynching and mob violence, Wells-Barnett was an outspoken race woman (Thompson, 1990). She had a reputation as an "Afro-American Agitator," a term coined by Henry Gady of the *Atlanta Constitution* to describe the more aggressive and militant African Americans of that era (ibid., p. 20).

For various reasons, Ms. Barnett had no graduate school training. Clearly, she had the ability to complete graduate studies, but her life circumstances, especially the early death of her parents, and perhaps her gender, precluded this accomplishment. Nevertheless, she had an illustrious career as a teacher, journalist, antilynching crusader, orator, and activist involved in civil rights and political and social issues.

Wells-Barnett's contributions to criminological thought are found in her research on lynching in the United States. She was one of the first individuals to call attention to the implications of lynching for both government and law and order in the late 1800s. She viewed lynching as a national crime and called attention to its deleterious impact on the administration of justice before and after the turn of the nineteenth century. Until very recently there has been a lack of information on Wells-Barnett's writings, activities, and accomplishments (Thompson, 1990). Consequently, her contributions to understanding crime and justice have not been included in the study of criminology. With few exceptions, she is still unknown to most criminologists.

Biographical Information

Wells-Barnett, the first of eight children, was born in Holly Springs, Mississippi, on 16 July, 1862 to Jim Wells and Lizzie Warrenton. Ida's father was the only son of his master, and his mother, Peggy, a slave. Thompson (1990) described Jim Wells as belonging to the favored class of blacks and thus was spared of some of the cruelties of slavery, including whipping and being sold. His father provided training as a carpenter for his son and apprenticed him to a contractor in Holly Springs. Wells-Barnett's mother was born a slave in Virginia. She was employed as a cook for the Holly Springs family where Jim Wells was apprenticed. The couple was married once as slaves and again after emancipation.

After emancipation the Wells family remained in Holly Springs. Thompson (1990) described Jim Wells as a good provider and Lizzie Wells as a religious woman who guided the children's housework, schoolwork, and religious service. In 1878 the Wells and one son were victims of a yellow fever epidemic that swept through the town. Ida was visiting with her grandmother at the time but returned immediately to care for her surviving brothers and sisters. At sixteen, Ida Wells became a surrogate parent to her five siblings, insisting that they be neither separated nor cared for by others.

As a result of her education (described below) at Shaw University (Rust College), Wells was hired as a teacher in Holly Springs and later moved to Memphis, Tennessee, to stay with an aunt. She left three of her siblings and took two sisters with her. For most of the 1880s she taught in Memphis. After losing her teaching appointment, she turned her attention to the newspaper of which she owned one-third, the *Free Speech and Headlight*. In 1892, her outspoken editorials (described below) resulted in her being exiled from Memphis.

After leaving Memphis, Wells-Barnett lived in New York City, working for the *New York Age,* edited by her colleagues T. Thomas Fortune and Jerome B. Peterson. She also lectured extensively, both nationally and abroad. She settled in Chicago in 1895, after marrying Ferdinand Barnett, a prominent Chicago lawyer and newspaper publisher. In 1896 Ferdinand Barnett was appointed assistant state's attorney (Thompson, 1990). The Barnetts were considered black leaders and belonged to the black social elite of Chicago. They were both journalists, politicians, and social activists.

Shortly after their marriage, Wells-Barnett assumed the responsibilities of editor of her husband's newspaper, the *Conservator.* Two years later, in 1897, Wells-Barnett gave up her duties and other activities to stay home with her children.

Academic Background and Experience

When Ida B. Wells was young, her father, Jim Wells, served on the board of Shaw University, a Freedman's school that included elementary, secondary, and college levels of learning. All the Wells children attended the school. Sometimes their mother would also attend classes to learn to read. At the time of the yellow fever outbreak, Ida had begun the college course, although she was unable to complete it. She also studied at Fisk University in Nashville, Tennessee, during several summers. Wells-Barnett passed the exam for country teachers in Holly Springs and taught there before relocating to Memphis to teach. In Memphis, she worked as both teacher and journalist. She relocated to Visalia, California, for a brief period to take a teaching position but resigned after a short stay (Thompson, 1990).

During the 1880s, Wells-Barnett contributed articles to several religious weeklies and other black and white newspapers using the name *Iola* (ibid., p. 15). She also belonged to Memphis' black literary circle and edited its weekly publication, the *Evening Star.* In 1889, she became a partner and joined the editorial staff of the *Free Speech,* an Afro-American newspaper. Eventually, her editorials criticizing the Memphis school system caused her to lose her reappointment as a teacher. This allowed her to devote more time to both editing and building up the circulation of the paper of which she was now co-owner (ibid., p. 19). Wells-Barnett's antilynching crusade began in the early 1890s. According to Thompson (1990), the lynching of three friends who owned a grocery store just outside of Memphis was a defining moment in Wells-Barnett's antilynching activities. Like most other Americans, she believed that lynching victims committed crimes, especially rape. However, the three blacks lynched in Memphis had not committed such crimes. Rather, they were victims of a scheme by a white grocer in the vicinity who was losing business to them. The circumstances of the lynching of her friends prompted her to investigate those that were supposedly related to rapes. After concluding that many of the rape stories were untrue, she penned her famous editorial that eventually led to the demise of *Free Speech.*

Her editorial on lynching that appeared on 21 May 1892 angered the leading business men of Memphis. Her statement, "Nobody in this section of the country believes the old thread bare lie that Negro men rape white women" (ibid., p. 29) prompted an editorial response in the white newspaper the *Daily Commercial.* That editorial noted "the fact that a black scoundrel is allowed to live and utter such loathsome and repulsive calumnies is a volume of evidence as to the wonderful patience of Southern whites" (Wells-Barnett, 1892/1969, p. 4). In reality, the leading citizens of Memphis were outraged. Within days, Mr. Fleming, the business manager and half-owner of *Free Speech* was forced to leave town, and Wells-Barnett was advised not to return from her participation in a church conference in Philadelphia and vacation in New York City. The *Free Speech* office was subsequently destroyed, taken by creditors and sold.

While exiled, Ms. Wells continued her antilynching writing and speaking. After a speech at a testimonial fund raiser sponsored by "two black club women" in New York City, she was able to finance her first publication on lynching, *Southern Horrors* (Thompson, 1990, p. 32). She lectured in the United States and in England at the request of both blacks and whites. Her lectures would also appear as newspaper articles. She was among the first to call for self-help against lynching among Afro-Americans. She supported economic boycotts, emigration, and self-armament to stamp out "lynch law, that last relic of barbarism and slavery" (ibid., p. 24).

CONTRIBUTIONS TO CRIMINOLOGICAL THOUGHT

> *Our country's national crime is lynching. It is not the creature of an hour, the sudden outburst of uncontrolled fury, or the unspeakable brutality of an insane mob. It represents the cool, calculating deliberation of intelligent people who openly avow that there is an "unwritten law" that justifies them in putting human beings to death without complaint under oath, without trial by jury, without opportunity to make defense, and without right of appeal.*
> —Ida B. Wells (1900, p. 15).

Wells-Barnett's research on lynching and mob violence was an outgrowth of both her personal experience in Memphis and her belief that no one else seemed to be defending Afro American victims against lynching during the 1890s. For over twenty years she was actively involved in efforts to understand the causes, extent, prevention, and control of lynching. Her research and writings presented the historical development of lynching, prevailing rationales, secondary data, case studies, and remedies. Yet her contributions were glaringly omitted. Here, Wells-Barnett's research on lynching and its acceptance by those responsible for upholding the law and the administration of justice are presented.

Although trained neither as a sociologist or a historian, Wells-Barnett utilized research methods common at the time, including content analyses of reports of lynching in newspapers, analyses of secondary data from the *Chicago Tribune,* and field research, usually after a lynching had occurred. She also published newspaper articles and three anti-lynching pamphlets, *Southern Horrors, A Red Record,* and *Mob Rule in New Orleans.* Her contributions to understanding lynching and mob violence are summarized below.

History and Rationale for Lynching

Historical information and the causes of lynching are important components of most of Wells-Barnett's antilynching writings. Like other early scholars, she acknowledges the roles of slavery, emancipation, and post-Reconstruction in the ongoing plight of blacks in America. She noted the effect of post-Reconstruction social, economic, and political conditions on the deteriorating status of the Negro. More specifically, she accused Southerners of depriving blacks (males) of the ballot, civil rights, redress in the courts, the fruits of their labor and of lynching them in efforts to maintain their power. One of her major contributions to understanding the causes of lynching is found in her rebuttal to the prevailing rationales, which she described as excuses for barbarism (Wells-Barnett, 1892/1969).

Wells-Barnett (1893) traced the origin of lynch law to Pittsylvania County, Virginia. In 1780 a group of citizens joined together to suppress horse thieves and counterfeiters who defied ordinary laws. A Colonel William Lynch drafted a constitution for the citizens' group, and since then the term *lynch law* has been used to refer to the infliction of punishment by private and unauthorized citizens. Wells-Barnett (1909) also noted that frontier lynch law was very popular in the far West until judicial apparatuses were established. However, in the South, even with the existence of a judicial process, lynch law continued. For fifteen years after emancipation, Negroes were lynched for trying to vote and attempting to rule whites.

Wells-Barnett (1892/1969) identified at least four causes or rationales for lynching during the late 1800s. Drawing on the writing of Frederick Douglass, Wells-Barnett noted that lynchings were justified by whites because they were used to prevent race riots, to prevent Negroes from voting, and to punish those who assaulted or attempted to assault white women. Another rationale she identified was an ongoing effort to eliminate blacks who were becoming too prosperous (Thompson, 1990).

Immediately after the civil war, until the early 1870s, lynchings were excused by propaganda that blacks were planning and participating in insurrections and riots. However, there was rarely any evidence to support this rationale. Wells-Barnett noted, "No insurrections ever materialized, no Negro rioter was ever apprehended and proven guilty, and no dynamite ever recorded the black man's protest against oppression and wrong" (Wells-Barnett, 1892/1969, p. 9). During Reconstruction, lynching to prevent voting began to occur. According to Wells-Barnett, "The southern white man would not consider that the Negro had any right which a white man was bound to respect, and the idea of a republican form of government in the southern states grew into general contempt" (ibid., p. 9). By 1882, the major reason for lynching was purported to be either attempting to or assaulting white women (Thompson, 1990, p. 195). Wells-Barnett refuted these causes/rationales/excuses for lynching on several grounds. First, she noted that in spite of the rationals given for lynching, in fact, blacks were lynched for almost any offense. Second, she argued that the term *rape* was used to describe any and all alliances between black men and white women, whether or not they met the legal definition of the crime of rape. Through her research, she discovered that many white women and black men were involved in voluntary relationships for which the male was lynched to uphold the honor of the woman (Wells-Barnett, 1892/1969).

Perhaps Wells-Barnett's most stinging argument against the rationale for rape/assault lynching is found in her comments on relationships between white females and black males and white males and black females during both slavery and the Civil War period. She specifically noted that during slavery and the Civil War, black males were not accused of rape but rather were the protectors of white women and children while white males fought the rebellion. Furthermore, she believed it hypocritical for white males to speak of chivalry when they themselves had fathered numerous biracial children in the South, usually by assault/rape of black female slaves.

Wells-Barnett's last rebuttal against the so-called causes of rape-related lynching was related to the role Northern white women played in educating former slaves after emancipation. She stated that these women were ostracized, insulted, and persecuted by the chivalrous white Southern men. More important, they spent most of their time with Negroes, in very remote areas, with little protection, and were not assaulted. Wells-Barnett believed that it was important for those outside the South to recognize the real facts about the morality and trustworthiness of the Negro.

Lynching Statistics

In order to give validity to her lynching facts, Wells-Barnett relied on the statistical compilations reported annually in the *Chicago Tribune*. In her pamphlets, she focused specifically on lynching of blacks and included the victims' names, the date and the location of incidents, and the offenses charged. Although she did not provide trend analyses, she did notice a steady increase in reported lynching and provided a breakdown by states for the years 1892, 1893, and 1894. In *Mob Rule in New Orleans* she focused more specifically on Negroes murdered by mobs between 1882 and 1899 (Wells-Barnett, 1900/1969).

Between 1880 and 1891, approximately one hundred Negroes were lynched annually. In 1892, the year that Wells-Barnett's friends were lynched in Memphis, lynching of black men reached an all time high of 160. The majority were lynched for murder (58) and rape (46). Others were lynched for attempted rape (11), incendiarism (6), race prejudice (6), and several other offenses (Wells-Barnett, [1895] 1969, p. 20). In 1893, 159 blacks were lynched for murder (44), alleged murder (6), alleged complicity in murder (4), rape (39), attempted rape (8), alleged rape (4), and other offenses (ibid., p. 19). In both years, the majority of victims were lynched in the Southern states.

Lynching Case Studies

Accounts of lynching, herein referred to as case studies, appeared in most of Wells-Barnett's antilynching writings. While some accounts were more detailed than others, each provided a glimpse of the facts surrounding lynching incidents. Her case studies were based upon content analyses of previously published articles as well as field visits to communities after a lynching. Her interest in understanding the situational characteristics of lynching increased after her friends were lynched in Memphis, Tennessee. As previously stated, even she had accepted the ideology of lynching until this incident.

After the deaths of her friends in Memphis in 1892, for three months (March–May) Wells-Barnett carefully researched the details of lynching incidents where the victims were accused of rape (Thompson, 1990). Based upon her findings, she challenged what is often referred to as the (lynching) "rape myth." This prompted her editorial that led to the destruction of *Free Speech* and her subsequent exile. Her accounts of the incidents she identified and that of the Memphis lynchings appeared in *Southern Horrors*. Additional accounts of rape lynchings and lynching of imbeciles and innocent men appeared in *A Red Record.*

The most detailed case study published by Wells-Barnett (1900/1969) described the mob lynchings of two black males in New Orleans, Louisiana, in July 1900. Based upon information reported in the *New Orleans Times Democrat* and the *New Orleans Picayune,* Wells-Barnett (ibid.) described the mob violence that lasted from Monday, 24 July to Friday, 28 July 1900. The mob brutality was provoked by an attempt by two New Orleans police officers, Officer Mora and Officer Cantrelle, to arrest two black men, which resulted in a shoot out, injuring one of the officers and one of the blacks. According to Wells-Barnett, Robert Charles and Leonard Pierce were resisting an unwarranted arrest and were victims of police harassment and brutality. Contrary to the depiction of the Negroes as desperadoes in the local papers, Wells-Barnett maintained that Charles, who killed Officer Mora, drew his weapon in self-defense. Although he was wounded, Charles escaped, and Pierce was taken into custody. Immediately, the mayor of New Orleans sanctioned Charles to be killed on sight and offered a $250 reward for his capture, dead or alive (ibid.). By Wednesday, 25 July, Charles was still at large, in spite of several attempts to capture him and his success in killing more police. Civil unrest that included rioting, assaults, and killings of blacks ensued. On Friday, the police were informed of Charles's location in a house, which they set on fire. After another shootout with the police, while the house was burning, Charles finally emerged and was riddled with bullets (ibid.).

Another case study of a double lynching in Cairo, Illinois, in November 1909, was reported by Wells-Barnett (1910). While the facts of the lynching incident are similar to the heinous and barbaric characteristics of other incidents, this one resulted in the governor's removal of the sheriff of Alexander County for failure to protect prisoners. This was believed to have had a profound impact on reducing lynching in the state (Thompson, 1990).

The Administration of Justice

> *Lynch Law has become so common in the United States that the finding of the dead body of a Negro, suspended, between heaven and earth to the limb of a tree, is of so slight importance that neither the civil authorities nor press agencies consider the matter worth investigating.*
> —Wells-Barnett (1900/1969, p. 44)

The lynching era in American history points to a breakdown in the administration of justice. First, lynching involved criminal behavior, including assaults, kidnapping, murder, riots, vigilantism, and other types of violence. Second, these acts often involved police officers and sheriffs and were tacitly condoned by those expected to uphold the law. Third, the majority of lynching victims were "along the color line" (Wells-Barnett, 1909, p. 261). Antilynching crusaders spoke out against the absence of law and order.

Cutler (1905, pp. 157–58) defined lynching as "the practice whereby mobs capture individuals suspected of crime or take them from the officers of the law or break open jails and hang convicted criminals with impunity." Wells-Barnett and other antilynching crusaders acknowledged that many of the black lynching victims had committed crimes. However, they called for the use of the judicial process in determining guilt and punishment and denounced vigilante justice.

Wells-Barnett (1909) viewed federal protection as the remedy for lynching since Americans were citizens of the country as well as its states. If state governments could not control the lawlessness of its citizens, she believed the federal government should.

Wells-Barnett was instrumental in establishing the utility of enfranchisement in preventing and controlling lynching. After the Cairo lynching, she petitioned Governor Charles Deneen, with the support of Cairo residents, to deny reappointment of the sheriff. In a legal brief prepared by her husband, Wells-Barnett argued that the sheriff acted in violation of the Anti-Mob Violence Statute of 1905 by his failure to protect his prisoners (Thompson, 1990).

CONCLUSION

As previously stated, Ida B. Wells-Barnett, an antilynching crusader, journalist, lecturer, militant, race woman, civil rights, political, and social activist, was well known both nationally and internationally. Her greatest contribution to criminology and to society is the detailed information about lynching she made available. Her work also laid the foundation for a better understanding of the reality of the problem of lynching as opposed to the hysteria it created. Wells-Barnett systematically dispelled many of the myths about both lynching and blacks and crime. She did not excuse the criminal behavior of those blacks who did commit crimes. Rather, she called into question the failure of the government and its agencies to prevent and control illegal lynching. Wells-Barnett also shaped public opinion and antilynching legislation during her antilynching campaign. Although lynching was not eradicated during her period of activism, other individuals and organizations, including the National Association for the Advancement of Colored People (NAACP), joined the antilynching movement in the early twentieth century.

Responses to both Wells-Barnett and her antilynching efforts were mixed. She was respected by some and disliked by others, both black and white, male and female. In the introduction to the reprint of Mrs. Wells-Barnett's antilynching pamphlets, August Meier described her as a propagandist even though she presented evidence of lynching that was factually accurate. Shortly after publishing her first pamphlet on lynching, entitled *Southern Horrors*, Wells-Barnett received a letter from Frederick Douglass thanking her for her knowledge and facts about "the lynch abomination" (Wells-Barnett, 1892/1969). Until his death in 1895, Douglass was a supporter of Wells-Barnett (Thompson, 1990). However, when Booker T. Washington and W. E. B. Du Bois ascended as spokespersons for blacks, Wells-Barnett was less prominent, due in part to her outspokenness and radical views.

More recently, Wells-Barnett has been recognized as the leader and heroine she always was. Fradin (2000) describes her as the mother of the civil rights movement. She is included in numerous publications that focus on outstanding Americans, black women, and women (Sterling, 1979; Thompson, 1990; Miller, 1995; Smallwood, 1998). Others continue to write about her life and antilynching crusade (Lisandrelli, 1998; McMurry, 1998; Welch, 1999). It is hoped that her contributions to criminological thought will receive more attention in the future.

References

Addams, J. & Wells-Barnett, I. (1977). In B. Aptheker (ed.), *Lynching and rape: An exchange of views* (pp. 22–34). New York: American Institute for Marxist Studies.

Cutler, J. E. (1905). *Lynch law: An investigation into the history of lynching in the United States.* New York: Longmans, Green. Reprinted., Montclair, NJ: Patterson Smith, 1969.

Duster, A. (ed.). (1970). *Crusade for justice: The autobiography of Ida B. Wells.* Chicago: University of Chicago Press.

Fortune, T. T. (1893). Ida B. Wells, A.M. In Lawson A. Scruggs (Ed.), *Women of distinction* (pp. 35–39). Raleigh, NC: La Scruggs.

Fradin, D. (2000). *Ida B. Wells: Mother of the civil rights movement.* New York: Clarion Books.

Hutton, M. (1975). *The rhetoric of Ida B. Wells: The genesis of the anti-lynching movement.* Ann Arbor, MI: University Microfilms International.

Lisandrelli, E. (1998). *Ida B. Wells-Barnett: Crusader against lynching.* Springfield, NJ: Enslow.

Logan, S. W. (1991). *Rhetorical strategies in Ida B. Wells's Southern horrors: Lynch law in all its phases.* Sage 8, no. 1.

McMurry, L. (1998). *To keep the waters troubled: The life of Ida B. Wells.* New York: Oxford University Press.

Miller, E. (1995). The other reconstruction: Where violence and womanhood meet in the writings of Ida B. Wells-Barnett, Angelina Weld Grimke, and Nella Larsen. *Dissertation Abstracts International.*

Smallwood, D. (1988). *Profiles of great African-Americans.* Lincolnwood, IL: Publishers International.

Sterling, D. (1979). *Black foremothers: Three lives.* Old Westbury, NY: Feminist Press.

Thompson, M. (1990). *Ida B. Wells-Barnett: An exploratory study of an American black woman, 1893–1930.* Brooklyn: Carlson Publishing Inc.

———. (1979). *Ida B. Wells-Barnett: An exploratory study of an American Black woman, 1893–1930.* Thesis. Ann Arbor, MI: University Microfilms International.

Walker, E. R. (1941). *Ida B. Wells-Barnett: Her contribution to the field of social welfare.* Master's (MSW) Thesis, Loyola University, 1941.

Welch, C. (1999). *Ida B. Wells-Barnett: Powerhouse with a pen.* Minneapolis, MN: Carolrhoda Books.

Wells-Barnett, I. B. (1893). *The reason why the colored American is not in the world's Columbian exposition.* In Hine (ed.), *Black women in United States History* (vol. 15, pp. 189–223). Brooklyn: Carlson Publishing Co.

———. (1900). Lynch law in America. *The Arena, 23,* 15–24.

———. (1909). Lynching: Our national crime. In *National Negro Conference: Proceedings,* pp. 174–79. 261–65). New York: Carlson Publishing Co.

———. (1892/1969). *Southern horrors.* New York: Arno Press.

———. (1895/1969) *A red record* New York: Arno Press.

———. (1900/1969). *Mob rule in New Orleans.* New York: Arno Press.

———. (1969). *On lynchings: Southern horrors [1892], A red record [1895], Mob rule in New Orleans [1900].* New York: Arno Press.

Ida B. Wells-Barnett
Selected References

Wells-Barnett, I. B. (1893). *The reason why the colored American is not in the world's Columbian exposition.* In Hine (ed.), *Black women in United States History* (vol. 15, pp. 189–223). Brooklyn: Carlson Publishing Co.

———. (1893). Lynch law in all its phases. *Our day,* 333–47.

———. (1900). Lynch law in America. *The Arena, 23,* 15–24.

———. (1909). Lynching: Our national crime. *National Negro Conference: Proceedings.* In Thompson, *Ida B. Wells-Barnett.* New York: Carlson Publishing Co.

———. (1910). How enfranchisement stops lynchings. *Original rights magazine* (June):42–53.

———. (1969). *On lynchings: Southern horrors [1892], A red record [1895], Mob rule in New Orleans [1900].* New York: Arno Press.

W. E. B. Du Bois
Courtesy of Moorland-Springarn Research Center
Howard University

Two

William Edward Burghardt Du Bois
(1868–1963)

Introduction

Of the African American scholars profiled in the historical era, W. E. B. Du Bois represents one who may be considered a "pioneer." In the case of Du Bois, along with his pioneering contributions to criminology/criminal justice, the label *pioneer* is also applicable to his contributions in other areas, including history, race relations, sociology, and civil rights activism (Broderick, 1974). While his primary criminological contributions span a five-year period (1899–1904), they nonetheless represent some of the earliest American contributions to the development of criminology as a discipline. As with the other authors in this volume, the bulk of Du Bois's writings focus on African Americans and the criminal justice system. His writings specifically focus on the causes, consequences, and potential remedies of African American crime. Writing during the height of the social Darwinist and eugenics movements, Du Bois envisioned using his broad educational training to carry out social scientific research that would refute these and other racist doctrines. Although Du Bois may have been naive in this belief, his vigilant pursuit of this aim resulted in his publication of several notable works on crime.

Biographical Information

William Edward Burghardt Du Bois was born on 23 February 1868 in Great Barrington, Massachusetts, to Alfred Du Bois and Mary Burghardt Du Bois. When Du Bois was young, his father left home, leaving Mary to raise "Willie" as a single parent. Fortunately, Mary was able to find odd jobs in town to help support her son. Additionally, townspeople were generous with assistance to the Du Bois family. Although Du Bois remembers only fifty out of the five thousand residents being black, he recalls primarily pleasant interactions with the white townspeople.

An outstanding student, Du Bois had a penchant for reading and served as a local correspondent to the *New York Age,* an African American newspaper. In 1884, after a notable high school career, Du Bois was the only African American graduate of Great Barrington High School. Following his graduation, Frank Hosmer, Du Bois's liberal- minded high school principal who regularly encouraged him, recommended that he pursue a liberal arts education vis-à-vis agricultural training or domestic service, which were the prevailing tracks for African Americans.

ACADEMIC BACKGROUND AND EXPERIENCE

Du Bois considered many schools; however, his heart was set on attending Harvard because "it was [the] oldest . . . largest and most widely known" (Du Bois, 1968, pp. 101–2). It was recommended that Du Bois defer applying and attending Harvard until the following year so that he could do additional preparation. Unexpectedly, in the fall of 1884, Du Bois's mother died. With no money of his own, Du Bois received considerable assistance from his family. By the fall of 1885, several churches had secured enough funds for Du Bois to attend Fisk University in Nashville, Tennessee (Du Bois, 1968, p. 105). Du Bois, however, still had his mind set on attending Harvard.

At Fisk, Du Bois became increasingly serious about his writing (he served as the editor of the school paper, the *Fisk Herald*) and public speaking. Of this period, he writes "I became an impassioned orator and developed a belligerent attitude toward the color bar. I was determined to make a scientific conquest of my environment which would render the emancipation of the Negro race quicker" (Du Bois, 1968, p. 125). Du Bois remembers Fisk as a place where he received "splendid inspiration" from professors who were little known—but were as good as the ones he had later at Harvard (Du Bois, 1968, p. 133).

After three years at Fisk, Du Bois graduated, cum laude, receiving an A.B. degree in philosophy. Following his plan, Du Bois applied and was accepted at Harvard. Since Fisk's requirements were behind Harvard's, Du Bois was accepted as a junior. Two years later Du Bois graduated, receiving another A.B. degree in philosophy.

At Harvard, Du Bois was influenced by several people, however, it was noted psychologist William James who had the biggest influence (Du Bois, 1968, p. 133). James steered Du Bois away from philosophy into a more "practical" course of study. This led Du Bois to pursue graduate studies in history, where he became a student of Albert Bushnell Hart. Working under Hart, Du Bois received his M.A. in 1890. With the encouragement of Hart, Du Bois enrolled in the Ph.D. program in history. After two years in this program, Du Bois felt a void in his academic training and pursued the possibility of studying at a German university. During this era, German training was widely regarded as the most respected available. Once Du Bois secured funding, he ventured to the University of Berlin, where he studied from 1892 through 1894.

While at the University of Berlin, Du Bois became a student of the Historical School of Economics. During the late 1890s, notable scholars, including Max Weber, were members of the school, which used the inductive, interdisciplinary approach to conduct research (Boston, 1991). Du Bois was particularly drawn to the leader of the school, Gustav van Schmoller. Under Schmoller's direction, Du Bois's future work became clearer; he would engage in social scientific research that would help shape national policy affecting African Americans. Du Bois was extremely focused in Berlin, having completed all the required course work and his thesis (under Schmoller) in two years. However, since Du Bois did not meet the residency requirement, he could not present his dissertation for defense (Du Bois, 1968, p. 175). His two years of study in economics likely helped shape some of his later writings on African Americans.

On his return to the United States, in 1894, Du Bois sought positions across the country, but to his surprise no major white university was ready to offer him an appointment. So, begrudgingly, he accepted a position at Wilberforce University in Ohio. In 1895, Du Bois completed his degree requirements with the completion of his dissertation, "The Suppression of the Slave Trade to the United States of America, 1638–1870," making him the first African American to receive a Ph.D. at Harvard. His dissertation was later published by Harvard (see Du Bois, 1896). Except for the completion of his doctorate and the meeting of future wife Nina, Du Bois considered his experience at Wilberforce an unpleasant one. In fact, he was relieved when he received an offer from the University of Pennsylvania to study the African American residents of the Seventh Ward in Philadelphia.

Du Bois accepted the position with the unusual title "assistant instructor in sociology." It was clear to Du Bois that they knew he was an able researcher, but they were not ready to accept Du Bois, an African American, as an equal (Du Bois, 1968, p. 194). In fact, they gave him no office, which insured that he had little interaction with students or faculty, and eventually removed his name from the university catalogue (Du Bois, 1968, p. 194). The final product of his efforts, *The Philadelphia Negro: A Social Study* (1899), is widely considered the first scientific study of an African American community. Du Bois's work in Philadelphia caught the attention of Horace Bumstead, president of Atlanta University, who was searching for someone to head the Sociology Department and to direct annual studies on various aspects of African American life.

From 1897 through 1910, Du Bois tirelessly carried out the annual studies that culminated with a conference that presented the findings from the yearly inquiry. Assorted luminaries regularly attended the conferences, which were highly regarded in the U.S. and abroad. During this period, Du Bois became a national figure because of his now classic debate with Booker T. Washington. Essentially, the debate centered around the future direction of the education and training of African Americans. Du Bois felt that while there was a need for industrial training, pursuing education in the liberal arts was also essential for African Americans. It was from this group of people ("the talented tenth") that Du Bois felt the leaders of the race would emerge. Washington felt that since the primary opportunities available for African Americans were in industrially oriented occupations, it was more appropriate for African Americans to fill this need at all costs, including the forfeiting of some rights (Harris, 1993).

During his tenure at Atlanta University, this debate became a hindrance to the attainment of funds since most philanthropists supported Washington's position. Because of this, Du Bois became increasingly disillusioned with the potential of academe to accomplish his objective of uplifting African Americans. So in 1905, Du Bois founded the Niagara movement. This radical movement called for "freedom of speech and criticism, manhood suffrage, the abolition of all distinctions based on race, the recognition of the basic principles of human fellowship, and respect for the working person" (Franklin and Moss, 1994, pp. 317–18). It represented Du Bois's move out of academe and into the world of activism. In 1909 Du Bois completed this move when the Niagara movement faltered and many of its members, including Du Bois, became founding members of the National Association for the Advancement of Colored People (NAACP). Du Bois resigned from Atlanta University in 1910 and accepted the position of director of publicity and research at the NAACP (Du Bois, 1968, pp. 231–32).

As director of publicity and research, Du Bois founded the NAACP's journal, the *Crisis*. Over the span of the next twenty-four years, Du Bois would use this publication to lash out against injustices of the day, particularly lynching. This position also contributed to making Du Bois one of the most recognized figures of the twentieth century.

In 1934, Du Bois resigned from the NAACP and returned to Atlanta University where he attempted to revive the Atlanta University studies. Shortly after his return to Atlanta, however, funding to conduct the annual studies again became a major concern. Therefore, Du Bois managed to only carry out a conference in 1943. The program was then transferred to E. Franklin Frazier at Howard University where only one additional conference was held, in 1944 (Du Bois, 1968, p. 324). This same year, Du Bois was forced to retire from Atlanta University, but was invited to return to the NAACP as Director of Special Research (Du Bois, 1968, p. 326).

During this second tenure at the NAACP, Du Bois became increasingly interested in world affairs. An early Pan-Africanist, Du Bois was particularly interested in world peace. His international interests, however, led Du Bois to become an admirer of communism. This interest eventually led to his removal from the NAACP in 1947. Not long after his removal, Du Bois, like noted African American Paul Robeson, became a victim of the McCarthy era witch hunts.

In 1951, Du Bois was indicted on frivolous charges related to a peace organization he and several others had founded. Essentially, these charges sought to silence Du Bois's opinions on international affairs—even after Du Bois was acquitted of the charges, he was denied a passport to travel overseas. Not until 1958 did Du Bois receive his passport, upon the receipt of which Du Bois embarked on a world tour during which he received numerous honorary degrees and awards. Two years after Du Bois returned to the United States, he joined the Communist Party of the United States. Soon thereafter, he accepted the invitation of Kwame Nkrumah, president of Ghana, Africa, to become a citizen of Ghana. Ironically, in 1963, on the eve of the historic civil rights march on Washington, Du Bois died at the age of ninety-five. This march is widely believed to have spurred the changes that Du Bois spent the better part of his ninety-five years pursuing.

CONTRIBUTIONS TO CRIMINOLOGICAL THOUGHT

Often the early publications of scholars anticipate some of their later important work. This premise holds true in the case of Du Bois. One of Du Bois's earliest publications on crime was written while he was a student at Harvard. As a graduate student at Harvard, Du Bois became interested in the slave trade and the enforcement of the laws prohibiting it. In 1891, Du Bois presented a paper titled "The Enforcement of the Slave Trade Laws" at the annual meeting of the American Historical Association. In this presentation, Du Bois examined the laws enacted to suppress the slave trade to the United States. He was particularly interested in the 1803 federal statute that prohibited the importation of slaves into America. Du Bois was interested in discovering how the laws were enforced. His findings showed that they were not enforced at all or, at best, were poorly enforced (Du Bois, 1891/1982, p. 21).

Discussing the laxity of enforcement by domestic and international governments, Du Bois commented that "not only was this negligence on the part of the government apparent abroad, but officials appeared to have been either careless or criminal at home. In spite of many convictions and numerous trials there are strangely few cases of severe punishment, and I have never found a record of the actual hanging of a slave trader for piracy" (Du Bois, 1891/1982, p. 25). This led Du Bois to conclude that "Northern greed joined to Southern credulity was a combination calculated to circumvent any law, human or divine" (Du Bois, 1891/1982 p. 27). This analysis of the slave trade laws and the reasons for their lack of enforcement provides the foundation through which Du Bois's insightful discussions on the convict-lease system may have later emerged.

Although much of Du Bois's later publications focused on African American crime, it is interesting that his first publication of relevance to criminal justice/criminology focused on "White" crime. While this early work is consistent with Du Bois's lifelong focus on African American concerns, he recognized that whites had laws (i.e., against the slave trade) that they did not enforce. In the case of the slave trade laws, Du Bois realized that whites did not enforce these laws because financially it was not in their best interest to do so. This critical analysis of the slave trade laws later evolved into Du Bois's doctoral dissertation and began his publications on the criminal justice system.

While Du Bois made statements on crime throughout his life, his primary thoughts on the subject were formulated early in his career. Therefore, our focus here is on his crime-related publications from 1899 to 1904. In 1899, Du Bois published two important works that included discussions on crime. The first, *The Philadelphia Negro*, though concerned with all aspects of the African American residents of the Seventh Ward in Philadelphia, includes discussions on crime throughout the text. The second, "The Negro and Crime" summarizes Du Bois's thoughts on African Americans and crime. In 1901, Du Bois felt it necessary to devote an entire article to the topic of the convict-lease system, which Du Bois believed was a major instigator on African American crime. In 1901 Du Bois also examined the state of African Americans in three northern cities. His findings provide further insight into African American crime in the North at the turn of the century. One of Du Bois's larger publications devoted to crime was the 1904 Atlanta University conference publication *Some Notes on Negro Crime, Particularly in Georgia*. This edited volume includes several discussions on crime by Du Bois. Our discussion begins with a review of *The Philadelphia Negro,* which is followed by a summary of his arguments in the latter publications.

The Philadelphia Negro

As noted earlier, Du Bois was hired by the University of Pennsylvania to conduct a detailed study of the residents of the Seventh Ward in Philadelphia. Outside observers clearly sensed that there were problems in the ward that warranted attention; however, they needed someone to collect the facts and make recommendations for the improvement of the ward. Since crime was a central part of the concern in the ward, Du Bois devoted two chapters—13, "The Negro Criminal," and 14 "Pauperism and Alcoholism"—to this subject. Additionally, chapters 15, "Environment of the Negro," and 17, "Negro Suffrage," include significant discussions on criminal classes and political and organized crime. After carefully reviewing the history of the city and the crime statistics for the ward, Du Bois composed the following explanation for African American crime:

> Crime is a phenomenon of organized social life, and is the open rebellion
> of an individual against his social environment. Naturally then, if men
> are suddenly transported from one environment to another; the result is
> lack of harmony with the new conditions; lack of harmony with the new
> physical surroundings leading to disease and death or modification of
> physique; lack of harmony with social surroundings leading to crime.
> (Du Bois, 1899a/1973, p. 235)

Du Bois supported this perspective on African American criminality with a detailed historical analysis of African American crime in Colonial America that revealed several occurrences that provided examples of the disorganization observable among African Americans due to their presence in a foreign land. Du Bois also pointed to several ordinances and legislative enactments created to quash disturbances by African Americans throughout the colonies. While these enactments did temporarily result in reduced disturbances, Du Bois writes that "little special mention of Negro crime is again met with until the freedmen under the act of 1780 began to congregate in the city and other free immigrants joined them" (Du Bois, 1899a/1973, p. 237). Soon thereafter, there were increasing incidents of thievery and assault. Several scholarly observers of this passage have suggested that it is reminiscent of the concept of social disorganization that was later popularized by the Chicago School of Sociology (see Frazier, 1949; Gabbidon, 1996; Young and Greene, 1995).

Following his statement on crime, Du Bois presented an analysis of the available crime and population statistics. Du Bois was surprised to find that "less than one-fourteenth of the population was responsible for nearly a third of the serious crimes committed" (Du Bois, 1899a/1973, p. 238). From this statement, one can conclude that Du Bois was concerned with the disproportionate number of African Americans in the crime figures.

Du Bois continued his analysis with an examination of the racial composition of Moyamensing prison. Here he reported that "in 1896 the Negroes forming 4 per cent of the population furnish 9 per cent of the arrests, but in 1850 being 5 per cent of the population they furnished 32 per cent of the prisoners received at the county prison" (Du Bois, 1899a/1973, p. 239). Attempting to explain this disproportionality, Du Bois wrote, "It must be remembered that the discrimination against the Negro was much greater then than now: he was arrested for less cause and given longer sentences than whites. Great numbers of those arrested and committed for trial were never brought to trial so that their guilt could be proven or disproven" (Du Bois, 1899b/1973, p. 239). Du Bois also pointed out the length of sentences for whites and African Americans: "[The] average length of sentences for whites in Eastern Penitentiary during [the past] nineteen years, [was] 2 years, 8 months, 2 days; for Negroes, [it was] 3 years, 3 months 14 days" (Du Bois, 1899a/1973, p. 239). With this passage, Du Bois made the important connection between the disparate justice administered to whites and African Americans and the latter's overrepresentation in the prison population.

A final analysis of the arrest figures in Philadelphia from 1864 through 1896 caused Du Bois to caution observers regarding their usefulness, considering "the varying efficiency and diligence of the police, by discrimination in the administration of law, and by unwarranted arrests" (Du Bois, 1899a/1973, p. 242). Du Bois then concentrated on the 541 African American criminals who were convicted of serious offenses. Du Bois explained the disproportionate representation of African-Americans in correctional institutions for the commission of serious offenses with the following passage:

> This of course assumes that the convicts in the penitentiary represent with a fair degree of accuracy the crime committed. The assumption is not wholly true; in convictions by human courts the rich always are favored somewhat at the expense of the poor, the upper classes at the expense of the unfortunate classes, and whites at the expense of Negroes. We know for instance that certain crimes are not punished in Philadelphia because the public opinion is lenient, as for instance embezzlement, forgery, and certain sorts of stealing; on the other hand a commercial community is apt to punish with severity petty thieving, breaches of the peace, and personal assault or burglary. (Du Bois, 1899a/1973, p. 249)[1]

Chapter 14 ("Pauperism and Alcoholism") of *The Philadelphia Negro: A Social Study* includes a section titled "The Causes of Crime and Poverty." Here Du Bois again emphasizes the effects of slavery and emancipation on Africans Americans. Throughout the chapter, Du Bois pointed to the strong influence of the social environment in the etiology on African American crime (Du Bois, 1899a/1973, 285–87). He concludes the chapter by suggesting that in order to get to the real causes of crime, and away from the symptoms, you must look at the environment of African Americans. In the next chapter, Du Bois did just that. His findings are reviewed below.

In chapter 15, "The Environment of the Negro," Du Bois focused on two important topics, the physical characteristics of the Seventh Ward and criminal classes. The former discussion focused on the dangers of the alleys of Philadelphia. Of these dangers, Du Bois wrote: "The inhabitants of the alley are at the mercy of its worst tenants . . . prostitutes ply their trade, and criminals hide" (Du Bois, 1899a, p. 294). Du Bois then turned to his concerns about the African American criminal class.

Criminal classes among African Americans represents a topic Du Bois began discussing prior to his work in Philadelphia (see Du Bois, 1898). However, he maintained an interest in this segment of the African American community right up to his death. In his discussion of social classes, Du Bois placed families into one of four grades. Those in the fourth grade constituted Du Bois's criminal class. He described members of this class as "[t]he lowest class of criminals, prostitutes and loafers; the 'submerged tenth'" (Du Bois, 1899a/1973, p. 311). Du Bois felt that this class had arisen since 1840 and that its members were typically involved in "shrewd laziness, shameless lewdness, cunning crime" (Du Bois, 1899a/1973, pp. 311–312). Speaking about loafers, a group included in his criminal class, Du Bois notes:

> Their nucleus consists of a class of professional criminals, who do not work . . . and migrate here and there . . . [T]hese are a set of gamblers and sharpers who seldom are caught in serious crime, but who nevertheless live from its proceeds and aid and abet it. The headquarters are usually the political clubs and pool rooms; they stand ready to entrap the unwary and tempt the weak. Their organization, tacit or recognized, is very effective, and no one can long watch their actions without seeing that they keep in close touch with the authorities in some way. (Du Bois, 1899a/1973, p. 312).

Du Bois concluded his analysis of the African American criminal class with a discussion of the primary group of female members of this class, prostitutes. While Du Bois acknowledged his difficulty in obtaining data on this segment of the criminal class, he did manage to obtain sufficient data to make some preliminary observations. Du Bois's sources revealed that there were about fifty prostitutes in the Seventh Ward who operated out of residences (Du Bois, 1899a/1973, p. 314). Additionally, he reported the presence of street walkers who serviced not only African Americans but also Italian immigrants (Du Bois, 1899a/1973, p. 314). Finally, Du Bois noted the presence of pimps: "they [prostitutes] usually have male associates whom they support" (Du Bois, 1899a/1973, p. 314).

In the following chapter, "Contact of the Races," Du Bois discusses the connection between race prejudice and crime. While Du Bois is hesitant to say that most

African-American crime is a result of race prejudice, he does suggest that it plays a role (Du Bois, 1899a/1973, pp. 350–51). On this issue, Du Bois provided an example of the potential connection:

> The connection of crime and prejudice is . . . neither simple nor direct. The boy who is refused promotion in his job as porter does not go out and snatch somebody's pocketbook. Conversely the loafers . . . and the thugs in the county prison are not usually graduates of high schools who have been refused work. The connections are much more subtle and dangerous; it is the atmosphere of rebellion and discontent that unrewarded merit and reasonable but unsatisfied ambition make. The social environment of excuse, listless despair, careless indulgence and lack of inspiration to work is the growing force that turns black boys and girls into gamblers, prostitutes and rascals. (Du Bois, 1899a/1973, p. 351)

Du Bois clearly felt that the prejudice encountered by lower-class African Americans "encouraged" African American criminality (Du Bois, 1899a/1973, p. 352).

Another important discussion by Du Bois, in *The Philadelphia Negro,* relates to political and organized crime. He devoted a chapter to "Negro Suffrage" to determine what effects, if any, the Fifteenth Amendment (the right to vote for all races) had on African Americans in Philadelphia. In the section "Some Bad Results of Negro Suffrage," Du Bois discusses political crimes such as bribery. Du Bois recognized that with the arrival of African American suffrage the vote of African Americans was for sale. In this area, Du Bois was specifically concerned about the role of political clubs as evidenced by the following passage:

> [A] political club is a band of eight or twelve men who rent a club house with money furnished them by the boss, and support themselves partially in the same way . . . The club is often named after some politician . . . and the business of the club is to see that its precinct is carried for the proper candidate, to get "jobs" for some of its "boys," to keep others from arrest and to secure bail and discharge for those arrested. (Du Bois, 1899a/1973, pp. 378–79)

Du Bois's research found that the leader of the club was the "boss of his district." These leaders were well acquainted with the policeman, who, "so long as the loafers and gamblers under him do not arouse the public too much he sees that they are not molested" (Du Bois, 1899a/1973, p. 379). His research also revealed that it was not only lower-class African Americans involved in bribery: There is of course a difference in the various clubs; some are of higher class than others and receive offices as bribes; others are openly devoted to gambling and receive protection as a bribe" (Du Bois, 1899a/1973, p. 379).

Moreover, Du Bois recognized that there were two other means to secure African American votes: "(a) contributions to various objects in which voters are interested, and (2) appointment to public office or to work of any kind for the city" (Du Bois, 1899a/1973, p. 380). According to Du Bois, the latter method used to secure African American votes was related to the general lack of opportunities afforded African Americans. Of this issue, Du Bois commented: "One class of well-paid positions, the city civil-service, was once closed to [Negroes], and only one road was open to them to secure these positions and that was unquestioning obedience to the 'machine' "(Du Bois, 1899a/1973, p. 380). Du Bois ends the chapter suggesting that in order for African Americans to advance away from crime, the links among gambling, crime, and city authorities must be broken (Du Bois, 1899a/1973, p. 384). From Du Bois's findings in this chapter, we can safely conclude that he was well aware of the existence of criminal organizations.

In the final chapter of *The Philadelphia Negro,* Du Bois makes some recommendations for the improvement of the Seventh Ward. Du Bois suggested that the city should invest resources in preventative agencies, such as schools and reformatories. Du Bois concludes his discussion on crime with two final comments. First, he points to the home as the place where crime prevention should begin. Second, he suggests that if whites continue to discriminate against African Americans in employment, "Negroes may drift into idleness and crime" (Du Bois, 1899a/1973, p. 395). An additional publication by Du Bois, in 1899, also highlights his views on crime. This article is discussed below.

"The Negro and Crime"

Recognizing the nationwide concern regarding the increasing involvement of African Americans in the criminal justice system, Du Bois devoted an entire publication to this subject. Du Bois prefaced his discussion of the causes of African American crime by suggesting that considering that African Americans had only recently been emancipated, it was surprising that there were not more African Americans in the criminal justice system (Du Bois, 1899b, p. 1355). Elaborating on this thought, he wrote:

> Indeed it is astounding that a body of people whose family life had been so nearly destroyed, whose women had been forced into concubinage, whose labor had been enslaved and then sent adrift penniless, that such a nation should in a single generation be able to point to so many pure homes, so many property-holders, so many striving law abiding citizens. (Du Bois, 1899b, p. 1355)

Besides the economic effects of emancipation, Du Bois pointed to four main causes of criminality among African Americans in the South: (1) convict-lease system; (2) attitude of the courts; (3) lawlessness and barbarity of the mobs; and (4) segregation.

Du Bois believed the convict-lease system, which was dependent on African Americans, led to the misuse of the law to "widen-the-net" so that there were enough bodies to meet the demand for laborers. The system allowed states to lease convicts to the public. Because of emancipation, land owners had a dire need for laborers, this labor shortage caused the criminal justice system to become a tool to secure the required labor (Du Bois's complete thoughts on the convict-lease system are discussed later).

The courts were another source of concern regarding African American criminality. Du Bois felt the Southern courts had two flaws: first, the leniency of the punishment administered to whites; and second, the severity of the punishment administered to African Americans. He noted that this double system of justice led to the over representation of African Americans in penal institutions. Therefore, any student of Southern penal institutions should be cautious in their inferences, based solely on prison statistics, regarding African American criminality (Du Bois, 1899b, p. 1356).

Du Bois also recognized that the increasing mob violence was an additional source of African American criminality. Specifically, Du Bois observed:

> [L]et a Negro be simply accused of any crime from barn-burning to rape and he is liable to be seized by a mob, given no chance to defend himself, given neither trial, judge nor jury, and killed. Passing over the acknowledged fact that many innocent Negroes have thus been murdered, the point that is of greater gravity is that lawlessness is a direct encouragement to crime. It shatters the faith of the mass of Negroes in justice; it makes race hatred fiercer; it discourages honest effort; it transforms horror at crime into sympathy for the tortured victim; and it binds the hands and lessens the influence of those race leaders who are striving to preach forbearance and patience and honest endeavor to their people. It teaches eight million wronged people to despise a civilization which is not civilized. (Du Bois, 1899b, p. 1357)

Du Bois's final cause of African American criminality was segregation. He believed that this practice was an exaggerated and unnatural separation of the races. Furthermore, he emphasized that "the drawing of the color line is not only silly but dangerous" (Du Bois, 1899b, p. 1357). Du Bois believed that the drawing of the color line led to false assumptions by members of both races and stymied any progress toward the solution of the causes of African American crime.

Immediately following the turn of the century, Du Bois published three additional works that included discussions on crime. Specifically, these works included an extensive analysis of the convict-lease system, a view of the conditions of African Americans residing in three Northern cities, and another general overview of African American criminality. The significant findings of each of these publications are discussed below.

Du Bois's article "The Spawn of Slavery: The Convict-Lease System in the South" represents one of his most theoretically relevant publications. This article focused on the convict-lease system that was regularly used to control African American labor. Attempting to describe the system, Du Bois wrote "The convict-lease system is the slavery in private hands of persons convicted of crimes and misdemeanors in the courts" (Du Bois, 1901a/1982, p. 110). Du Bois prefaced his discussion of the system with a history of the punishments administered before and after the Civil War.

His analysis began with the observation that prior to the Civil War punishments in the South were similar to those in the North. However, Du Bois recognized that in the South crime was less prevalent. He believed that this was a direct result of the system of slavery, primarily because slaves could not be criminals under the law, and the master often served as the police, judge, and jury (Du Bois, 1901a/1982, p. 110).

Du Bois also reported that during the slave era, masters regularly worked together to control the slave population. This cooperation was established because of the rampant fear of insurrections, such as the ones by Cato, Gabriel, Vesey, Turner, and Toussaint (Du Bois, 1901a/1982, p. 110). On this cooperation among masters, Du Bois wrote, "[T]he result was a system of rural police, mounted and on duty chiefly at night, whose work it was to stop the nocturnal wandering and meeting of slaves. It was usually an effective organization, [to] which all white men belonged, and were liable to active detailed duty at regular intervals" (Du Bois, 1901a/1982, pp. 110–111).

Following emancipation, Du Bois believed the South was determined to keep the slave labor (Du Bois, 1901a/1982, p. 111). To accomplish this objective, the South enacted, "[e]laborate and ingenious apprentice and vagrancy laws . . . designed to make the freedmen and their children work for their former masters at practically no wages" (Du Bois, 1901a/1982, p. 111). This practice was gradually slowed after the development of the Freedmans Bureau and other government interventions. However, even with these measures, Du Bois noted that "careless and untrained Negroes" still received severe sentences (Du Bois, 1901a/1982, p. 111). Discussing this period, Du Bois wrote that "[t]he courts and jails became filled with the careless and ignorant, with those who sought to emphasize their new-found freedom, and too often with innocent victims of oppression. The testimony of a Negro counted for nothing in court, while the accusation of white witnesses was usually decisive" (Du Bois, 1901a/1982, p. 111).

Because of the dramatic increase in the prison population, the space available to house criminals became inadequate. Du Bois recognized that the state had no real intention of housing these offenders. Soon thereafter, the Southern states passed laws authorizing the lease of convict labor to the highest bidder (Du Bois, 1901a/1982, p. 112). The lessee then worked the convict, with little or no intervention from the state. With the advent of this system, Du Bois believed "a new slavery and slave-trade was established" (Du Bois, 1901a/1982, p. 112).

Once established, Du Bois describes how the innocent, guilty, and "depraved" men, women, and children were turned over to irresponsible men who were out to make as much money as possible (Du Bois, 1901a/1982, p.112). As a result of this system, Du Bois noted, "the innocent were made bad, the bad worse; women were outraged and children tainted; whipping and torture were in vogue, and the death-rate from cruelty, exposure, and overwork rose to larger percentages" (Du Bois, 1901a/1982, p. 112).

Du Bois also expressed concern about the wretched living conditions of the leased convicts. In one case, he found that sixty-one men slept in one room. Du Bois felt that because of the state involvement in this system, "the state became a dealer in crime, profited by it so as to derive a net annual income for her prisoners. The lessees of the convicts made large profits also" (Du Bois, 1901a/1982, p. 112). Another concern of Du Bois's were the chain gangs. He felt they were "schools of crime" that led to the involvement of African Americans in more serious offenses (Du Bois, 1901a, p. 113). Du Bois felt that the creation of the more serious African American offenders was ironic since whites had long utilized the criminal courts to put African Americans to work by conviction of petty thieving and other minor crimes; however, they were not ready for the more bold and violent crimes (Du Bois, 1901a/1982, p. 113). Du Bois acknowledged that there had been improvements in the administration of the system; however, the system remained intact just under tighter state control (Du Bois, 1901a/1982, p. 114).

While Du Bois endorsed the idea of prisoners working, he did so under a different premise: "The correct theory is that the work is for the benefit of the criminal—for his correction, if possible. At the same time, his work should not be allowed to come into unfair competition with that of honest laborers, and it should never be an object of traffic for pure financial gain" (Du Bois, 1901a/1982, pp. 114–15)

In regard to juvenile offenders, Du Bois expressed concern with them being housed with adult offenders. Du Bois felt the commingling of adult and juvenile offenders "manufactured" additional criminals (Du Bois, 1901a/1982, p. 115). A final concern expressed by Du Bois was the treatment of white criminals. He was firm in the belief that while African American criminals were unfairly severely punished, white criminals remained free and dangerous. He argued for the development of additional preventative measures (i.e., reformatories) for African Americans as well as whites (Du Bois, 1901a/1982, p. 116). Du Bois closed his analysis of the convict-lease system with the following statement:

> Above all, we must remember that crime is not normal; that the appearance of crime among Southern Negroes is a symptom of wrong social conditions—of a stress of life greater than a large part of the community can bear. The Negro is not naturally criminal; he is usually patient and

law-abiding. If slavery, the convict-lease system, the traffic in criminal
labor, the lack of juvenile reformatories, together with the unfortunate
discrimination and prejudice in other walks of life, have led to that sort
of social protest and revolt which we call crime, then we must look for
remedy in the sane reform of these wrong social conditions, and not in
intimidation, savagery, or the legalized slavery of men. (Du Bois,
1901a/1982, p. 116)

From this publication, it is clear that Du Bois was an early conflict criminologist. He understood that the strategic enactment of assorted vagrancy laws (commonly referred to as the "black codes") by the Southern oligarchy was based not on
criminal justice considerations but on economic ones. Emancipation left such a
shortage of laborers that the rulers of the South used their power to insure that there
would be an ample supply of cheap laborers.

Du Bois also addressed the notion of crime among African Americans being
normal. He plainly disagreed with Durkheim's earlier assessment that crime was
normal (see Durkheim, 1895/1964). According to Du Bois, crime in the African
American community was an inevitable product of the terrible social conditions to
which many of them were exposed. In 1901, Du Bois also examined the lives of
African Americans living in three Northern cities. His observations in New York,
Boston, and Philadelphia are discussed in the next section.

African American Crime in Northern Cities

In 1901, Du Bois published *The Black North in 1901*, which was a compilation of
several articles he wrote for the *New York Times*. The publication overviewed the
conditions of African Americans in three Northern cities: New York, Philadelphia,
and Boston. Since his findings in Philadelphia were similar to those presented in our
earlier review of *The Philadelphia Negro* (1899), this review will highlight his observations in New York and Boston.

Du Bois's first discussion on crime came in his analysis of the African Americans in New York. As in his previous publications, Du Bois begins by attempting to
determine the amount of African American crime. In relying on available records to
track African American criminality in New York, Du Bois noted that crime statistics
were not available before 1827. The 1827 figures showed that while African Americans were only 1 percent of the population, they constituted 25 percent of the New
York state convicts (Du Bois, 1901b, p. 14). Du Bois reported that these figures
decreased twenty years later to 15 percent and forty years later to 6 percent. Du Bois
also found that from 1870 to 1885 African Americans furnished about 2 percent of
the arrests, and from 1885 through 1895, Du Bois noted increases from 2½ to the
then figure of 3½ percent (Du Bois, 1901b, p. 15). Du Bois provided two primary
reasons for this increase in crime; first, he attributed it to the increase in the African
American population; additionally, he offered the following explanation:

The larger portion of the increase in arrests is undoubtedly due to migration—the sudden contact of newcomers with unknown city life. From the mere record of arrests one can get no very good idea of crime, and yet it is safe to conclude from the fact that in the state in 1890 every 10,000 Negroes furnished 100 prisoners that there is much serious crime among Negroes. And, indeed, what else should we expect? What else is this but a logical result of bad homes, poor health, restricted opportunities for work, and general social oppression? That the present situation is abnormal all admit. That the Negro under normal conditions is law-abiding and good-natured cannot be disputed. We have but to change conditions, then, to reduce Negro crime. (Du Bois, 1901b, p. 15)

Du Bois's commentary on crime in Boston was briefer because of the favorable conditions in this city. However, he cautioned the reader, stating, "[I]t would be wrong to suppose that beneath the fair conditions described there was not the usual substratum of crime and idleness" (Du Bois, 1901b, p. 37). Du Bois noted that seventy years earlier African Americans accounted for 14 percent of the convicts in Massachusetts and constituted 1 percent of the population (Du Bois, 1901b, p. 37). He was encouraged by the fact that presently the Negro was 2 percent of the population and only constituted 2¼ percent of the prisoners and 3½ percent of the penitentiary convicts (Du Bois, 1901b, p. 37).

Du Bois concluded pointing readers to the census, crime statistics, and municipal misgovernment as proof that "the exclusion of honest Negro workmen from earning a living in the North means direct encouragement to the Northward migration of Negro criminals and loafers" (Du Bois, 1901b, p. 45). In addition, Du Bois, reiterating his belief that crime, at least among African Americans, was not normal, stated, "The crime of Negroes in New York is not normal. It is the crime of a class of professional Negro criminals, gamblers, and loafers, encouraged and protected by political corruption and race prejudice" (Du Bois, 1901b, p. 37). The following section highlights Du Bois's contributions to Atlanta University's Ninth Conference for the Study of the Negro Problems, which focused on crime.

Some Notes on Negro Crime

In the spring of 1904, the Ninth Conference for the Study of Negro Problems convened at Atlanta University. The conference proceedings were later published as *Some Notes on Negro Crime, Particularly in Georgia* (1904). There were several contributing authors, including Frank Sanborn, Monroe Work (see chapter 3), H. H. Proctor, A. G. Combs, and L. D. Davis. It was Du Bois, however, who made the largest contribution to the publication. Relying upon several official and unofficial sources, Du Bois, along with the other conference participants, sought to grasp the extent of African American crime primarily in the state of Georgia. Some of Du Bois's contributions to the publication are discussed below.

Du Bois's first contribution to the publication, "Crime and Slavery," is a slightly altered version of the previously discussed publication on the convict-lease system. His second contribution to the publication, "Extent of Negro Crime" provided a detailed presentation of United States prisoner characteristics (i.e., race of the offender, literacy level, gender of offender, type of offense committed, etc.).

From the data, Du Bois provided the following observations regarding the disproportionate involvement of African Americans in certain offenses:

1. Almost half of African American prisoners were confined for crimes against property. Du Bois attributed this to "imperfect ideas of property ownership inseparable from a system of slavery" (Du Bois, 1904, p. 16). Essentially, Du Bois believed that the system of slavery caused African Americans to crave property, which after slavery they were unable to legally obtain. However, many former slaves felt they were deserving of the stolen property because of their free labor during slavery.

2. Du Bois also reported that a quarter of African American prisoners were confined for crimes against a person. He addressed fighting among African Americans with the following explanation: "Fighting is to be expected of ignorant people and people living under unsettled conditions" (Du Bois, 1904, p. 16). As for rape, Du Bois partially attributed the 578 African Americans in prison (out of 1,392) to public opinion, which often caused African Americans to be more easily convicted and given longer sentences than whites. Additionally, Du Bois again pointed to the system of slavery, having stated: "Notwithstanding all these considerations there is no doubt a large prevalence of sexual crimes among Negroes. This is due to the sexual immorality of slavery, the present defenselessness of a proscribed caste, and the excesses of the undeveloped classes among Negroes" (Du Bois, 1904, p. 16).

As part of his investigation into African American crime, Du Bois sent out surveys to all police chiefs in Georgia and various public officials. His aim was for them to provide commentary on the extent of African American crime in their jurisdiction. Their responses (see Du Bois, 1904, pp. 35–48) showed that while crime among African Americans in Georgia was increasing in a few counties, overall, most counties reported that African American crime was on the decline.

At the close of the publication, Du Bois provided the resolutions of the conference. These resolutions noted that while crime among African Americans in Georgia was high, it was on the decline. Further, Du Bois and the conference participants pointed to six explanations as to why crime was so high among African Americans: (1) transition stage between slavery and freedom; (2) race prejudice; (3) less legal protections than whites; (4) vagrancy laws associated with the convict-lease system and crop-lien system; (5) unfair court system; (6) punishment that encourages crime (lynching) (Du Bois, 1904, p. 65).

As for the remedies for African American crime, Du Bois and the conference participants suggested that "moral uplift and inspiration among Negroes" was a key component to any significant reduction in African American crime. Four agencies were called upon to assist in this moral uplift and inspiration: the church, the school, institutions for rescue work (outreach organizations), and juvenile reformatories (Du

Bois, 1904, p. 66). Recognizing the key role that whites would have to play if there was to be any significant reduction in African American crime, the conference participants made the following appeal to whites:

> [T]his conference appeals to the white people of Georgia for six things: Fairer criminal laws; justice in the courts; the abolition of state traffic in crime for public revenue and private gain; more intelligent methods of punishment; the refusal to allow free labor to be displaced by convict labor; and finally a wider recognition of the fact that honest, intelligent, law-abiding black men are safer neighbors than ignorant, unpaid serfs, because it is the latter class that breeds dangerous crime. (Du Bois, 1904, p. 66)

Du Bois's influence on the resolutions of the conference are clear. In fact, most of them mirror earlier statements by Du Bois on African American crime. A discussion of Du Bois's contribution to criminology is incomplete without a discussion of his pioneering use of social scientific methodologies. The final section discusses Du Bois's methodological contributions.

Methodological Contributions

Over the years, the research methods used by Du Bois in his pioneering studies have been the focus of several publications (see, for example, Broderick, 1958a; Broderick, 1958b; Montiero, 1994; Rudwick, 1957). Observers have been particularly interested in the research methods used by Du Bois in his research for *The Philadelphia Negro* and the research model he used later at Atlanta University. This period is also the focus of our review.

Early in *The Philadelphia Negro,* Du Bois discussed his "Methods of Inquiry" and "The Credibility of Results" (see Du Bois, 1899a/1973, pp. 1–4) A close examination of these sections shows that Du Bois used several research methods to conduct the research, including surveys, statistical analyses, historical analyses, general observation, participant observation, and content analysis.

Du Bois used an assortment of surveys to capture detailed information on the Seventh Ward residents. For example, he used a family survey (demographics of family), home survey (described interior of home), street survey (discussed physical characteristics of the streets and alleys), institutional survey (for organizations and various institutions), individual survey (demographics on individual residents of the home), and a house servant survey (demographics on live-in house-servants) (Du Bois, 1899a, p. 2). Du Bois also noted, "Through out the study . . . official statistics and historical matters as seemed reliable were used, and experienced persons, both white and colored, were freely consulted" (Du Bois, 1899a/1973, p. 2). To illustrate the types of crimes being committed by African Americans, Du Bois used content analysis to extract excerpts on African American incidents of crime from various newspapers (see Du Bois, 1899a/1973, pp. 259–68). Finally, Du Bois used general observation as well as participant observation (he lived in the ward throughout the duration of the study).

Although Du Bois used an assortment of research techniques, he was still aware of the limitations of his study:

> The best available methods of sociological research are at present so liable to inaccuracies that the careful student discloses the results of individual research with diffidence; he knows that they are liable to error from the seemingly ineradicable faults of the statistical method, to even greater error from the methods of general observation, and above all, he must ever tremble lest some unconscious trend of thought due to previous training, has to a degree distorted the picture in his view. (Du Bois, 1899a 1973, p. 3)

Much like researchers of today, Du Bois used multiple research methods to reduce the amount of error in his research (now referred to as "triangulation").

Du Bois used the methods previously described throughout his life, and especially while at Atlanta University where every year from 1897 through 1910 he directed the annual Atlanta University studies. Under Du Bois's guidance, students annually conducted research on a preselected subject. After the research was completed, a conference was held to present the findings. The papers from the conference were then compiled and later published by Atlanta University Press.

In 1903, Du Bois wrote about his model in Atlanta. The article begins with Du Bois pointing to the location of Atlanta University as an ideal one to study African American problems. He reasoned that since there was a significant African American population, the city served as an ideal "laboratory" to investigate their concerns.

At Atlanta University, Du Bois required juniors and seniors to participate in some sociological research, while postgraduates worked on the research conducted for the Atlanta University conferences (Du Bois, 1903/1982, p. 158). About the undergraduate curriculum, Du Bois wrote that "the undergraduate courses in sociology are simply an attempt to study systematically conditions of living right around the university . . . For this purpose . . . two years is taken up principally with a course in economics . . . Here the methods of study are largely inductive, going from fieldwork and personal knowledge to the establishment of the main principles" (Du Bois, 1903/1982, pp. 158–59).

An avid user of statistical methods (always, however, noting their shortcomings), Du Bois insured that his students were adequately trained in their use; furthermore, he required students to know vital statistics on African Americans (Du Bois, 1903/1982, p. 159). A testament to the quality of the work produced by Du Bois's students is that several of their works were published in professional journals and for government agencies. Even with this promising program, Du Bois consistently had difficulty securing funds to conduct his work. On a yearly budget of five thousand dollars, Du Bois paid himself, conducted the research, and held an annual conference (Du Bois, 1903/1982, p. 159). Recently, Gabbidon (1999a), evaluating Du Bois's work in Atlanta, has concluded that while Du Bois was at Atlanta he founded one of the first "schools" of social scientific research in the United States.

CONCLUSION

The criminological writings of W. E. B. Du Bois clearly represent some of the earliest and most insightful publications that focus on African Americans and crime. His writings anticipate later theoretical perspectives such as social disorganization and conflict theory. Du Bois concluded that African American crime in the North could be explained by the disorganization that resulted when Southern-born African Americans arrived in the unfamiliar urban environment. Besides the effects of this "social revolution," as Du Bois called the mass migration of African Americans to the North, he believed the wretched social conditions they were forced to live in also contributed to the disproportionate involvement of African Americans in the criminal justice system.

In the South, Du Bois felt African American criminality could be traced to four factors: (1) the convict-lease system; (2) the attitude of the courts; (3) lynchings of African Americans; (4) segregation. Predominant among the causes were the first two of Du Bois's explanations. That is, the convict-lease system and the attitudes of the court were the primary causes of the disproportionate representation of African Americans in the Southern criminal justice system. The passage of the black codes by the rulers of the South insured that the convict-lease system would have an ample supply of cheap laborers to do work formerly done with slave labor. Du Bois, however, realized the central role the courts played in this system. He observed it was necessary for the courts to "fix" the judgments so that African Americans were insured a trip to the state correctional system, which then leased them to eagerly awaiting Southern white landowners.

Finally, while Du Bois's writings recently have been the subject of some scholarly discourse, primarily by African Americans criminologists (see, for example, Hawkins, 1995; Gabbidon, 1996; Young and Greene, 1995), his writings and early use of numerous social scientific methodologies are pioneering and, we believe, should be viewed by a wider audience. In sum, as it has been stated elsewhere, "an accurate history of American criminology is incomplete without a discussion of W. E. B. Du Bois" (Gabbidon, 1999b)

References

Boston, T. D. (1991). W. E. B. Du Bois and the historical school of economics. *American Economics Association Papers and Proceedings* (May), 303–7.

Broderick, F. L. (1958a). German influence on the scholarship of W. E. B. Du Bois. *Phylon, 19*, 367–71.

———. (1958b). The academic training of W. E. B. Du Bois. *The Journal of Negro Education, 27*, 10–16.

———. (1974). W. E. B. Du Bois: History of an intellectual. In J. E. Blackwell & M. Janowitz (eds.), *Black sociologists: historical and contemporary perspectives* (pp. 25–55). Chicago: The University of Chicago Press.

Du Bois, W. E. B. (1898/1980). *The Negroes of Farmville, Virginia: A social study.* Washington, DC: The Department of Labor. In H. Aptheker (ed.), *Contributions by W. E. B. Du Bois in government publications and proceedings.* Millwood, NY: Kraus-Thomson Organization.

———. (1899a/1973). *The Philadelphia Negro: A social study.* Millwood, NY: Kraus-Thomson Organization Limited.

———. (1899b). The Negro and crime. *The Independent, 51* (May 18): 1355–57.

———. (1901a/1982). The spawn of slavery: The convict-lease system in the South. *The Missionary Review of the World, 14,* 737–45. In H. Aptheker (ed.), *Writings in periodical literature edited by others vol. 1 (1891–1909).* Millwood, NY: Kraus-Thomson Organization Limited.

———. (1901b/1969). *The black North in 1901: A social study.* New York: Arno Press and the New York Times.

———. (1903/1982). The laboratory in sociology at Atlanta University. *Annals of the American Academy of Political and Social Sciences, 21* (May):160–63. In H. Aptheker (ed.), *Writings in periodical literature edited by others vol. 1 (1891–1909).* Millwood, NY: Kraus-Thomson Organization Limited.

———. (ed.). (1904). *Some notes on Negro crime, particularly in Georgia.* Atlanta: Atlanta University Press.

———. (1968). *The autobiography of W. E. B. Du Bois.* International Publishers.

Durkheim, E. (1895/1964). *The rules of sociological method.* New York: The Free Press.

Franklin, J. H. & Moss, A. A. (1994). *From slavery to freedom: A history of African-Americans* (7th ed.). New York: McGraw-Hill.

Frazier, E. F. (1949). *The Negro in the United States.* NY: Macmillan Co.

Gabbidon, S. L. (1996). An argument for the inclusion of W. E. B. Du Bois in the criminology/ criminal justice literature. *Journal of Criminal Justice Education, 7* (1), 99–112.

Gabbidon, S. L. (1999a). W. E. B. Du Bois and the Atlanta school of social scientific research: 1897–1913. *Journal of Criminal Justice Education, 10* (1), 21–38.

———. (1999b). W. E. B. Du Bois on crime: American conflict theorist. *The Criminologist, 24* (1), 1, 3, 20.

Green, D. (1973). *The truth shall make ye free: The sociology of W. E. B. Du Bois.* Unpublished doctoral dissertation, University of Massachusetts, Amherst.

Harris, T. E. (1993). *Analysis of the clash over the issues between Booker T. Washington and W. E. B. Du Bois.* New York: Garland Press.

Hawkins, D. F. (1995). Ethnicity, race, and crime: A review of selected studies. In D. F. Hawkins (ed.), *Ethnicity, race, and crime: Perspectives across time and place* (pp. 11–45). Albany: SUNY Press.

Montiero, T. (1994). The revolutionary and scientific legacy of W. E. B. Du Bois. *Political Affairs* (February): 1–9.

Rudwick, E. M. (1957). W. E. B. Du Bois and the Atlanta University studies on the Negro. *The Journal of Negro Education, 26,* 466–76.

Young, V. D., & Greene, H. T. (1995). Pedagogical reconstruction: Incorporating African-American perspectives into the curriculum. *Journal of Criminal Justice Education, 6,* 85–104.

W. E. B. Du Bois
Selected References

Du Bois, W. E. B. (1896 /1986). *The suppression of the African slave-trade to the United States of America 1638–1870.* New York: Literary Classics of the United States.

————. (1899a/1973). *The Philadelphia Negro: A social study.* Millwood, New York: Kraus-Thomson Organization Limited.

————. (1899b). The Negro and crime. *The Independent, 51,* 1355–57.

————. (1900). The problem of Negro crime. *Bulletin of Atlanta University,* (February). In H. Aptheker (ed.), *Writings in periodical literature edited by others vol. 1 (1891–1909).* Millwood, NY: Kraus-Thomson Organization Limited.

————. (1901a). The spawn of slavery: The convict-lease system in the South. *The Missionary Review of the World, 14,* 737–45. In H. Aptheker (ed.), *Writings in periodical literature edited by others vol. 1 (1891–1909).* Millwood, NY: Kraus-Thomson Organization Limited.

————. (1901b/1969). *The black North in 1901: A social study.* New York: Arno Press and the New York Times.

————. (1902). Crime and our colored population. *The Nation, 75,* 499. In H. Aptheker (ed.), *Writings in periodical literature edited by others vol. 1 (1891–1909).* Millwood, NY: Kraus Thomson Organization Limited.

————. (1903). The laboratory in sociology at Atlanta University. *Annals of the American Academy of Political and Social Sciences, 21* (May), 160–63. In H. Aptheker (ed.), *Writings in periodical literature edited by others vol. 1 (1891–1909).* Millwood, NY: Kraus-Thomson Organization Limited.

————. (ed.). (1904). *Some notes on Negro crime, particularly in Georgia.* Atlanta: Atlanta University Press.

————. (1914). Lynching. *The Crisis, 7,* 239. In H. Aptheker (ed.), *Selections from* The Crisis. White Plains, NY: Kraus-Thomson International.

————. (1915a). Logic. *The Crisis, 9,* 132. In H. Aptheker (Ed.), *Selections from* The Crisis. White Plains, NY: Kraus-Thomson International.

————. (1915b). The lynching industry. *The Crisis, 9,* 196–98. In H. Aptheker (Ed.), *Selections from* The Crisis. White Plains, NY: Kraus-Thomson International.

————. (1915c). The clansman. *The Crisis, 10,* 33. In H. Aptheker (Ed.), *Selections from* The Crisis. White Plains, NY: Kraus-Thomson International.

———. (1917). Votes for women. *The Crisis, 15.* In W. E. B. Du Bois (ed.), *An ABC of color.* New York: International Publishers.

———. (1919). Rape. *The Crisis, 18,* 12–13. In H. Aptheker (Ed.), *Selections from* The Crisis. White Plains, NY: Kraus-Thomson International.

———. (1920). Extradition cases. *The Crisis, 20,* 5. In H. Aptheker (ed.), *Selections from* The Crisis. White Plains, NY: Kraus-Thomson International.

———. (1921). Crime. *The Crisis, 22,* 57.

———. (1923). A university course in lynching. *The Crisis, 26,* 55. In H. Aptheker (ed.), *Selections from* The Crisis. White Plains, NY: Kraus-Thomson International.

———. (1926a). The Shape of Fear. *North American Review, 223,* 291–304. In H. Aptheker (ed.), *Writings by W. E. B. Du Bois in periodicals edited by others (vol. 2 1910–1934).* Millwood, NY: Kraus-Thomson, Organization.

———. (1926). Crime. *The Crisis, 32,* 286–87. In H. Aptheker (ed.), *Selections from* The Crisis. White Plains, NY: Kraus-Thomson International.

———. (1927a). Negro crime. *The Crisis, 34,* 105. In H. Aptheker (ed.), *Selections from* The Crisis. White Plains, NY: Kraus-Thomson International.

———. (1927b). Lynchings. *The Crisis, 34,* 207. In H. Aptheker (ed.), *Selections from* The Crisis. White Plains, NY: Kraus-Thomson International.

———. (1927c). Mob tactics. *The Crisis, 34,* 204. In H. Aptheker (ed.), *Selections from* The Crisis. White Plains, NY: Kraus-Thomson International.

———. (1927d). The terrible truth. *The Crisis, 34,* 276. In H. Aptheker (ed.), *Selections from* The Crisis. White Plains, NY: Kraus-Thomson International.

———. (1931). Criminals. *The Crisis, 38,* In H. Aptheker (ed.), *Selections from* The Crisis. White Plains, NY: Kraus-Thomson International.

———. (1932a). Lynchings. *The Crisis, 39,* 58. In H. Aptheker (ed.), *Selections from* The Crisis. White Plains, NY: Kraus-Thomson International.

———. (1932b). Courts and jails. *The Crisis, 39.* In W. E. B. Du Bois (ed.), *An ABC of color.* New York: International Publishers.

———. (1932c). Crime. *The Crisis, 39* (July): 234–35.

———. (1936). Socialized law. *Pittsburgh Courier* (April 18). In H. Aptheker (ed.), *Newspaper columns/ by W. E. B. Du Bois (vol. 1 1883–1944).* White Plains, NY: Kraus-Thomson Organization.

———. (1941). Economic illiteracy. *Amsterdam News* (February 15). In H. Aptheker (ed.), *Newspaper columns/ by W. E. B. Du Bois (vol. 1 1883–1944).* White Plains, NY: Kraus-Thomson Organization.

———. (1942). Prisoners. *Amsterdam News* (May 30). In H. Aptheker (ed.), *Newspaper columns/ by W. E. B. Du Bois (vol. 1 1883–1944).* White Plains, NY: Kraus-Thomson Organization.

———. (1943a). Riots. *Amsterdam News* (July 3). In H. Aptheker (ed.), *Newspaper columns/ by W. E. B. Du Bois (vol. 1 1883–1944).* White Plains, NY: Kraus-Thomson Organization.

———. (1943b). Unrealistic charge. *Amsterdam News* (July 10). In H. Aptheker (ed.), *Newspaper columns/ by W. E. B. Du Bois (vol. 1 1883–1944).* White Plains, NY: Kraus-Thomson Organization.

. (1943c). On the riots. *Amsterdam News* (August 21). In H. Aptheker (Ed.), *Newspaper columns/ by W. E. B. Du Bois (vol. 1 1883–1944)*. White Plains, NY: Kraus-Thomson Organization.

Du Bois, W. E. B. & Dill, A. G. (1913). *Morals and manners among Negro Americans: Report of a social study made by Atlanta University under the patronage of the trustees of the John F. Slater Fund; with the proceedings of the 18th annual conference for the study of the Negro problems.* Atlanta: Atlanta University Press.

Notes

1. Green (1973, p. 374) and Gabbidon (1996, p. 101) have both concluded that Du Bois was close to conceptualizing white-collar crimes. He was clearly aware of the dissimilar treatment of "street crimes" and white-collar offenses (i.e., embezzlement, forgery, etc.). According to Du Bois, the dissimilar treatment of these two types of offenses should cause observers to be cautious when making assertions from available crime figures.

Monroe N. Work
Courtesy of Tuskegee University Archives

THREE

MONROE NATHAN WORK
(1866–1945)

I have undertaken to write you in detail in regard to Mr. Work because I think the qualities he has shown are so rare and so exceptional that they deserve to be recognized, and because I think it is important that you should know the sort of man you have working for you.
—Robert E. Park in a letter to Booker T. Washington, 18 October 1909, Guzman (1949, p. 441).

INTRODUCTION

Monroe Work, described by McMurray (1985) as a pioneer African American sociologist, lived during a time of widespread acceptance of racial doctrines supporting white supremacy and black inferiority. In the late 1800s and early 1900s, a few African Americans, including Work, were admitted to (white) undergraduate and graduate programs, but they were rarely accepted as scholars or hired to teach within the academic community. Rather, they were viewed as Negro scholars studying Negroes (ibid., p. 6). These early African American intellectuals also struggled with their acceptance of either W. E. B. Du Bois's perspective on the role of the educated "talented tenth," or Booker T. Washington's accomodationist approach emphasizing industrial work and farming.

Work was one of very few African Americans of his era to have an opportunity to work with both Du Bois and Washington. For over forty years he documented the Negro experience as founder and director of the Department of Records and Research at Tuskegee Normal and Industrial Institute, headed by Washington. However, Work attributed his early contact as a student with Du Bois with contributing to the development of his own belief in the importance of sociology. After working with Du Bois on a study of African American churches in Illinois for the 1903 Atlanta conference, Work realized the importance of sociological research in eliminating prejudice and misunderstandings (McMurray, 1985). For Work, gathering information and compiling exact knowledge concerning Negroes was paramount (Guzman, 1949, p. 435).

Most of the information about Negroes was made available in the *Negro Yearbook* that he founded and edited between 1912 and 1938. Throughout the 1900s, this publication was widely used as a reference for historical and sociological information pertaining to the Negro in the United States and abroad (Guzman, Jones, Hall, 1952). Work also contributed scholarly research on crime, health, and African studies to numerous journals.

Work's research and scholarly contributions, including his pioneering research on Negro crime, criminals, lynching, and social control, are summarized here. His discussions of these concepts are significant to understanding the economic, historical, social, and political context of African Americans, crime, and justice. His biographical and academic background, contributions to criminological thought, and other research topics are presented in this chapter.

BIOGRAPHICAL INFORMATION

Monroe Nathan Work was born on 15 August 1866 in Iradell County, North Carolina (McMurray, 1985, p.8). His father, Alexander Work, mother, Eliza Hobbs, and eight siblings were slaves; Monroe and two other siblings were born after emancipation (ibid., p. 8–9). Guzman (1949, p. 428) reported that Work's grandfather, Henry Work, had obtained his freedom before the Civil War ended and had purchased most of his children, but not Work's father. Work's parents worked for the Poston family until emancipation. After emancipation, his father migrated to Illinois and was joined by his wife and children in Cairo in 1867 (ibid., p. 429).

Alexander Work was part of the first wave of African American exodusters to stake a claim in Kansas. The Holmstead Act of 1860 offered land to U.S. citizens who were willing to migrate. In 1876, the family relocated to the 160-acre homestead in Sumner County (McMurray, 1985, p. 13). Eventually, Monroe would have the full responsibility of operating the family farm after his parents could no longer do so and his other siblings had moved away. Work remained on the farm until his mother died in 1889 (Guzman, 1949, p. 429).

Work's education began in Illinois and continued in Kansas. However, his high school education was delayed until he was twenty three, due in part to his responsibilities on the farm. Shortly after graduation, Work unsuccessfully sought teaching positions in Arkansas City, Kansas, and among the Creek and Cherokee Indians (McMurray, 1985, p.15). Although hired by neither, he did teach briefly at a private school, for room and board. Later that year, Work pastored an African Methodist Episcopal Church in Wellington, Kansas, for a few months before deciding to stake his own claim in Oklahoma. Still unable to acquire a teaching job, and although he was a capable farmer, Work decided to return to the ministry and continue his education in Chicago (described below).

After completing his studies in Chicago, Work met his future wife, Florence E. Hendrickson, while teaching at Georgia State Industrial College in Savannah, Georgia. They were married on 27 December 1904 and stayed together until Work's death in 1945. Although they had no children, their nieces and nephews often visited and lived with them (McMurray, 1985, p. 35).

ACADEMIC BACKGROUND AND EXPERIENCE

In 1895, when Work entered the Chicago Theological Seminary, his intent was to acquire advanced training in religion. Work soon discovered that he might not succeed as a preacher and that a theological education was too limited. However, while at the seminary and enrolled in Christian Sociology, taught by Graham Taylor, he realized the possibility of studying sociology. Under Taylor's guidance, Work studied Negro crime in the city of Chicago while enrolled in the course.

At the turn of the century, there was a close link between the Chicago Theological Seminary, the Sociology Department, and the divinity school at the University of Chicago (Young and Taylor Greene, 1995, p. 89). In 1891, the university was founded as a Baptist school endowed by John D. Rockefeller. The Sociology Department established in 1892 was the first such program in the nation. Its founder, Albion Small, was a Baptist minister. William Graham Taylor, chairman of the first Department of Christian Sociology established at the seminary in 1892, later taught part time in the Sociology Department at the University of Chicago (McMurray, 1985, p. 18, 19). Work, as a student at the seminary and the Sociology Department, was able to work with both Taylor and Small, both pioneers in American sociology.

In 1898, Work entered the University of Chicago and earned the bachelor of philosophy degree in 1902. McMurray (1985, p. 21) noted that "Work's metamorphosis into a sociologist paralleled the emergence of the discipline itself . . . . and thus [he] became one of the first African American sociologists, sharing that honor with W. E. B. Du Bois, Kelly Miller and Richard Wright, Jr."[1] Work also enrolled in the graduate program and was the first Negro to earn a master of arts degree from the University of Chicago Department of Sociology in June, 1903 (ibid., p. 30, Guzman, 1949).

Work's thesis, entitled "The Negro Real Estate Owners of Chicago," was a study of the evolution of Negroes owning property in the city that utilized both historical and sociological research methods. According to McMurray (1985, p. 29), Work asserted that Baptist Point de Saille was the first African American to own real estate in Chicago in 1790. Work interviewed the city's African Americans and included maps to illustrate the value and location of black real estate holdings. He also addressed the effect of segregation of African Americans and social disorganization on housing problems (ibid., p. 29).

Upon completion of his graduate studies, Work had the choice of a position being created for him at Langston University in Oklahoma or a position at Georgia State College (Guzman, 1949, p. 433). David R. Boyd, who had persuaded Work to continue his high school studies when he had serious thought about quitting, wanted him to take a position at Langston University that would be created for him. Boyd hoped that Work would subsequently become president of the university (ibid., p. 433). Work chose Georgia State (Industrial) College in Savannah[2] for several reasons. First, Richard Wright Sr., president of the college, was the father of one of Work's classmates at Chicago, Richard Wright Jr. (ibid.). Second, Wright Sr., a graduate of Atlanta University and a trustee, had been instrumental in implementing the Atlanta studies. Third, since Work had previously worked with Du Bois and the Atlanta studies, he was excited about the opportunity to be close to Du Bois and his research (McMurray, 1985, p. 30).

Like many other African American intellectuals, Work was deeply committed to his people. McMurray (1985, p. 30) described this as a "sense of racial responsibility that drew other members of the Talented Tenth to the Deep South." Another reality was the segregation in higher education that limited employment opportunities outside of the South. Even in the South, whites usually controlled the boards responsible for managing African American colleges and universities. While Work may have been initially excited about relocating to the South, his teaching experience was disappointing. Georgia State Industrial College, a land-grant school, was opened in 1891. At that time, the focus was on industrial education, and teaching Greek, Latin, or higher mathematics was forbidden. During the five years (1903–1908) Work taught there, he became discouraged with teaching. It did not pay well; it took up too much of his time; and the lack of adequate library facilities impeded his research interests. He was also disappointed when Savannah passed Jim Crow laws in 1906 that signaled the reversal of progress between the races in Savannah (McMurray, 1985).

Booker T. Washington, founder and principal of Tuskegee Normal and Industrial Institute in Alabama, had an interest in establishing a sociological research program as early as 1899. However, it was nine years later that members of the institute's Board of Trustees suggested that Washington be encouraged to hire someone to provide him with accurate data. In May 1908 Washington requested a meeting with Work when his train passed through Savannah on his way to deliver a speech in Beaufort, South Carolina. One month later, Work arrived at Tuskegee without a title, to study Tuskegee graduates. Work viewed his new position as an opportunity both for advancement and to focus on his research and analytical skills. However, according to McMurray (1985, p. 53), "Work discovered that a number of obstacles blocked the development of the kind of research program he had envisioned when he accepted the offer." The biggest problem confronting work and Washington was the necessity of placating the local whites who did not want the institute to threaten them. Thus, there was very little public discussion of Work's research responsibilities.

Over time, Work would transform the "Division"[3] of Records and Research into a nationally recognized resource center on Negroes. Stokes (1931) described the major functions of the Department of Records and Research as obtaining and classifying information on Negroes, publishing the results, and providing answers to questions. It was a clearing house for information on the status and developments of Negroes in America and abroad (ibid.).

CONTRIBUTIONS TO CRIMINOLOGICAL THOUGHT

Work used both historical and sociological methods to explore social problems of the early 1900s. His research interests clearly were shaped by two factors: (1) his educational background in both divinity (also referred to as the social gospel) and sociology, and (2) his interest in providing accurate facts on Negroes. One of Work's earliest research studies began in 1897 as a term paper for the Christian sociology course taught by Graham Taylor. A version of the paper, entitled "Crime among the Negroes of Chicago," was published in the *American Journal of Sociology*. This was the first article by a Negro appearing in the journal. Work was also initially involved as a student with the Atlanta University studies and conferences. He coauthored a study with Du Bois of African American churches in Illinois for the 1903 Atlanta conference (McMurray, 1985, p. 28). In 1904, he contributed two papers, entitled "Crime in Cities" and "Crime in Savannah as Compared with Chicago, Illinois" (Du Bois, 1904).

Guzman (1949) provides a comprehensive listing of Work's research publications (and professional affiliations) compiled from the Work Papers in the Department of Records and Research at Tuskegee Institute. Most of his research appeared in *The Negro Yearbook*, which he edited between 1912 and 1938. These yearbooks provided extensive information on ninety eight topics, including lynchings and health, two social problems Work was especially concerned about.

During his Tuskegee years, Work compiled facts related to Negroes in America and Africa from several sources, including books, newspapers and periodicals, government reports, special reports, and questionnaires. All information received was classifed and filed alphabetically by year (McMurray, 1985, pp. 73–74). He also traveled to Europe to collect references on Negroes in Africa.

In addition to his work for the Research Department, Work continued to conduct historical and sociological research on Negroes. He was particularly interested in (1) race and class issues in the South (Work, 1913, 1915, 1920a, 1920b, 1936, 1937), (2) Africa studies (Work, 1906, 1907, 1908, 1909, 1916), and (3) the race problem (Work, 1924, 1925). His works often appeared in the *Journal of Negro History, Social Forces,* and *Southern Workman.*

Like Du Bois, Work was one of the first African American scholars to study Negro crime, including its causes, extent, control, race and class differences, delinquency, and lynching. His contributions to criminological thought are found in his two classic writings, "Crime among the Negroes of Chicago," and "Negro Criminality in the South," as well as in the publications of the *Eighth Atlanta Conference, Ninth Atlanta Conference,* and an article entitled "Problems of Adjustment of Race and Class in the South." He also prepared resource materials on black laws, crime, Negro police, incidents of police brutality, race riots, and discrimination in legal penalties for *The Negro Yearbook* and *A Bibliography of the Negro in Africa and America.*

According to Young and Taylor Greene (1995), Work and most African American scholars emphasize several major themes in their research, including social disorganization, the impact of the administration of justice on crime, African American criminals as a special group of African Americans, the use of statistics, and economics and crime. Additionally, Work (and Du Bois) pioneered the importance of including a historical framework for understanding Negro crime.

Negro Crime

As previously mentioned, Work (1900) first studied Negro crime as a student in Chicago. This research described (1) Negro crime in the United States utilizing prisoner statistics from the Eleventh Census, (2) the Negro population in Chicago, (3) Negro crime in Chicago utilizing police records, data for the Chicago house of correction, and (4) a brief discussion of the causes of Negro crime. Not surprisingly, Work found an increase in the proportion of Negroes arrested and confined in Chicago. However, the average per cent of Negro arrests changed very little during the 1888 through 1892 (9.41 percent) and 1893 through 1897 periods (9.50 percent). Work also provided a comparative analysis of Negro arrests between 1890 and 1897 in Chicago; Charleston, South Carolina; New York City; Richmond, Virginia; and Washington, DC. He concluded that "[the proportion of] negro arrests in Chicago is from two to five times as great as the proportion of negro arrests to negro population in these cities" (Work, 1900, p. 210).

Interestingly, Work presented a description of the gender and age of persons arrested as well as information on the types of offenses committed. Last, Work (1990, p. 222) challenged the prevailing racial doctrine, which posited that the excess of crime was due to "negro retrograding." He noted that if Negroes were making progress, there were other causes of crime, including economic stress and their transitional state. He believed that Negroes in Chicago were in a poorer economic condition, which accounted for their excess of crime (ibid., p. 223).

One of Work's greatest contributions to criminological thought is his emphasis on the historical context of crime. In "Negro Criminality in the South" (1913), he examined Negro crime prior to and after emancipation, in an effort to better understand the problem. He notes that prior to the Civil War there were "severe" laws for dealing with Negro criminals, although there were few criminals. After the war, the increase in Negro crime was affected by the breakdown of social control and the migration by Negroes from rural to urban areas and from the South to the North. While there were more Negro criminals after emancipation, Work (1987, p. 64) notes that the majority of "freedmen" were not "lawless."

Work described the increase in Negro criminals by analyzing 1858 prisoner statistics for Georgia and United States census data on prisoners for 1858, 1870, 1880, 1890, and 1904. He found that while the number of Negro prisoners had steadily increased in both the North and the South, the prisoner rate was higher in the North than in the South and higher for Negroes than for whites. This was due at least in part to the age of persons who migrated to the North and the conditions they confronted in the cities. Work also described prison commitments by nationality. Here he noted that Negroes had a lower prison commitment rate than Mexicans, Italians, Austrians, French, Canadians, and Russians. In the conclusion of his 1913 article, he recommended several strategies to prevent and control crime including the formation of Negro law and order leagues, interracial Christian civic leagues, adoption of principles of prison reform, and abolition of convict lease systems.

The Administration of Justice, the Convict Lease System, and Social Control

The administration of justice was an important theme in Work's publications. He believed that the use of the law to punish and restrain rather than protect Negroes resulted in their fear, and evasion of, and lack of respect for it. The law often imposed severe sanctions and unjust sentences for misdemeanors, petty offenses, and vagrancy (Young & Taylor Greene, 1995). Work (1913) noted Judge Thomas's comments at the Southern Sociological Congress in Nashville (1912) that disparities in punishment could lead to distrust of its administration.

Work (1913), like Du Bois earlier, criticized the convict-lease system in Southern prisons. Shortly after the Civil War, convicts were a source of revenue to states that leased them to those needing labor. According to Young and Taylor Greene (1995, p. 91), Work argued that "the number of convicts increased because of the financial benefits of the convict-lease system. The implication is that the criminalization of Negroes, the major contributors to the convict-lease system, and their movement into the system in large numbers can be attributed to more than just their behavior."

Social Control

Social control is another theme appearing in Work's research (1913, 1937). In 1913 he attributed Negro criminality in the South to the "confusion and disorder" that resulted from the removal of old forms of social control. Work was particularly concerned with the economic, moral, and political context of race and class in the South. He noted the problems of adjustment caused by the transition from an agricultural to an industrial-commercial economy and provided an overview of social control during the antebellum (agricultural) period (Work, 1937).

Work (1937) identified three classes of whites in the antebellum South: the upper class, consisting primarily of planters; the middle class, consisting of farmers and others; and a third class, poor whites. Social control was achieved through political manipulation and domination of the middle-class and poor whites as well as the Negroes. External and internal social controls were useful for conserving and promoting the economic, political, and social interests of the planter class. The planter class manipulated the other whites by emphasizing the superiority of whites and inferiority of Negroes and creating a fear complex. Additionally, the moral order was used to conserve the interests of the planter class. Slavery was believed to be morally justified by Divine authority.

What is more important, during this era, the law was used to "keep the Negro in his place, protect the Negro as long as he remained in his place, . . . make justice severe, sure and swift" (Work, 1937, p.111). Work viewed this role of the law (in social control) as the origin of differences in the application of the law to whites and Negroes.

Lynching

Another more controversial aspect of social control, or racial control, that received considerable attention in Work's research was lynching. After the Civil War, for various reasons, lynchings of Negroes increased. Work, Du Bois, Wells-Barnett, and numerous others were involved in the antilynching campaign during the early 1900s. Work became actively involved in the antilynching movement by collecting and disseminating the *Tuskegee Lynching Report* (Work, n.d.). This semiannual report provided statistics on number of lynchings, race of the victims, nature of their reported offenses, percentage of lynchings for rape, and a breakdown of lynchings by state. Later, Work added information on antilynchng laws and statistics on the indictments, convictions, and sentences of lynchers (McMurray, 1985, p. 122).

The *Tuskegee Lynching Report* (Work, n.d.) was one of the three leading sources of lynching data in the early 1900s; the *Chicago Tribune* and the National Association for the Advancement of Colored People (NAACP) also published lynching statistics. The Tuskegee reports were widely accepted as accurate, especially in the South, and frequently included in other publications, including the *American Year Book,* the *International Yearbook,* and the *World Almanac.*

Criminology and Criminal Justice Reference Sources

Work, through the publications of the Department of Records and Research, provided the primary source of information on numerous topics including Negro crime. Most of the information appeared, over the years, in *The Negro Yearbook* and *A Bibliography of the Negro in Africa and America.*

In the first yearbook, the black laws of several states before 1865 were summarized. These laws were designed to define and restrict the position of free persons of color. Interestingly, several states, including Iowa, Illinois, Indiana, Ohio, Louisiana, Missouri, Maryland, Georgia, and Kentucky, prohibited free Negroes from entering. Delaware allowed immigration of free Negroes from Maryland only. Virginia required that any emancipated slave had to leave the state within 12 months or forfeit his freedom.

The yearbooks also provided descriptive information on the race riots occurring between 1915 and 1921. The descriptive summaries identify several sources of riots, including influx of Negroes from the South (Chester, PA, 1918), moving into segregated neighborhoods (Philadelphia, PA, 1918), friction between city police and Negro soldiers (Houston, TX, 1917), bad political conditions, (Tulsa, OK, 1921), drowning of a Negro youth (Chicago, 1919), and alleged attacks by Negroes on white women (Washington, DC, 1919). The yearbooks also identified complaints of Negroes after the riots such as their disarming by the police and harsher sentences by the courts (*The Negro Yearbook,* 1918–1919, 1921–1922).

In the 1921 through 1922 edition of *The Negro Yearbook,* information on Negro policemen, policewomen, and probation officers is provided. The 1931 through 1932 yearbook contained a section on Negro crime that included crime and delinquency rates, reported police brutality incidents, and disparities in sentencing of Negroes and whites.

Work compiled a reference list on Negro crime that identified publications on crime and the Negro, the convict systems and the Negro, and Negro juvenile delinquency by both white and African American scholars. These references, along with others on lynching and riots, appeared in *A Bibliography of the Negro in Africa and America.*

CONCLUSION

Monroe Nathan Work, one of the leading authorities of information and facts on Negroes in the United States and Africa, labored for over forty years to develop the collection of the Department of Records and Research at Tuskegee Institute. During this time, he remained actively involved in scholarly research and professional associations, including the American Negro Academy, the Association for the Study of Negro Life and History, and sociological associations and was often invited to speak at conferences (Guzman, 1949). Work compiled reference materials related to African studies during his Tuskegee years. He and his wife also traveled to Europe to identify additional reference sources to include in *A Bibliography of the Negro in America and Africa.*

The department was an important research center, visited frequently by other African American scholars and utilized by the United States Bureau of Education, the Census Bureau, the NAACP Bureau of Research, and several universities, including the Universities of Chicago, Pennsylvania, Virginia, and California (McMurray, 1985, p. 74). It was also supported financially by philanthropic individuals and foundations such as the Carnegie Corporation, the Phelps Stokes Fund, the Rockefeller Foundation, and the Rosenwald Fund (Guzman, 1949, p. 446).

While the focus here is on crime-related research, Work was also actively involved in research related to many other topics. Two of his special interest areas were Negro health and African studies. His first efforts in the area of health began in Savannah, Georgia, when he established Negro Health Week in 1905. At the 1914 Tuskegee Negro Conference, Work prepared a series of charts to illustrate the status of Negro Health (Guzman, 1949, p. 452). In 1915 Booker T. Washington placed Work in charge of National Negro Health Week, to be held the first week of February. Shortly thereafter, Work was instrumental in involving the United States Public Health Services in the national negro health movement (ibid., p. 453–454). Although Work did not publish very much health-related research, he is credited with bringing the issue to the forefront in America and with increasing the life expectancy of African Americans (Guzman, 1949; McMurray, 1985).

His contributions to criminological thought are significant because he provided historical information on the causes and extent of crime among Negroes. His analyses of arrest data and prisoner statistics were comprehensive, providing comparative studies of African Americans in cities in the North and South, as well as comparing their crime rates to native born whites and immigrant whites. The resource information on various criminal justice topics available in the *Negro Yearbook* and *A Bibliography of the Negro in Africa and America* were unparalleled at the time they were published.

Before his death, Monroe Work had a national reputation for his contributions to understanding Negroes, their progress, and their problems. He was also recognized for his accomplishments by the Harmon Foundation of New York, the Alumni Association of the University of Chicago, and Howard University, where he received an honorary degree in 1943 (McMurray, 1958, p.142). He was among the first to recognize the importance of collecting facts in an effort to create a more realistic African American identity (Williams, 1997).

McMurray (1958, p. 101) concluded that Work subscribed to the views of both Du Bois and Washington. Like Du Bois, he believed in the obligation that educated Negroes had to their race. Like Washington, he believed in self-help but also recognized the barriers confronted by African Americans, especially in the criminal justice system. Williams (1997) notes Work's influence on Washington as well. He credits Work with being instrumental in changing Washington's negative views of Africans, which provided a more logical foundation for Washington's belief that blacks could be self-reliant.

Like other early African American scholars, Work was a generalist. His writings on crime were only part of his overall contributions. Nevertheless, he is important because he was among the first African American scholars to call into question ideologies that centered on race, heredity, and black degeneracy that had direct implications for explaining crime, especially among African Americans.

References

Du Bois, W. E. B. (1903). *Eighth Atlanta conference.* Atlanta, GA: Atlanta University.
————. (1904). *Ninth Atlanta conference.* Atlanta, GA: Atlanta University.
Guzman, J. (1949). Monroe Nathan Work and his contributions. *Journal of Negro History, 34,* 428–61.
Guzman, J. Jones L.N. & Hall, W. (1952). The *Negro yearbook.* Tuskegee, AL: Tuskegee Institute.
McMurray, L. (1985). *Recorder of the black experience A biography of Monroe Nathan Work.* Baton Rouge: Louisiana State University Press.
Stokes, A. (1931). *Tuskegee Institute, the first fifty years.* Tuskegee, AL: Tuskegee Institute Press.
Williams, V. (1997). Monroe N. Work's contribution to Booker T. Washington's nationalist legacy. *The Western Journal of Black Studies, 21,* 85–91.
Work, M. (1900). Crime among the Negroes of Chicago. *American Journal of Sociology, 6,* 204–23.

————. (1906). Some parallelisms in the development of Africans and other races. *Southern Workman* November, 614–621.

————. (1907). The African medicine man . *Southern Workman,* October, 561–564.

————. (1908). An African system of writing. *Southern Workman,* October, 518–526.

————. (1909). The African family as an institution. *Southern Workman,* June, July, August, 343–353, 391–397, 433–440.

————. (1912–1938). *The Negro yearbook.* Tuskegee, AL: Tuskegee Institute Press.

————. (1913). Negro criminality in the South. *Annals of the American Academy of Political and Social Sciences, 49,* 74–80.

————. (1915). The South and the health of Negroes. *Proceedings of the Southern Sociological Congress,* 412–421.

————. (1916). The passing tradition and the African civilization. *Journal of Negro History,* 1, 34–41.

————. (1920a). Some Negro members of Reconstruction conventions and legislatures and of Congress. *Journal of Negro History,* 5, 63–119.

————. (1920b). The South's labor problem. *South Atlantic Quarterly,* XIX, 1–8.

————. (1924). The race problem in cross section: The Negro in 1923. *Social Forces,* 2, 245–252.

————. (1925). Aspects and tendencies of the race problem. *Proceedings of the American Sociological Society,* vol. 19.

————. (1936). Racial and economic forces in land tenure in the South. *Social Forces,* 205–15. Presented at the meeting of the Southern Sociological Society in Atlanta, Georgia, 17–18 April 1936.

————. (1937). Problems of adjustment of the race and class in the South. *Social Forces, 16,* 108–17. Presented at the meeting of the Southern Sociological Society in Birmingham, Alabama, 3 April 1937.

————. (n.d.). *Tuskegee lynching report.* Tuskegee, AL: Tuskegee Institute.

Young, V. & Taylor Greene, H. (1995). Pedagogical reconstruction: Incorporating African-American perspectives into the curriculum. *Journal of Criminal Justice Education,* 6, 85–104.

Monroe N. Work
Selected References

Work, M. (1900). Crime among the Negroes of Chicago. *American Journal of Sociology,* 6, 204–23.

————. (1903). *The Negro Real Estate Owners of Chicago.* Master's Thesis, Chicago: University of Chicago.

————. (Ed.). (1912–1938). *The Negro Yearbook.* Tuskegee, AL: Tuskegee Institute.

————. (1913). Negro criminality in the South. *Annals of the American Academy of Political and Social Sciences, 49,* 74–80.

————. (1916). The passing tradition and the African civilization. *Journal of Negro History* 1916.

————. (1924). The race problem in cross section: The Negro in 1923. *Social Forces,*

————. (1924). Taking stock of the race problem in cross section: A statistical review and interpretation of the facts at the end of the year 1923. *Opportunity.*

————. (1925). Aspects and tendencies of the race problem. *Proceedings of the American Sociological Society* volume 19.

————. (1925). *The law versus the mob.* New York: Federal Council of the Churches of Christ in America, Commission on the Church and Race Relations.

————. (1936). Racial and economic forces in land tenure in the South. *Social Forces,* 205–15. Presented at the meeting of the Southern Sociological Society in Atlanta, Georgia, 17–18 April 1936.

————. (1937). Problems of adjustment of the race and class in the South. *Social Forces,* 108–17. Presented at the meeting of the Southern Sociological Society in Birmingham, Alabama, 3 April 1937.

————. (n.d.). *Tuskegee lynching report.* Tuskegee, AL: Tuskegee Institute.

Notes

1. Du Bois was not trained as a sociologist.

2. The college is now known as Savannah State University.

3. The term *division* was used so as not to imply too much status to the unit or the person in charge. The title was changed to *department* in 1919.

E. Franklin Frazier
Courtesy of Moorland-Springarn Research Center
Howard University

Four

E. Franklin Frazier
(1894–1962)

There has been a rather widespread feeling or belief that studies of the Negroes did not have the same academic status or did not require the same intellectual maturity or discipline as the study of other sociological problems . . . As a consequence of this attitude, the study of vitally important social problems, for which the Negro provided incomparably valuable materials, was left to anyone who might occupy himself with such lowly sociological materials. It is only recently that the sociological study of the Negro has acquired the academic status of studies of other groups and has attracted the serious attention of sociologists.
—E. Franklin Frazier, The Presidential Address, American Sociological Society, Chicago, Illinois, December 1948 (Frazier, 1949c)

INTRODUCTION

E. Franklin Frazier was a pioneer in African American studies and sociology. He was an outspoken scholar, militant, and race man and was viewed as an "improper" Negro for his time.[1] He purposely chose to be a scholar and not a leader in an effort to devote his time and energy to intellectual achievements. According to Drake (1967), Frazier viewed his scholarly work as a contribution to shattering the myth of Negro inferiority. During his career he authored several classics including, *Black Bourgeoisie, The Negro Family in Chicago, The Negro Family in the United States, The Negro in the United States,* and *Race and Culture Contacts in the Modern World.*

Frazier was well known, both nationally and internationally. In the early 1920s, he was a research fellow of the American Scandinavian Foundation (their first Negro candidate) and studied in Denmark. In 1940 Frazier received a fellowship to study the Negro family in Brazil and the West Indies from the John Simon Guggenheim Foundation. In 1948, Frazier became the first African American to head a national scholarly organization when he served as president of the American Sociological Association.[2] In the 1950s Frazier visited both England and France. He was invited to England to deliver three "Special University Lectures in Sociology" at the University of London in May 1953 (Edwards, 1968a). Between 1951 and 1953, Frazier worked for UNESCO in Paris, France. Two years later, *Bourgeoisie Noire* was published in France. Throughout the 1950s Frazier's research examined race relations in the Caribbean and Africa.

Like other early African American scholars, Frazier's writings on crime and delinquency are especially important temporally. His contributions to criminological thought are found in his analyses of basic sociological concepts such as acculturation, the family, race relations, social disorganization, and social processes. His specific focus upon systems of social relationships contributed greatly to understanding criminality in a sociological context. He also provided some research on crime in African American communities during the early twentieth century. At the time, they were significant contributions and later provided the foundation for future research.

BIOGRAPHICAL INFORMATION

E. Franklin Frazier was born in Baltimore, Maryland, on 24 September 1894 to James H. and Hattie (Clark) Frazier. His father was a bank messenger, described by Edwards (1968a, p. ix) as "intensely race-conscious." Frazier's father, the son of slaves, never attended school but taught himself to read and write. He encouraged his children to get an education so they would not have to experience the humiliation he endured (Davis, 1962).

Frazier attended segregated public schools and graduated from high school in 1912 (Edwards, 1982, p. 241). He was awarded a scholarship to Howard University by his high school (Davis, 1962). According to Frazier, "my curiosity to learn everything was at fever heat, my course of study embraced a wide range of courses, including mathematics and physical science, literature, Latin, Greek, French, German, as well as social sciences (in Odum, 1951, pp. 233–34). Although sociology was not in the curriculum, Frazier was interested in social problems during his college days. He was also a member of the Intercollegiate Socialist Society and president of both the German and the political science clubs.

Davis (1962) relates an experience during Frazier's senior year that had a lasting impact on the young student. Woodrow Wilson, an educator and former college president, had invited universities and colleges to participate in the inaugural parade. Howard was given a position at the end of the Negro section, which came last in the parade. Frazier and other students petitioned the Inaugural Committee to place Howard with other American colleges in alphabetical order. The request was denied, although Howard was allowed, as a compromise, to march at the end of the white college section. While other committee members accepted the compromise, Frazier refused to participate.

Frazier graduated cum laude from Howard University in 1916 (Edwards, 1968a; 1968b). Upon graduation, he joined a small group of college educated Negroes confronted with the reality of their unique status in a segregated American society. Decades later, Drake (1967, p. viii) described Frazier as an ambivalent son of the "crossways," a term used to describe dilemmas that characterize the transition for youth from a southern rural to a middle states urban way of life.

In 1922, Frazier married Marie Ellen Brown, the daughter of a Baptist preacher and leader in North Carolina. Although they had no children of their own, they often were visited by (Mrs. Frazier's) nieces and nephews (Davis, 1962).

ACADEMIC BACKGROUND AND EXPERIENCE

Davis (1962), Edwards (1968a, 1982), and Odum (1951) provide in-depth information on E. Franklin Frazier's academic background and teaching experiences. Upon completion of his undergraduate studies at Howard University, Frazier taught a range of subjects, including sociology and social work, at Negro public, private, and church-related (high) schools for three years. He taught mathematics at Tuskegee Institute, summer school at Fort Valley High and Industrial School, math and history at Baltimore High School, and English and history at St. Paul's Normal and Industrial School in Lawrenceville, Virginia (Davis, 1962; Odum, 1951; Edwards, 1968a, p. ix).

In 1919, Frazier received a scholarship to Clark University in Worcester, Massachusetts. Under Professor Frank H. Hankins, he began his career as a sociologist (Odum, 1951, p. 234). According to Drake (1967, p. x), "Frazier's ideological and intellectual orientation took form in the crisis period that followed World War I . . . [W]hen race riots erupted throughout the United States in 1919, his attention became focused upon the people of the Great Migration to the North."

After obtaining his master's degree in 1920, Frazier was a research fellow at the New York School of Social Work (1920–1921) and a fellow of the American-Scandinavian Foundation at the University of Copenhagen in Denmark (1921–22) (Odum, 1951, p. 235; Edwards, 1968a, p. xi). In 1922, Frazier was an instructor in sociology at Morehouse College and later became director of the Atlanta School of Social Work. While in Atlanta, Frazier published a controversial article, entitled "The Pathology of Race Prejudice," that compared the mechanisms of prejudice behavior to those of mental illness. As a result, his life was threatened, and he was forced to leave the city (Edwards, 1968a).

In 1928, Frazier went to Chicago to pursue doctoral studies in sociology at the University of Chicago. He was awarded the Ph.D. in 1931, and his dissertation was published a year later as *The Negro Family in Chicago* (Edwards, 1982, p. 242). Drake (1967, p. xi) noted that "there were no posts available at white universities for brilliant Negro scholars in those days, so Frazier accepted a position at Fisk University in Tennessee."

Frazier stayed at Fisk until 1934 when he returned to his alma mater, Howard University. Shortly after his arrival at Howard, he completed a study of Negro youth in Washington, D.C., and Louisville, Kentucky, for the Negro Youth Commission. At Howard he was known for his radicalism, and criticism of the black bourgeoisie. Nevertheless, he served as head of the Department of Sociology until his death in 1962. During his career, he also taught at the New York School of Social Work,

Columbia University, New York University, Carleton College, Sarah Lawrence College, and the University of California at Berkeley (Edwards, 1982, p. 243, Odum, 1951, p. 235–36). Additionally, he served as chief of the Division of Applied Social Science of UNESCO in the early 1950s.

Contributions to Criminological Thought

Criminality, which thrives among Negroes in an environment of poverty and social disorganization, has its roots in juvenile delinquency.
—Frazier (1949a, p. 649)

As previously stated, Frazier is considered a pioneer in American sociology due to his substantial contribution to the sociological body of knowledge. As a student of the Chicago School of Sociology, he was influenced by and utilized its concepts and methods. For example, the ecological approach and concept of social disorganization appeared in many of his studies (Frazier, 1932, 1937a, 1937b, 1939a, 1939b, 1940). At the same time, his critique of theoretical approaches and research methods of the Chicago School and other American sociologists is one of his major contributions to sociological research. For example, Frazier criticized the absence of analyses of human interaction involving social definitions and communication in the study of human ecology (Frazier, 1953).

G. Franklin Edwards (1968a, p. vii), a friend and colleague of Frazier, states in the introduction to *E. Franklin Frazier on Race Relations* that two major themes characterize Frazier's work: "the historical development, structure, and functions of the Negro family . . . , and the problems and processes of race relations." Frazier's research also includes studies of urbanization and social change that included crime and delinquency, the Negro middle class, desegregation, and comparative analyses of race relations and the family in Brazil, the Caribbean, and Africa. According to Edwards (ibid, p. viii),

> Central to his concern with urbanization was the manner in which this process produced changes in Negro life primarily in the family and in forms of social and economic status, and secondarily in individual behavior. It was the influence of the larger community forces upon the institutions of Negro life, and, conversely, the impact made by the presence of the Negro upon the larger society of which he was a part that were the central foci of Frazier's research interests.

Frazier contributed to the epistemology of sociology by challenging traditional approaches to both theory and research methods. Frazier's theoretical and methodological contributions are evident both in his research on the family and race

relations and in his theoretical writings (Frazier, 1947, 1953). In an age of quantitative and empirical research, he was well known and often criticized for his nonquantitative methods. One of Frazier's major contributions to sociological methods was his
study of systems of social relationships in the context of their natural history. For
example, Frazier emphasized the historical factors that shaped the Negro family in his
research. This required qualitative methods that he not only utilized but strongly
encouraged others to use as well. He also believed that both economic and political
factors were critical to sociological inquiry. As previously stated, Frazier also challenged the ecological approach and attitudinal studies. Frazier was particularly concerned with the absence of analyses of social relationships in sociological research. He
was critical of both attitudinal and quantitative research methods that were devoid of
analyses of social definitions and communication in human relations. This was due to
his belief in an organic rather than an atomistic conception of social life.

According to the organic view, the acts of individuals are meaningful in the
context of the organization of the behavior of individuals. It is different from the
atomistic conception that views society as an aggregate of individuals with similar
behaviors and attitudes. Frazier believed that social behavior involved both interaction and communication, which had subjective meanings. In order to better understand collective living, institutions, and other structured behavior, sociologists had to
examine ecological patterns of human association (symbiosis), as well as social definitions and communication (Frazier, cited in Edwards, 1968a, p. 4).

Frazier's literature reviews related to his research on African Americans are also
important. He provided in-depth analyses of literature available on the African
American family (Frazier, 1939a), African Americans in the United States (Frazier,
1949b/1957), crime and delinquency (Frazier, 1949), and race relations (Frazier,
1947). His review of the literature on African Americans and crime (described below)
was the first to include research by both African American and white scholars.

Frazier's contributions to criminological thought are extensive in spite of the
fact that crime and explaining crime were never the primary foci of his research. His
research on crime and delinquency is found in *The Negro Family in the United States,*
The Negro in the United States, "Theoretical Structure of Sociology and Sociological
Research," "Negro Harlem: An Ecological Study," and *Negro Youth at the Crossways.*
His historical research examined the social control of African Americans before and
after slavery. He also provided one of the most comprehensive reviews of the literature
on African American crime and delinquency (Frazier, 1949a). In the Chicago School
tradition, he examined the ecology of crime and delinquency among Negroes in
Chicago, Illinois; Harlem, New York City; Nashville, Tennessee; and Washington,
D.C. His research often presented crime statistics and trends, but he viewed them as
contributing little to understanding either crime or delinquency. Instead, he studied
the problems of crime and delinquency in the context of family and community
social systems. Using qualitative methods, he provided insight into the social and
economic aspects of crime and delinquency among Negroes by providing narratives

from his field studies. He also used the participant-observer method to provide detailed information on the nature and causes of crime, delinquency, and dependency. His contributions are described in more detail below.

African American Crime

Frazier's most important contribution to criminological thought is his review of explanations of African American crime and delinquency in the first half of the twentieth century. This review is found in chapter 25 in *The Negro in the United States*. Unlike other sociologists, Frazier (1949) not only included the writings of both white and African American scholars but also focused specifically on studies and explanations of Negro criminality during slavery, and emancipation, before the mass migration North, between the world wars, and during the 1940s. While there were several early studies of Negro crime during slavery, most of the research reviewed by Frazier attempted to interpret the high rate of Negro criminality in the United States after emancipation.

Interestingly, there were opposing viewpoints about the extent of crime among Negroes during slavery. Some erroneously believed there was no crime, while others described the slaves' involvement in crime as retaliations against whites. According to Frazier (1949a), several white scholars attributed Negro criminality to their lack of respect, childlike and primitive race, and psychical characteristics during the late 1800s and early 1900s. African American scholars were more likely to explain Negro criminality as a function of social disorganization following emancipation, urban conditions, and the age of Negroes who migrated to the North.

Frazier reviewed the work of Sellin (1928), who noted that while both white and African American scholars accepted the higher criminal rate among Negroes as true, there were many problems with the statistical data upon which rates were based. Racial discrimination, irresponsibility of police in the South, harsher sentences, and other social factors (unemployment, gambling, etc.) contributed to the apparent criminality rates, although not necessarily to the real criminality rates. Frazier also cited case studies of Negro prisoners and crime among Negroes in Harlem to support Sellin's argument.

Frazier also reviewed the work of Johnson (1941), who analyzed causes of Negro crime in relation to the administration of justice. Unlike other early white scholars, Johnson dismissed the significance of race in explaining criminality. Rather, he analyzed the lower caste position of the Negro to explain its role in Negro criminality. Last, Frazier reviewed the work of Myrdal, who also considered the lower caste position of the Negro, as well as historical, social, and economic factors that influence both legal injustice and criminality.

Social Control and Crime

Frazier addresses social control in several of his writings (1937b, 1947, 1949a, 1953). He traces the origins of social control of African Americans to the history, economics, and politics of the plantation system in the South. He argued that the economic exploitation of slaves required a system to maintain order that was often both informal and extralegal. Although the plantation was an industrial institution, it became a type of social institution with its own traditions, customs, and system of social control that included both physical force and punishment (Frazier, 1953, p. 12). After emancipation, social control was maintained both formally and informally through a system of castes and divisions along racial lines. Eventually, racial prejudice, described by Frazier as an emotional attitude, was utilized to preserve the traditional order. Frazier also discussed the absence of "communal controls" as one of the causes of crime and delinquency. In an article entitled "Negro Harlem: An Ecological Study,"[3] and in "Crime and Delinquency," Frazier alluded to the immoral and illegal behaviors that were found in Harlem, primarily as a result of the removal of normal social restraints. Frazier (ibid., p. 645) was referring to the lack of economic power that often resulted in an increased availability of "vicious and antisocial behavior" in Harlem for both whites and Negroes.

Frazier (1949a) viewed the family and other community institutions, such as the church, as agents of social control. The importance of the family in social control is found in his ecological research in Chicago and Harlem. He specifically focuses on the role of the family in social control in his juvenile delinquency research presented below.

Juvenile Delinquency

> *The incidence of juvenile delinquency is closely tied up with the organization of the community. Juvenile delinquency flourishes in those areas where the Negro, because of his poverty and cultural backwardness, is forced to find a dwelling-place. In the slum areas of Negro communities, because of the numerous broken homes and the employment of the mother, the children lack parental control which is sometimes able to offset the influence of the vicious environment.*
> —Frazier (1939b, p. 280)

Frazier explored the problem of juvenile delinquency in "Negro Harlem: An Ecological Study," *The Negro Family in the United States, Negro Youth at the Crossways,* and *The Negro in the United States.* He conducted field research and provided case studies of delinquents and delinquency in Harlem (New York City), Nashville, Tennessee; Washington, D.C.; and Chicago, Illinois. Frazier often included adult and youth narratives to contextualize the problem of delinquency. He also presented juvenile court statistics compiled by the U.S. Children's Bureau to describe the extent and trends of Negro delinquency during the first half of the twentieth century. The major focus of his delinquency research was the role of the family in delinquency, specifically the social disorganization of Negro families. He also utilized the ecological approach to describe the patterns of delinquency in Chicago and Harlem.

Frazier reported similarities in delinquency in his comparative analyses of delinquent Negro youth in Chicago, Harlem, and Nashville (Frazier, 1939b). He noted that in Harlem and Nashville, the majority of delinquents were males, between the ages of ten and sixteen, and were most often arrested for larceny and burglary. Girls were usually charged with incorrigibility. In the communities Frazier studied, Negro delinquency rates were higher than that of white youth, although there was no identifiable trend among Negroes (Frazier, 1939b).

In chapter 17 of *The Negro Family in the United States,* entitled, "Rebellious Youth," Frazier (1939b, p. 268) states, "The disorganization of Negro family life in the urban environment, together with the absence of communal controls, results in a high delinquency rate among Negro boys and girls." In this study, Negro boys and girls were younger that white youth brought before the courts. Frazier included vignettes of the circumstances of youth charged in Nashville to identify social factors contributing to delinquency in the South. Evidence of broken families, immorality, ineffective socialization, and the breakdown and/or absence of standards in the urban environment that were available in the rural environment were often cited in the vignettes.

"Rebellious Youth" (1939b) and "Crime and Delinquency" (1949a) both include delinquency data and an overview of delinquency and community disorganization that had previously appeared in other Frazier writings. A comparative analysis of delinquency in both Harlem and Chicago was often presented. He emphasized the ecological approach and often noted the decline in delinquency rates as social disorganization diminished.

Other Contributions to Criminological Thought

Frazier's research on the family, race relations, and the middle class also contributes to our understanding of crime and criminal behavior. The role of the family is central to many psychological and social process theories of delinquency (Aichorn, 1963; Hirschi, 1969; Nye, 1958; Reckless, 1961). Frazier understood the importance of the family in society and devoted a considerable amount of research to understanding African American families, often neglected or viewed as pathological by majority scholars. For Frazier, race relations defined the problems of African Americans in our society. This continues to be an important issue in the study of criminology and criminal justice due to the overrepresentation of African Americans as offenders and as victims of police violence. Research on the middle class is also important today. Frazier's research on the family, race relations, and the middle class is summarized below.

Research on the Family

Frazier viewed the study of the family important because (1) it enlightened the study of race and culture contacts by providing insights on acculturation and assimilation, and (2) it helped understand sociological aspects of family dynamics. According to Edwards (1968a), Frazier first began writing on the Negro family while working in Atlanta, Georgia. Later, at the University of Chicago, he studied Negro families in Chicago. According to Edwards (1968a, p. xii–xiii), he was the first to combine two methodological tools—human ecology and personal documents—in his study of the Chicago Negro community. Frazier viewed the family as a social system that was affected by historical, social, economic, and political factors, including "the break-down of the African heritage, slavery, emancipation, urbanization . . . race prejudice and discrimination" (ibid., p. xvi). His primary focus was on the Negro family in the context of the Negro community and in interaction with the larger American society. Frazier's first contribution to the study of the family culminated in his dissertation and a book entitled *The Negro Family in Chicago*. Perhaps his greatest contribution to the study of the family appeared in 1939 in his seminal work entitled *The Negro Family in the United States*. Noted sociologist Ernest Burgess described Frazier's book "as the most valuable contribution to the literature on the family in twenty years" (Drake, 1967, p. xi).

Frazier's research on the Negro family contributed to the body of knowledge in numerous ways. First, it identified the disorganizing effects of urban areas on Negro families. Second, it identified stable as well as what would be described today as "dysfunctional" family units in Negro communities. Third, it influenced social work approaches to dealing with Negro families. Fourth, it offered an alternative to the prevailing ideology of biological explanations for Negro family life. Last, it provided the foundation for comparative analyses of Negroes in the United States, Brazil, and Africa (Edwards, 1968a). Frazier believed that the study of the family offered the best approach to understanding assimilation and acculturation in the study of race relations.

Research on Race and Culture Contacts

Frazier's research on race relations in the United States and abroad is extensive (Frazier, 1924, 1927, 1940/1967, 1942, 1947, 1949d, 1953, 1957a, 1957b, 1958, 1959, 1961). His study of the system of race relations was based on an organic view of social life in which human interaction involving social definitions and communication is paramount (Frazier, 1953; Edwards, 1968a). For Frazier, the sociological explanation of race relations required an understanding of economic and political factors, especially class conflict among whites in the South, the restoration of white supremacy after emancipation, and racial separation and disfranchisement of the Negro. He identified several stages that provided an analytical framework for under-standing the changing character of race relations in the United States and abroad. These stages included biological determinism, economic exploitation, an extralegal system of social control, and the hierarchical racial division of society (Frazier, 1953).

Frazier also presented one of the first literature reviews on the study of race relations in sociology. He summarized and critiqued the prevailing perspectives of the "fathers" of American sociology, described the "caste and class" approach, and suggested the need for a dynamic sociological theory of race relations. Frazier acknowledges the substantial contribution of Park to race relations theory but viewed his approach as initially "static" and therefore overlooking changes (dynamics) in race relations over time (Frazier, 1947).

In 1948 in his presidential address before the American Sociological Society, Frazier emphasized the need for sociologists to study race and culture contacts in the context of social relationships that had undergone rapid changes. He noted that the study of race and culture contacts had to take into consideration "the behavior of men as members of social groups" and the effect of urbanization on both race and class (Frazier, 1949c). Frazier also noted that the sociological study of Negroes was viewed as either a social problem or a problem of intergroup relations. What is more important, Negro studies had not acquired the appropriate status or attention within the discipline.

Research on the African American Middle Class

Frazier's research on the African American middle class was an outgrowth of his interest in the Negro family and urbanization (Frazier, 1925, 1955a, 1955b, 1957a). His first article on the subject appeared in 1925 and described the African American middle class in Durham, North Carolina (Frazier, 1925). At the time, the middle-class was viewed by Frazier as a new group of Negroes comprised of doctors, teachers, dentists, government employees, preachers, and others. Frazier described these Negroes as distinguishable from others by their income, social status, education, and morality. At the time, middle-class Negroes were described by Frazier as holdovers from the social structure of Southern plantations, a mixture of both peasant and gentleman.

Thirty years later, Frazier (1955b) described the "New Negro Middle Class." The size of this group had grown substantially and included persons in more occupations. However, Frazier was very critical of the new middle class, describing the members as attempting to escape from themselves, isolated in American society, and plagued by feelings of inferiority.

His classic *Black Bourgeoisie* offered a radical perspective on the new middle class. Frazier described the members of this group as very different from the old middle class in their members, as well as their values. The new middle class was more concerned with conspicuous consumption and mobility and provided evidence of a breakdown in Negro family life (Edwards, 1968a, p. xviii).

CONCLUSION

Frazier's contributions in sociology are well known. More recently, his research on crime and delinquency has also received attention in criminology (Taylor Greene,

1979; Young & Taylor Greene, 1995; Taylor Greene, 1997). As previously stated, his contributions to criminological thought are embedded in his sociological research on the African American, the African American family, and race relations. His most important contribution is an in-depth analysis of the early research on African Americans and crime. His analyses of juvenile delinquency, social control, and the role of the family in social control are also significant.

Frazier's research is important to both sociology and criminology for several reasons. Along with others, he challenged the reliance on physical and moral deficiency explanations of crime and delinquency, turning instead to social structure factors, including economics and social conditions (Frazier, 1949). His research that often included case studies of African American delinquents facilitated a better understanding of these boys and girls in several jurisdictions. Although national studies of African American delinquent youth were rare at the time, Frazier provided a foundation for future studies in this area. Unlike other early scholars studying delinquency, Frazier included females in his writings.

Along with Frazier, several African American scholars, including Moses (1947) and Blue (1948), studied the ecology of delinquency in African American communities (Taylor Greene, 1997). In 1959 a decade after Frazier's research on delinquency, the *Journal of Negro Education* devoted an entire issue to Negro delinquency that included research by both whites and African Americans. Although Frazier did not have an article in the special issue, his works were more widely known because of his notoriety and the publication of his research in both majority and African American journals and periodicals.

Frazier (1949, p. 653) described his research on African American delinquency as part of a "new understanding." The following statement about this knowledge was quite prophetic:

> But whether this knowledge will be utilized to reduce Negro crime and juvenile delinquency will depend partly upon the extent to which the Negro is integrated into American life and partly upon the measures which the American community adopts to deal with these problems. (ibid.)

While Frazier often commented on the problem of family dysfunction and delinquency, he devoted little attention to the problem of delinquency in two-parent families who also resided in socially disorganized areas. He, like others, ignored delinquency in the middle-class except for noting that delinquency was least likely in middle-class communities. Unlike most early scholars, Frazier did include black females in his delinquency research.

Although Frazier's contributions to understanding crime and delinquency have been overlooked, his research on the family has received considerable attention and caused great controversy. Three years after his death, Daniel P. Moynihan (1965) published *The Negro Family: The Case for National Action*, better known as the

Moynihan Report, and acknowledged his intellectual debt to Frazier (Platt, 1991). Posthumously, Frazier was criticized for contributing to a pathology model of the black family. Platt (1987, 1989, 1991) argues that Frazier's research on the family was often taken out of social and historical context and thus distorted. What is more important, Frazier would not have agreed with Moynihan's findings about the black family (Platt, 1987). It is interesting that Platt does not address Frazier's contributions to understanding the family and delinquency, especially in light of (1) the importance of the family in understanding delinquency and (2) Platt's own research on delinquency. In spite of his critics and admirers, Frazier's research on both the family and delinquency is still relevant and worthy of further analyses.

References

Aichorn, A. (1963). *Wayward youth.* New York: Viking.

Blue, J. T. (1948). The relationship of juvenile delinquency, race, and economic status. *Journal of Negro Education, 17,* 469–77.

Davis, A. (1962). E. Franklin Frazier: A profile. *Journal of Negro Education, 31,* 430–35.

Drake, St. C. (1967). Introduction. In E. Franklin Frazier, *Negro youth at the crossways* (pp. v–xx). Washington, DC: American Council on Education.

Edwards, G. F. (1968a). *E. Franklin Frazier on race relations.* Chicago: The University of Chicago Press.

———. (1968b). Frazier, E. Franklin. In D. Sills (Ed.), *International encyclopedia of the social sciences* (vol. 5, pp. 553–54). New York: MacMillan.

———. (1982). Frazier, E. Franklin. In R. W. Logan and M. R. Winston (Eds.), *Dictionary of American Negro biography* (pp. 241–44). New York: W. W. Norton.

Frazier, E. F. 1920. New currents of thought among the colored people of America. M.A. Thesis. Worcester, MA: Clark University.

———. (1924). Social work in race relations. *Crisis, 29,* 254.

———. (1925). Durham: Capital of the black middle class. In Alain Locke (ed.), *The new Negro* (pp. 333–40). New York: C. Boni Company.

———. (1927). The pathology of race prejudice. *Forum, 70,* 856–62.

———. (1931). *The Negro family in Chicago.* Doctoral Dissertation. Chicago: University of Chicago.

———. (1932). *The Negro family in Chicago.* Chicago: University of Chicago Press.

———. (1937a). The impact of urban civilization upon Negro family life. *American Sociological Review (August), 2,* 609–18.

———. (1937b). Negro Harlem: An ecological study. *American Journal of Sociology, 43,* 72–88.

———. (1939a). *The Negro family in the United States.* Chicago: University of Chicago Press.

———. (1939b). Rebellious youth. In *The Negro family in the United States* (pp. 268–80). Chicago: University of Chicago Press.

————— (1939c). Roving men and homeless women. In *The Negro family in the United States* (pp. 209–33). Chicago: University of Chicago Press.

—————. (1940/1967). *Negro youth at the crossways.* Washington, DC: American Council on Education.

—————. (1942). Some aspects of race relations in Brazil. *Phylon,* 284–95.

—————. (1947). Sociological theory and race relations. *American Sociological Review, 12,* 265–71.

—————. (1949a). Crime and delinquency. *The Negro in the United States* (Ch. 5, pp. 638–53). New York: Macmillan Co.

—————. (1949b/1957). *The Negro in the United States.* New York: The Macmillan Company.

—————. (1949c). The presidential address. *American Sociological Review, 14,* 1–11.

—————. (1949d). Race contacts and social structure. *American Sociological Review, 14,* 1–11.

—————. (1953). Theoretical structure of sociology and social research. *British Journal of Sociology, 4,* 293–311.

—————. (1955a). *Bourgeoisie noire.* Paris, France: Librairie Plon.

—————. (1955b). The new Negro middle class. In Division of Social Sciences (ed.), *The new Negro thirty years afterward* (pp. 26–32). Washington, DC: Howard University Press.

—————. (1957a). *Black bourgeoisie.* Glencoe, IL: The Free Press.

—————. (1957b). *Race and culture contacts in the modern world.* New York: A. A. Knopf.

—————. (1958). Areas of research in race relations. *Sociology and Social Research, 4,* (4), 24–29.

—————. (1959). The present state of sociological knowledge concerning race relations. In Milan and Stressa (eds.), *Transactions of the Fourth World Congress of Sociology.*

—————. (1961). Racial problems in world society. In J. Masuoka and P. Valien (eds.), *Race Relations Problems and Theory: Essays in Honor of Robert E. Park* (pp. 38–50) Chapel Hill: The University of North Carolina Press.

Hirschi, T. (1969). *Causes of delinquency.* Berkeley. University of California Press.

Johnson, G. (1941). The Negro and crime. *The Annals of the American Academy of Political and Social Science, 217,* 93–104.

Moses, E. (1947). Differentials in crime rates between Negroes and whites based on comparisons of four socio-economically equated areas. *American Sociological Review, 12,* 411–20.

Moynihan, D. (1965). *The Negro family: The case for national action.* Washington, DC: Government Printing Office.

Nye, F. (1958). *Family relationships and delinquent behavior.* New York: John Wiley.

Odum, H. (1951). *American sociology.* New York: Longmans, Green and Co.

Platt, A. (1987). E. Franklin Frazier and Daniel Patrick Moynihan: Setting the Record Straight. *Contemporary-Crises,* 265–77.

—————. (1989). E. Franklin Frazier reconsidered. *Social Justice, 16,* 186–95.

—————. (1991). *E. Franklin Frazier reconsidered.* New Brunswick, NJ: Rutgers University Press.

Reckless, W. (1961). A new theory of delinquency and crime. *Federal Probation, 25,* 42–46.

Sellin, T. (1928). The Negro criminal. *The Annals of the American Academy of Political and Social Science, 140,* 52–64.

Taylor Greene, H. (1979). *A comprehensive bibliography of criminology and criminal justice literature by black authors from 1895–1978.* Hyattsville, MD: Ummah Publications.

———. (1997). Teaching delinquency: Incorporating research by black scholars into undergraduate courses. *Teaching Sociology, 25,* 57–64.

Thompson, C. (ed.). (1959). Juvenile delinquency among Negroes in the United States. *Journal of Negro Education, 28* (3).

Young, V. & Taylor Greene, H. (1995). Pedagogical reconstruction: Incorporating African-American perspectives into the curriculum. *Journal of Criminal Justice Education, 6,* 85–104.

E. Franklin Frazier
Selected References

Frazier, E. F. (1920). *New currents of thought among the colored people of America.* M.A. Thesis. Worcester, MA: Clark University.

———. (1924). Social work in race relations. *Crisis, 29,* 254.

———. (1925). Durham: Capital of the black middle class. In Alain Locke (ed.), *The new Negro* (pp. 333–40). New York: C. Boni Company.

———. (1927). The pathology of race prejudice. *Forum, 70,* 856–62.

———. (1932). *The Negro family in Chicago.* Chicago: University of Chicago Press.

———. (1937). The impact of urban civilization upon Negro family life. *American Sociological Review, (August) 2,* 609–18.

———. (1937). Negro Harlem: An ecological study. *American Journal of Sociology, 43,* 72–88.

———. (1939). *The Negro family in the United States.* Chicago: University of Chicago Press.

———. (1939). Rebellious youth. In *The Negro family in the United States* (pp. 268–80). Chicago: University of Chicago Press.

———. (1939). Roving men and homeless women. In *The Negro family in the United States* (pp. 209–33). Chicago: University of Chicago Press.

———. (1940/1967). *Negro youth at the crossways.* Washington, DC: American Council on Education.

———. (1949). Crime and delinquency. *The Negro in the United States* (ch. 5, pp. 638–53). New York: The Macmillan Company.

Notes

1. Brown (1962) contrasts a "proper" Negro and "improper" Negro in an article about Frazier published shortly after his death. Frazier is described as improper because of his intellect, scholarship, nonconformity, and protests, which were viewed as "improper" for Negroes of his time.

2. At the time the organization was known as the American Sociological Society.

3. Frazier collected information for this article as part of Mayor LaGuardia's Commission on Conditions in Harlem in 1935.

Part II
Contemporary Scholars

Overview

We begin the contemporary perspectives with the decade of the 1960s. Over the last thirty-five years African Americans became even more heavily involved in the study of crime and the criminal justice system. This was a direct result of increased educational opportunities and the desegregation of colleges and universities. Of equal importance were the civil rights movement and the black power movement. These two movements further instigated the interest of African Americans in the criminal justice system. For example, the civil rights movement openly showed the brutality of the police toward African Americans, while the black power movement revealed the role of police as agents of oppression. Along with the actions of the police, the social, economic, and political conditions of the inner cities were key instigators of the riots in Harlem, Watts, Newark, and Detroit (National Advisory Commission on Civil Disorders, 1968, p. 206).

The modern civil rights struggle gained momentum with the *Brown v. Board of Education* victory by Thurgood Marshall that ended the "separate but equal" notion rendered in the 1896 *Plessy v. Ferguson* decision. On the heels of the landmark *Brown* decision, the civil rights movement under the direction of several high-profile organizations, including the Southern Christian Leadership Conference (SCLC) (under the leadership of Martin Luther King, Jr.), the Congress of Racial Equality (CORE), and the Student Non-Violent Coordinating Committee (SNCC), became major players in the struggle for civil rights. As these civil rights organizations became more influential, opponents of the movement, often with the assistance of law enforcement officials, intimidated and brutalized nonviolent civil rights workers and activists (Bullard, 1993).

While the 1960s did bring significant legislation (most notably, the 1964 Civil Rights Act and the 1965 Voting Rights Act), dissension remained among urban African American residents who saw little improvement in their condition. Out of this dissension rose the call for "black power." The main thrust of the black power movement included three core ideas: self-determination, self-respect, and self-defense (Karenga, 1993). Frustrated with what they viewed as minimal progress, which in their eyes was too little too late, followers of this movement were convinced "that whites would never concede complete equality to African-Americans" (Franklin & Moss, 1994, p. 518). Therefore, at a 1967 black power conference, they suggested that the United States be divided into two parts—with half being a homeland for whites and the other a homeland for African Americans (ibid., 1994, p. 518). Although unrealistic, this call exemplified the dissatisfaction among participants of the movement.

At the same time in Oakland, California, the Black Panther Party for Self-Defense was rising in prominence. With Huey P. Newton, Bobby Seale, and Eldridge Cleaver leading the way, the organization primarily monitored the actions of the Oakland police, who were known for their brutality in the African American community. They eventually expanded their mission with the call for "full employment, decent housing, black control of the black community, and an end to every form of repression and brutality" (Franklin & Moss, 1994, p. 520). Though the movement was later undermined by the actions of the FBI's notorious counterintelligence (COINTELPRO) program, which monitored and disrupted the activities of several black power and civil rights organizations (Karenga, 1993, p. 179–80), both movements had already had a tremendous influence on the African American scholars profiled here.

Part 2 profiles Coramae Richey Mann, William Julius Wilson, Lee P. Brown, Darnell F. Hawkins, Daniel E. Georges-Abeyie, and Vernetta D. Young, contemporary scholars who have made significant contributions to criminology/criminal justice. The lasting influence of the sixties can be seen in the research of each scholar. During the 1960s and 1970s, several of these scholars engaged in theses or dissertations directly related to the events of the sixties. For example, Lee Brown, a police officer in San Jose, California, devoted both his master's thesis and his doctoral dissertation research to police-community relations (Brown, 1968, 1970).

In 1970, Darnell Hawkins completed his M.A.T. thesis at Wayne State University, which, according to him "drew heavily from the social sciences and was a critique of notions of 'cultural deprivation' as used in the educational literature" (Hawkins, 1997). And Daniel E. Georges-Abeyie completed his doctoral program in geography with a dissertation based on the 1967 Newark riot (Georges-Abeyie, 1974). The events of the sixties also caused William Julius Wilson, a student during the decade, to later develop a specialty in the area of race relations (Wilson, 1988). Ironically, Wilson has become one of the most acclaimed sociologists of the contemporary era because of his publications in this area.

During the 1960s, Coramae Richey Mann was serving on the front lines in a variety of positions, which she suggests would have classified her as an "urban sociologist" (Mann, 1995). The youngest of the contemporary scholars, Vernetta Young was probably least influenced by the events of the sixties. Young became interested in the subject matter as an undergraduate in the late 1960s because of her enrollment in a sociology class where the instructor was discussing theories that might explain African American criminality (Young, 1998).

As we begin our profiles of the contemporary scholars, it is important to note that we admittedly left out many noteworthy African American scholars who easily could have been included. Therefore, as in the historical overview, we provide a table that presents a sampling of the most recent publications of contemporary African American scholars not profiled in this volume (see table 2). For a more complete list of scholarship by African American criminologists from 1970 through 1998, we refer readers to Ross (1998).

Table 2 African American Scholarship on Crime and Justice, 1962–1998

SCHOLAR	DATA	RESEARCH TOPIC
Holden, M.	1962	Police-Community Relations
Vontress, C.	1962	Segregation, Discrimination, and Crime
Willie, C. V.	1965	Race and Delinquency
Epps, E.	1967	Juvenile Delinquency
Jackson, G.	1970	Prison Life
Pickney, A.	1972	History of Violence in America
Pouissant, A.	1972	Black-on-Black Violence
Staples, R.	1974	Internal Colonialism and Black Violence
Houston, C. H.	1975	Racial Discrimination in Sentencing
Wright, B.	1975	Black Youth and the Courts
Perry, R. L.	1976	Black Matriarchy and Delinquency
Debro, J.	1977	Institutional Racism in Corrections
Pierson, G.	1977	Institutional Racism in Policing
Napper, G.	1977	Perceptions of Crime
Swan, A.	1977	Delinquency Among black Youth
Anderson, E.	1978	Street Life
Austin, R. L.	1978	Race, Father Absence, and Female Delinquency
Taylor Greene, H.	1979	Black Perspectives on Crime
Taylor-Gibbs, J.	1981	Depression and Suicide
Pouissant, A.	1983	Black-on-Black Homicide
Wilson, G. P.	1983	Halfway House Programs
Wright, B. E.	1984	AfricanAmerican Suicide
Peterson, R.	1985	Discrimination in Legislation
Covington, J.	1986	Self-Esteem and Deviance
Simms, M. & Myers, S.	1988	Economics, Race, and Crime
Oliver, W.	1989	Afrocentric Socialization of Black Males
Anderson, E.	1990	Street Life
Wilson, A. N.	1990	Black-on-Black Violence
Quimby, E.	1990	Drug Trafficking and the Caribbean Connection
Coston, C. T.	1992	Race and Fear of Crime among Homeless Females
Ebbie, O.	1992	Juvenile Delinquency in Nigeria
Edwards, W. J.	1992	Predicting Juvenile Delinquency
Johnson, I. M.	1992	Battered Women
McGee, Z. T.	1992	Adolescent Drug Use
McIntyre, C.	1992	Free Blacks and the Criminal Justice System
Russell, K. K.	1992	Black Criminology
Wilson, A. N.	1992	Black Adolescent Male Violence
Bailey, F.	1993	Vigilantism
Taylor, C.	1993	Girls, Gangs, Women, and Drugs
Heard, C. A.	1993	Managing Inmate Population
McMurry, H. L.	1993	Parolees Transition to Community
Anderson, E.	1994	Code of the Streets
Oliver, W.	1994	Black Male Violence
Scott, E.	1994	African American Males in the Criminal Justice System
Tatum, B.	1994	The Colonial Model
Taylor, D. L.	1994	Family and Delinquency

Table 2 continued

SCHOLAR	DATA	RESEARCH TOPIC
Bing et al.	. 1995	African American and White Experiences in Criminal Justice Education
Conley, D.	1995	Explaining Racial Disproportionality in the Juvenile Justice System
Henriques, Z.	1995	African American Women
Joseph, J.	1995	African American Juvenile Delinquency
Dulaney, M.	1996	Blacks in Policing
Jackson, J. E.	1996	Credit Card Fraud
Jones, J.	1996	Crime Prevention in Urban Areas
Pettiway. L. E	1996	Street Life, Gay African Americans, and Crime
Ross, L. E.	1998	African American Criminologists
Russell, K. K	1998	African American and White Crime

References

Anderson, E. (1978). *A place on the corner.* Chicago: The University of Chicago Press.

————. (1990). *Streetwise: Race, class, and change in an urban community.* Chicago: The University of Chicago Press.

————. (1994). The code of the streets. *Atlantic Monthly* (May), 80–94.

Austin, R. (1978). Race, father-absence, and female delinquency. *Criminology, 15,* 487–504.

Bailey, F. (1993). Getting justice: Real life vigilantism and vigilantism in popular film." *The Justice Professional, 8,* 33–51.

Bing, Robert., Heard, C & Gilbert, E. (1995). The experiences of African-American and whites in criminal justice education: Do race and gender differences exist? *Journal of Criminal Justice Education, 6,* 123–45.

Brown, L. (1968). *The development of a police-community relations program: An assessment of the San Jose project.* M.A. Thesis, University of California at Berkeley.

————. (1970). *Evaluation of a police-community relations program.* Ph.D. Dissertation, University of California at Berkeley.

Bullard, S. (1993). *Free at last: A history of the civil rights movement and those who died in the struggle.* New York: Oxford University Press.

Conley, D. (1995). Adding color to a black and white picture: Using qualitative data to explain racial disproportionality in the juvenile justice system. *Journal of Research in Crime and Delinquency, 31,* 135–48.

Coston, C. (1992). The influence of race in urban homeless females' fear of crime. *Justice Quarterly, 9,* 721–30.

Covington, J. (1986). Self-esteem and deviance: The effects of race and gender. *Criminology, 24,* 105–36.

Debro, J. (1977). Institutional racism within the structure of American prisons. In R. L. Woodson (ed.), *Black perspectives on crime and the criminal justice system*. Boston: G. K. Hall.

Dulaney, M. (1996). *Black police in America*. Bloomington: Indiana University Press.

Ebbie, O. (1992). Juvenile delinquency in Nigeria: The problem of application of Western theories. *International Journal of Comparative and Applied Criminal Justice, 16*, 353–70.

Edwards, W. (1992). Predicting juvenile delinquency: A review of correlates and a confirmation by recent research based on an integrated theoretical model. *Justice Quarterly, 9*, 553–84.

Epps, E. (1967). Socioeconomic status, race, level of aspiration and juvenile delinquency: A limited empirical test of Merton's conception of deviation. *Phylon, 28*, 16–27.

Franklin, J. & Moss, A. (1994). *From slavery to freedom: A history of African Americans,* 7th Edition. New York: McGraw-Hill.

Georges-Abeyie, D. (1974). *The ecology of urban unrest in an American city—Newark New Jersey, A case study in collective violence*. Ph.D. Dissertation, Syracuse University.

Hawkins, D. (1997). Biographical data furnished to the authors.

Heard, C. (1993). Forecasting models for managing a changing inmate population: Implications for public policy. *Criminal Justice Review, 18*, 77–95.

Henriques, Z. (1995). African American women: The oppressive intersection of gender, race, and class. *Women and Criminal Justice, 7*, 67–81.

Houston, C. (1975). Racial discrimination in sentencing. It is interesting that Platt does not address Frazier's contributions to understanding the family and delinquency. *Judicature, 59*, 121–25.

Jackson, G. (1970). *Soledad brother: The prison letters of George Jackson*. New York: Coward McCann, Inc.

Jackson, J. (1996). Fraud masters: Professional credit cards criminals and crime. *Criminal Justice Review, 19*, 24–55.

Johnson, I. (1992). Economics, situational, and psychological correlates of the decision-making process of battered women. *Families in Society, 73*, 168 76.

Jones, J. (1996). *Non-Violent models in violent communities: A crime prevention model for African-American urban neighborhoods*. Bethesda, MD: Austin & Winfield, Publishers.

Joseph, J. (1995). Juvenile delinquents among African-Americans. *Journal of Black Studies, 25*, 475–91.

Karenga, M. (1993). *Introduction to black studies*. 2nd Edition. Los Angeles: The University of Sankore Press.

Mann, C. (1995). Seventeen white men and me. In A. Goetting and S. Fenstermaker (eds.), *Individual voices, collective visions: Fifty years of women in sociology* (pp. 273–83). Philadelphia: Temple University Press.

McGee, Z. (1992). Social class differences in parental and peer influence on adolescent drug use. *Deviant Behavior: An Interdisciplinary Journal, 13*, 349–72.

McIntyre, C. (1992). *Criminalizing a race: Free blacks during slavery*. Queens, NY: Kayode Publications.

McMurray, H. (1993). High risk parolees in transition from institution to community life. *Journal of Offender Rehabilitation, 9,* 145–61.

Napper, G. (1977). Perception of crime: Problems and implications. In R.Woodson (Ed.), *Black perspectives on crime and the criminal justice system* (pp. 5–22). Boston: G. K. Hall.

Oliver, W. (1989). Black males and social problems prevention through Afrocentric socialization. *Journal of Black Studies, 20,* 15–39.

———. (1994). *The violent social world of black men.* New York: Macmillan.

Perry, R. (1976). The black matriarchy controversy and black male delinquency. *Journal of Afro-American Issues, 4,* 362–72.

Pickney, A. (1972). *The American way of violence.* New York: Random House.

Pierson, G. (1977). Institutional racism and crime clearance. In Robert L. Woodson (ed.), *Black perspectives on crime and the criminal justice system* (pp. 107–22). Boston: G. K. Hall.

Peterson, R. (1985). Discriminatory decision making at the legislative level: An analysis of the Comprehensive Drug Abuse Prevention and Control Act of 1970. *Law and Human Behavior* 6:243–69.

Pettiway, L. (1996). *Honey, honey, miss thang: Being black, gay, and on the streets.* Philadelphia: Temple University Press.

Poussaint, A. (1972). *Why blacks kill blacks.* New York: Emerson Hall.

———. (1983). Black on Black homicide: A psychological-political perspective. *Victimology, 8,* 161–69.

Quimby, E. (1990). Drug trafficking and the Caribbean connection: Survival mechanisms, entrepreneurship and social symptoms. *Urban League Review, 14,* 61–70.

Report of the national advisory commission on civil disorders. (1968). New York: Bantam Books.

Ross L. E. (1998). *African-American criminologists, 1970–1996.* Westport, CT: Greenwood Press.

Russell, K. K. (1992). Development of a black criminology and the role of a black criminologist. *Justice Quarterly, 9,* 667–83.

———. (1998). *The color of crime: Racial hoaxes, white fear, black protectionism, police harassment, and other macroaggressions.* New York: New York University Press.

Scott, E. (1976). Black attitudes toward crime and crime prevention. In L. E. Gary & L. P. Brown (eds.), *Crime and its impact on the black community* (pp. 155–64). Washington, DC: Howard University Institute for Urban Affairs and Research.

Simms, M. & Myers, S. (1988). *The economics of race and crime.* New Brunswick, NJ: Transaction Publications.

Staples, R. (1974). Internal colonialism and black violence. *Black World, 23,* 16–34.

Swan, A. (1977). Juvenile delinquency, juvenile justice and black youth. In R. L. Woodson (ed.), *Black perspectives on crime and the criminal justice system* (pp. 55–79). Boston: G. K. Hall.

Tatum, B. (1994). The colonial model as a theoretical explanation of crime and delinquency. In A. T. Sulton (Ed.), *African-American perspectives on: Crime causation, criminal justice administration, and crime prevention* (pp. 33–52). Englewood, CO: Sulton Books.

Taylor, C. S. (1993). *Girls, gangs, women and drugs.* East Lansing: Michigan State University Press.

Taylor, D. L. (1994). Family and delinquency: African American female headed households and chronic maladaptive behavior of juveniles. In A. T. Sulton (Ed.), *African-American perspectives on crime causation, criminal justice administration, and crime prevention* (pp. 123–38). Englewood, CO: Sulton Books.

Taylor-Gibbs, J. (1981). Depression and suicide behavior among delinquent females. *Journal of Youth and Adolescence, 10,* 159–67.

Taylor Greene, H. (1979). *A comprehensive bibliography of criminology and criminal justice literature by black authors from 1895 to 1978.* Hyattsville, MD: Ummah Publications.

Vontress, C. E. (1962). Patterns of segregation and discrimination: Contributing factors to crime among Negroes. *Journal of Negro Education, 31,* 108–16.

Willie, C. V. (1965). Race and delinquency. *Phylon, 26,* 240–46.

Wilson, A. N. (1990). *Black on black violence: The psychodynamics of black self-annihilation in service of white domination.* New York: Afrikan World Infosystems.

———. (1992). *Understanding black adolescent male violence: Its remediation and prevention.* New York: Afrikan World Infosystems.

Wilson, G. P. (1983). Halfway house programs for offenders. In L. F. Travis III (ed.), *Probation, parole, and community corrections: A reader* (pp. 151–64). Prospect Heights, IL: Waveland Press.

Wilson, W. J. (1988). Academic controversy and intellectual growth. In M.W. Riley (Ed.), *Sociological lives* (pp. 79–90). Beverly Hills: Sage Publications.

Wright, B. E. (1984). Black suicide: Lynching by any other name is still lynching. In B. E. Wright (ed.), *The psychopathic racial personality and other essays* (pp. 17–23) Chicago: Third World Press.

Wright, B. (1975). Bangs & whimpers: Black youth and the courts. *Freedomways, 15,* 178–87.

Young, V. (1998). Interview with the authors.

Coramae Richey Mann

FIVE

CORAMAE RICHEY MANN
(1931–   )

INTRODUCTION

A latecomer to the world of academe at the age of forty-five, Coramae Richey Mann has made up for her late start with tremendous scholarly productivity. Over the past twenty plus years, Mann has been a consistent contributor to the criminology/ criminal justice literature in primarily three areas: female crime and delinquency, violence, and minorities and crime. Because of her significant efforts in these areas, she is generally viewed as one of the leading African American scholars of the contemporary era. Mann has also served as an advocate and mentor to countless African American and white graduate students and professors. We believe that in the future this contribution will be viewed as being as important as her scholarly endeavors.

BIOGRAPHICAL INFORMATION

The last of two children of Edward and Louise Richey, Coramae Richey Mann was born in a segregated Chicago hospital on a January morning in 1931 (Mann, 1995a). Although her family resided in Ohio, Louise Richey wanted to be with her mother in Chicago for the birth of her second child. Mann's mother, a homemaker, gave up an opportunity for a career in the arts to raise Mann and her older brother. Her father was a teacher at a segregated high school in Dayton, Ohio, where he also coached several athletic teams (Mann, 1995a, p. 273). At the time of Louise's death in 1987, the Richeys had been married sixty-three years.

Mann has vivid recollections of her childhood. Early in her youth she decided that she wanted to be an artist or a writer. Exhibiting talents in both areas, she completed her first oil painting before she attended school. And later, while in grammar school, Mann would write and illustrate her first poem "Rabbit Tracks" (Mann, 1995a, p. 274). The Richeys lived in a predominantly white neighborhood, where Mann regularly had white playmates. On one occasion, after winning a child-hood game with her white playmates, Mann recalls being called a "chocolate drop." This remark was so hurtful that Mann ran home to her mother in tears. Although her mother attempted to put a positive spin on the incident, Mann "knew something cruel and wrong had occurred" (Mann, 1995a, p. 274).

One of only two African American students in her integrated Ohio grammar school, Mann and her African American classmate were the best students in the class. On track for an outstanding future, two untimely family deaths had an impact on Mann's life course. In 1943, Mann's brother, Edward, passed away. His death was followed by that of Mann's maternal grandfather the following year. Without her brother, Mann no longer had anyone to "protect her." After the death of her grandfather, the family decided to move to Chicago. While Mann's mother inherited all of her grandfather's vast estate, the Richeys were leery of the bad influences awaiting Mann in the segregated African American schools of Chicago, so they sent her South to the Palmer Memorial Institute in North Carolina.

At the Institute, however, Mann was taken under the guidance of two "big sisters" who taught her about boys. This discovery contributed to Mann engaging in uncharacteristic behavior. Now a status offender, Mann's parents removed her from the institute and sent her to live with her aunt in Minneapolis, Minnesota. This, too, turned out to be a bad move. In Minneapolis, Mann became best friends with a "shoplifter" who taught her all the tricks of the trade. Mann was eventually caught by her aunt, who insisted she take all her "loot" back to the store and apologize to the sales clerks in each of the departments where she had stolen. This summarily ended her delinquent activities.

Amazingly, Mann still managed to maintain an A average. In fact, during her senior year of high school, Mann was selected for the prestigious class yearbook editor position. However, after running home to call her parents to tell them the good news, the following day Mann's teacher informed her that the school was not ready for an African American editor; therefore, she would have to be co-editor with a white classmate. Extremely disappointed over this incident, Mann invoked her revenge by ensuring that her African American face appeared early and often throughout the publication. Following her stint as editor of the yearbook, she was asked to pose for some pictures, one of which ended up as an early cover of *Ebony* magazine. Though she would later model again, she ended her career after being told by a prospective employer that she "photographed too white" (Mann, 1995a, p. 277). These two race-related incidents exemplify some of the obstacles Mann has endured for much of her life.

Finishing fourth out of her 350 classmates, Mann applied to three colleges all of which accepted her. She decided to enroll at the University of Chicago so that she could be near friends and family. During her first year, however, Mann almost flunked out because of her card playing and drinking activities. Mann also eloped after her first year. After the marriage faltered, Mann decided to resume her studies at Howard University in Washington, D.C. Of her experience at Howard, Mann states, "The three years I spent at Howard were clearly the most important in my educational life" (Mann, 1995a, p. 278). This, according to Mann, had quite a bit to do with the wonderful African American instructors she had.

While at Howard Mann majored in English with a specialty in short-story writing. She studied eagerly under noted African American author and poet Sterling

Brown. During her studies under Brown, Mann became interested in the writings of O. Henry and Henry James, whose works encompassed heavy psychological foundations. Since she wanted to write similar types of stories, Mann enrolled in the psychology course of Dr. Charles Sumner. Mann was profoundly impressed with Sumner. She became a protege of Sumner and "lived and breathed clinical psychology." After his unexpected death, Mann returned to Chicago, where she enrolled in Roosevelt University.

In 1956, Mann received a B.A. in clinical psychology. Six years later she would also earn an M.A. in clinical psychology at Roosevelt. In the interim, however, Mann would work in a variety of jobs she believes would have classified her more as an urban sociologist rather than a clinical psychologist. Some of these positions include vocational counselor, planner and community action trainer, and planned parenthood administrator. Also, several years after completing her M.A., Mann accepted an adjunct teaching position at Roosevelt. Mann loved teaching and decided to enroll in a Ph.D. program. She was admittedly more interested in psychology than sociology/criminology, but since there were long waiting lists at the more desirable clinical psychology programs, Mann enrolled in the sociology program at the University of Illinois at Chicago. She completed her dissertation, "The Female Delinquent in the Judicial Process," in 1976.

Upon completion of her doctorate, Mann accepted a position in the School of Criminology at Florida State University. During much of her tenure at Florida State University, Mann was the lone female and African American faculty member. As a result:

> I had to appeal the denial of my tenure, make salary inequity a formal
> issue twice, and challenge my male colleagues for not receiving doctoral
> directive status. I won each of these battles by using gender, not race, as
> the basis of my arguments. I could have gone either way, but I reasoned
> that gender was the less explosive argument. (Mann, 1995, p. 281)

Twelve years after joining the Florida State University faculty, Mann accepted an appointment as professor of criminal justice at Indiana University in Bloomington, Indiana. She is presently professor emerita at both Florida State University and Indiana University.

In recent years, Mann's contributions to criminology and criminal justice have been recognized with her receipt of the Bruce Smith Sr. Award from the Academy of Criminal Justice Sciences (ACJS) in 1995, and the following year Mann was selected to be a fellow of the ACJS. The Division of Women and Crime of the American Society of Criminology (ASC) also acknowledged Mann's accomplishments by selecting her for their Distinguished Scholar Award in 1995. In 1998, Mann was chosen to serve as the Wayne C. Basler chair of excellence at East Tennessee State University. And more recently, in 1999, she was selected as an ASC fellow and awarded the Distinguished Scholar award by the ASC Division on People of Color and Crime (the award is now called the Coramae Richey Mann Distinguished Scholar Award).

CONTRIBUTIONS TO CRIMINOLOGICAL THOUGHT

Much of Mann's early research focused on female delinquency (Mann, 1979a, 1979b, 1980a, 1980b). An outgrowth of her dissertation, this research was based on an observational study of a midwestern juvenile court. Making use of systematic observation, Mann observed dispositional hearings of male and female runaways during a three-month period. She investigated the potential differences in treatment between males and females, as well as the effects of other extralegal factors in juvenile court dispositions. Mann used quota sampling to observe fifty male and fifty female runaway disposition hearings. Some of her findings are presented below.

Girls more often than boys were sentenced to the most severe penalty for runaways (commitment to the Department of Children and Family Services). Males received the least serious penalty (supervision) more than females. Six out of the fifty female runaways were requested to undergo a physical examination, while no males were similarly requested. As for parental involvement in the disposition hearings, Mann found that in cases where either parent was present, the juvenile typically received the least severe penalty. An examination of time spent on each case showed that about two more minutes were spent on male cases than female ones. Other extralegal variables of relevance to Mann's research included appearance, demeanor, dress, and walk (Mann, 1980b, p. 46). She operationalized each of these variables and then observed their impact on the judicial dispositions (pp. 46–47). Mann's results showed that "none of . . . [these] variables . . . appeared to be associated with, or influenced upon, the judge's decision" (p. 50).

The aforementioned results were in agreement with the prevailing literature on the treatment of females in court (see, for example, Chesney-Lind, 1977). For example, Mann's finding that girls received the most severe sentence more often than boys speaks to the "paternalistic" attitudes of some judges. This is further evidenced by judges having referred six female runaways for physical examinations (Mann, 1979b, p. 42). Of these referrals, Mann concluded that "sexual misbehavior appeared to be presumed by the court as the justification for this medical scrutiny" (Mann, 1979b, p. 47), something that was obviously not presumed in the case of a single male runaway. Her early research on female criminality culminated in the publication of *Female Crime and Delinquency* (1984), which is a comprehensive text on female criminality that reviews data on the experience of females at every stage of the criminal justice system. Mann's subsequent research can be categorized under two themes: violent female criminality and minorities and crime.

Violent Female Criminality

Much of the research reviewed under this subheading is from a field study conducted by Mann over a two-year period (1985–86). She conducted field research in six U.S. cities whose homicide rates were at or higher than the national rates for the years 1979 and 1983 (Mann, 1988). She randomly selected 296 cleared female homicide cases from Chicago, Houston, Atlanta, Los Angeles, New York, and Baltimore. According to Mann (ibid., p. 34), the 296 homicides represented 43 percent of the female homicides in 1979 and 42 percent of the female homicides in 1983. Mann recorded information from both the police homicide files and the criminal court records, which included photographs, autopsy reports, and other related information. She then created a seven-page schedule to record demographic information on the offender and victim and any other pertinent information. This research was completed during the one to two weeks Mann spent in each city between 1985 and 1987. From this research, Mann has contributed significantly to the violent female crime literature. Her principle areas of focus have been domestic violence (Mann, 1988), female-on-female homicide (1993a), African American female violence (Mann, 1987, 1990a, 1991, 1992), and maternal filicide (Mann, 1993b).

Female-on-Female Violence

In the publication "Sister against Sister: Female Intrasexual Homicide," Mann investigates two central questions: (1) what is the profile of a female who kills another female? and (2) are women who kill other women different from women who kill men? Using a subsample of the aforementioned data set, Mann examined fifty-seven female homicide offenders whose victims were also females (Mann, 1993a, p. 200). Her data showed that, much like previous studies on female-on-female homicide (see Goetting, 1988), the offenders tended to be predominantly black, undereducated, unemployed, have prior arrest records, and commit their offenses in residences (Mann, 1993a, p. 202).

   Contrary to Goetting's earlier research, Mann found that the offenses had the same possibility of occurring on a weekend as a weekday (Mann, 1993a, p. 204). She also found that the homicides occurred primarily during the daytime to early evening period. Many of the offenders denied responsibility for the homicide by invoking explanations such as self-defense and the notion that the homicide was accidental. As for Mann's comparison of homicide characteristics (such as offender profile, role, motive, extent of violence, influence of "southernness," prior criminality of the offender, and criminal justice outcome for the murder) by gender of the victim, she found that "[n]one of . . . the characteristics significantly distinguished women who killed women from women who killed men, which suggests that perhaps the process of violence may be identical for men and women" (Mann, 1993a, p. 219). After generally addressing female homicide, Mann conducted a separate analysis of African American females and homicide.

African American Female Homicide

While Mann had previously examined the patterns of African American female criminality (see Mann, 1984a, 1984b), the dearth of research studies on African American female homicide resulted in her publication of several articles/chapters on the topic (Mann, 1987, 1990a, 1991). Much of Mann's research drew from her rich data on female homicide. An early publication on the topic reviewed fifteen empirical studies (from 1958–1984) that focused on female homicide. Of the fifteen studies, Mann conducted an analysis of twelve to determine the sociodemographics of African American female homicides. Her review of the studies showed that "[b]lack women are the most frequently arrested female offenders in cleared murder cases; they also make up the largest proportion of women incarcerated for criminal homicide" (Mann, 1987, p. 160). She adds: "With the exception of two studies . . . blacks tend to predominate among the homicide offenders in every study where the proportion of black female offenders is known" (Mann, 1987, p. 161).

Other important findings from her review of the literature include the following: the typical African American female homicide offender tends to be older with less than normal education and intelligence; they tend to come from intact households; prior to their offense, African American female homicide offenders were either unemployed or employed in an unskilled occupation (Mann, 1987, pp. 165–66). As for the victim characteristics, Mann found that, like white female homicide offenders, African American females primarily kill family members. They are more likely than whites to kill friends and acquaintances, however (Mann, 1987, p. 182). And they are less likely than whites to premeditate their homicides.

Following the publication of the aforementioned studies, Mann published two additional papers on African American female homicide (Mann, 1990a, 1991). Both papers rely on the previously discussed data collected by Mann in Houston, Atlanta, Baltimore, Chicago, Los Angeles, and New York. One paper focused on African American females who killed a loved one (1991), while the other was an overview of African American female homicide (1990a). Mann's overview analyzes data on the 230 African American female homicide offenders in her data set (Mann, 1990a, p. 180). Her aim was essentially to determine if the findings from her earlier survey of the literature held true in the six cities included in her study. By and large, much of Mann's findings corroborated with those of earlier studies; therefore, our focus here is her research on African American females who killed a loved one.

This research compared whether those African American women who killed a loved one were any different than those who killed a nonfamily member. Mann also investigated other subgroup comparisons, such as whether a woman who kills her partner is characteristically similar to one who kills a child (Mann, 1991). Out of her data set, Mann identified 150 African American females who had killed a loved one (study group) and 77 who had killed someone other than a loved one (comparison group). Mann noted that her study group members "tend to be about five years older . . . have attained higher level of education, have slightly more children, and are more likely to be employed [than the comparison group]" (Mann, 1991, p. 132). Mann aptly concluded that the study group members are more representative of our "familial society." As for victim characteristics, Mann reports that the victims of the study group members were generally over the age of twenty-five, while the victims of the comparison group were under twenty-five. Interestingly, while both groups tended to kill other African Americans, the comparison group members were more likely to kill whites (10 percent of their victims) (Mann, 1991, p. 132).

As one may expect, both groups indicated that their motive for the killing was self-defense. Women who killed a family member were more likely to report that the homicide occurred during an emotional encounter (76 percent). These types of homicides typically involved lone offenders. However, murders involving women in Mann's comparison group tended to be premeditated and involve an accomplice (Mann, 1991, p. 132). Mann's results also showed that those offenders in her comparison group were more likely to be under the influence of alcohol, have a criminal record, and receive a more severe sentence (longer prison term) than those women in the study group. As a part of this study, Mann also examined maternal filicide (a mother killing her child) offenders. Her comparison of the punishment for the various offenses showed that filicide offenders only averaged 3.8 years in prison (Mann, 1991, p. 142).

Mann concluded this paper by calling for the elimination of "poor education, unemployment, poverty, and many other indicators of social disorganization contributing to the anger and violence that lead black women to kill their children and others whom they love" (Mann, 1991, p. 145). Interestingly, while much of Mann's findings in this study were consistent with prior research, she still felt a need to further investigate the issue of maternal filicide.

Maternal Filicide

Using a subsample from her original data set (Mann, 1988), Mann investigated the crime of maternal filicide. Her subsample included ten filicide cases in 1979 and fifteen cases in 1983. While this event historically was not found in the African American community (Mann, 1988), Mann's results show that African American children were twice as likely to be victims of filicide. Furthermore, as in the past, little girls tended to be the victims of filicide (60 percent). Many of the filicide offenders had previous records (40 percent). And 90 percent of the offenders in cases where the filicide victims were older (ages 2–5) had child abuse histories. Of these disturbing figures, Mann observed: "It would seem that the early identification of these woman as child abusers and the utilization of some type of therapeutic intervention might have prevented the subsequent filicide" (Mann, 1988, p. 237).

As noted earlier, the filicide offenders received very lenient sentences as compared to other homicide offenders. For example, although "all of the filicide offenders [in Mann's study] were initially charged with some form of murder (84 percent) or manslaughter (16 percent) . . . only 19 percent . . . were finally charged with murder (Mann, 1988, p. 238). And only 40 percent of the convicted women were sentenced to prison.

Mann's focus on maternal filicide speaks to the depth of her concern about female violence. Moreover, her exploration into areas in need of research, such as maternal filicide, has been responsible for welcome additions to the criminal justice/

criminology literature. Another area of research that Mann has taken the lead in is minorities/race and crime. From very early on, she has paid close attention to the treatment of minorities in the criminal justice system (see, for example, Mann, 1984a, 1984b). Over the last decade, she has remained at the fore of the minorities and crime dialogue (see Mann, 1989, 1990b, 1994, 1995b, 1995c, 1997). Additionally, her book *Unequal Justice: A Question of Color* (1993) has been referred to as possibly "the most significant examination of race and crime in over two decades" (Bowman, 1994, p. 1104). Her debates concerning the "discrimination thesis" (DT) (cf. Mann, 1993) and William Wilbanks's "no discrimination thesis" (NDT) (see Wilbanks, 1987) have become legendary. In the process, however, Mann has contributed mightily to the advancement of knowledge in this area. We review some of her contributions in this area below.

Minorities and Crime

As previously noted, Mann has always addressed the plight of minorities in her research. However, with the publication of William Wilbanks's book, *The Myth of a Racist Criminal Justice System* (1987), Mann delved even further into this subject. Immediately following the publication of Wilbanks's book, Mann was asked to respond to his NDT. Summarizing his NDT, Wilbanks (1990, p. 5) wrote:

> I take the position that the perception of the criminal justice system as racist is a myth. This overall thesis should not be misinterpreted. I do believe that there is racial prejudice and discrimination *within* the criminal justice system, in that there are individuals, both white and black, who make decisions, at least in part, on the basis of race. I do not believe that *the system* is characterized by racial prejudice or discrimination *against* blacks.

After her initial written response to the NDT, Mann, along with Wilbanks, was invited to debate the issue at the 1988 American Society of Criminology meeting, which was followed by another appearance in the spring of 1989 at Illinois State University (Mann, 1990b).

Although Mann acknowledged that this ongoing dialogue was healthy for the discipline, she remained particularly concerned about those "silent" supporters of the NDT. As she put it: "I am fearful of the thoughts festering in them and the nature and content of their instruction to students and colleagues that stem from those thoughts" (Mann, 1990, p. 16). As a result of this fear, Mann took the lead in challenging the NDT. In 1989, Mann began her quest to the fore of the minorities/race and crime discourse with an article on minority women in the criminal justice system (Mann, 1989). In the article, which discussed the "double bind" that minority women are faced with because of their minority and female status, Mann follows a review of the acute statistics of minority women in the criminal justice system with a detailed review of the literature that addressed their experience at every stage of the system (ibid., 1989, pp. 97–104). After this review, Mann made the following recommendations:

1. Indeterminate sentencing exclusively applied to women should be eliminated;
2. Prostitution should be decriminalized, particularly since such laws have a discriminatory effect against minority women, while ignoring the male customer who is usually white;
3. Other victimless crimes, such as drug and alcohol abuse, should be viewed as the diseases they are and decriminalized;
4. Educational programs should be initiated to orient both Native Americans and criminal justice personnel to the rights of Native Americans and the discretion and powers of tribal laws and courts; translators should be provided at every level of the criminal justice system for those minorities who are not English speaking; and
5. More women and minority judges and other administrators should be installed at every level of the judicial system. (Mann, 1989, pp. 106–7)

This publication was followed with a direct response to Wilbanks's NDT (Mann, 1990b). As previously noted, while Wilbanks does acknowledge that there is prejudice and racial discrimination in the criminal justice system, he does not feel "the whole barrel is rotten" (ibid., p. 16). However, Mann takes the stance that "racism in the criminal justice system has become institutionalized in the same way that it has in other organizational segments of the nation such as education, politics, religion, and the economic structure; and the barrel *is* rotten" (p. 16). And while she noted the insufficiency of the available research to "prove" one position over the other, she criticized Wilbanks for his dependency on primarily large statistical studies to support his thesis. Mann specifically takes Wilbanks to task for "discount[ing] both qualitative, and observational research and minority personal experiences as 'ignorant' and invalid measures to study racism in the system" (p. 19).

For the five years leading up to 1993, Mann continued to respond to supporters of the NDT, while also writing her strongest challenge to the thesis. In 1993, Mann published *Unequal Justice: A Question of Color,* which is likely the most comprehensive volume written on race and crime in the twentieth century. While others have published volumes on the topic before (see, for examples, Bonger, 1943; Flowers, 1990; Georges-Abeyie, 1984; Wilbanks, 1987; Wolfgang and Cohen, 1970) and after Mann's work (see, for examples, Free, 1996; Miller, 1996; Russell, 1998; Tonry, 1995; Walker, Spohn, and De Lone, 1996), few, if any, approach the depth of Mann's investigation of the subject.

Unequal Justice includes a thorough review of the available studies on criminal justice and American minorities. Additionally, Mann reviewed the historical experiences of each minority group. From her review of these experiences, Mann noted:

The exploitation of African Americans, Asian Americans, and Hispanic Americans as sources of slave or cheap labor in the history and ongoing development of this country and the original siezure of the country from the indigenous Native Americans clearly indicate the manifest politico-economic underpinnings of a once patent, but now more subtle pattern of racial discrimination. In order to maintain their hegemony, Euro-Americans, who at first simpy enslaved, misemployed, or through cunning and duplicity seized the property of these racial groups, later turned to more meticulous manipulations of the law itself to accomplish the original plan. (1993c, p. ix)

She follows a review of minority experiences with a discussion of the so-called minority crime problem. Here she discussed both the Uniform Crime Reports (UCR) and the National Crime Victimization Survey (NCVS), noting the limitations of each. After reviewing crime patterns for all minority groups and whites, Mann thoughtfully conducted a comparative analysis of within-group proportions of UCR arrest offenses for whites, African Americans, Hispanics, Native Americans, and Asians. From this analysis, she concluded that, while the extent of minority crime is disproportionate,

> minority status notwithstanding, persons are arrested in this country for essentially the same crimes. A look within each subgroup's arrest portfolio has demonstrated that the proportions of each type of crime do not vary substantially between minorities, or between minorities and whites. (Mann, 1993c, p. 45)

Following her analysis of arrest statistics, Mann reviewed the many theoretical perspectives commonly used to explain minority crime.

A notable contribution in this section is Mann's focus on minority theorists and their explanations for minority crime. While not exhaustive, her review of minority scholarship speaks to the unique perspective minority scholars can bring to the study of minority crime (something we have highlighted throughout this text). Since many minority scholars are familiar with these communities, which incidentally are constantly the focus of crime-related and other research, Mann is adamant in her belief that "[m]inority scholars have been systematically and effectively denied the opportunity to initiate funded research on minority crime . . . Only in the past decade have a few minority researchers been awarded major grants to address any research subject, much less studies of minorities like themselves" (Mann, 1993, p. 72). We review Mann's thoughts in this area again later in this chapter.

In the remainder of *Unequal Justice,* Mann dissects the criminal justice system by thoroughly analyzing the available relevant literature on each stage of the criminal justice system. This analysis clearly shows how all phases of the criminal justice system are biased against minorities.

Since the publication of *Unequal Justice*, Mann has remained active, having published two additional books (Mann, 1996, Mann and Zatz, 1998). It is clear, however, that in her retirement, she has devoted a large part of her time to the vigorous pursuit of public policy changes she believes will reduce minority involvement in the criminal justice system. A recent publication by Mann summarizes some of her proposed policy changes (Mann, 1997). We review her policy recommendations below.

Minorities, Criminal Justice, and Public Policy

In her article "We Need No More Wars" (1997) Mann presents some old and new policy recommendations for the criminal justice system. After presenting the often-cited figures from recent research on African American involvement in the criminal justice system, Mann states that the primary beneficiaries of this research are the researchers. This is the case because, as she correctly notes, researchers benefit "by adding publications to their resumes, aiding in their promotion and tenure process, and bringing them renown and celebrity" (Mann, 1997, p. 565). She acknowledges that some have changed the system, but primarily by enacting more punitive policies. According to Mann, another detrimental effect of these studies is that they perpetuate negative stereotypes of minorities, which contribute to white fear. Because of her views, Mann's first policy recommendation to solve the problems of gangs, drugs, and violence requires "the cessation of state and federally funded research to study minority crime and delinquency unless the researchers are minorities" (ibid.).

Mann proposes the aforementioned policy for two reasons. First, as she alluded to earlier in *Unequal Justice,* since minorities are often familiar with these communities, many having lived in them previously, they would bring "reality to the research" (Mann, 1997, p. 565).

Second, because of the limited number of minority researchers who have received funding for research on minorities, Mann believes they should be given priority in funding situations. Mann recommends this action taking into consideration that, in her opinion: "[t]he hundreds of grants funded to Caucasians over the last two decades to 'study' minority crime produced a picture of minority crime that is biased, inaccurate, and certainly not intended to address, much less eliminate, the problems they purport to identify" (Mann, 1997, p. 565). Under a later section devoted entirely to Mann's proposed policies, she addresses drug policy, research policy, revisiting antipoverty programs, strengthening social institutions, and new law recommendations by African American scholars.

In the area of drug policy, Mann calls for the legalization of drugs. She believes, as do other scholars, that drug addiction is a medical problem and should be treated as such. She advocates "the treatment of registered drug users through the regulation and control of the substance" (Mann, 1997, p. 572). As for her criminal justice research policy recommendation, Mann adds to her previously stated policy recommendation by noting that since we know enough about the problems of the inner city, we should not fund any more research devoted to this area. Instead, the money that would normally have been spent on researching minority youths and adults in the inner cities should be redirected to drug treatment and rehabilitation programs (ibid.). Mann closes her discussion of research policy by encouraging researchers who do not agree with her position to work with state and federal agencies "to adopt a more realistic research focus, one centered on the primary drug users—white Americans" (ibid.).

An admirer of the 1960s "war on poverty," Mann believes that we should revisit some of the approaches from the program. In her eyes, "[t]his was the only 'war' that made sense, but also had the potential for introducing major changes in U.S. social institutions. Unfortunately, with few exceptions like Headstart and the Job Corps, the war effort was prematurely abandoned" (Mann, 1997, p. 573). In a similar vein, she suggests that since discrimination is so much a part of American society, the country is in need of "a mammoth program of social and economic reform involving the inclusive restructuring of *all* of our social institutions" (ibid.). Only through this restructuring does Mann see any potential for change in regard to minority involvement in the criminal justice system.

A final issue Mann addresses is recent laws proposed by African American scholars. In this area, Mann points to the recent scholarship by Butler (1995) and Russell (1996), who propose legislation on "jury-nullification" and "racial hoaxes." Both scholars provide insights into proposed legislation that has the potential for improving the "justice" minorities receive in the criminal justice system. Their publications are illustrative of the alternative views of minority scholars, which Mann believes are essential if American society is serious about reducing the involvement of minorities in the criminal justice system.

CONCLUSION

Over the past twenty years, Coramae Richey Mann has accomplished what most scholars strive to achieve in careers that typically span thirty to forty years. She has become a leading criminologist whose publications and opinions are widely respected. Her research, particularly in the areas of female crime and delinquency, violent female criminality, and minorities and crime have notably advanced the discipline in each of these areas. More specifically, Mann's pioneering research on female homicide in six major U.S. cities resulted in the publication of numerous articles focusing on several aspects of female violence. And with the publication of her already classic book *Unequal Justice,* Mann has quieted the NDT supporters for now. We suspect that it will take several more years for them to produce a response equal to Mann's treatise.

References

Bonger, W. A. (1943). *Race and crime.* New York: Columbia University Press.

Bowman, P. (1994). Race and criminal justice: Research, theoretical, and policy issues. *Contemporary Psychology, 39,* 1104–5.

Butler, P. (1995). Racially based jury nullification: Black power in the criminal justice system. *Yale Law Journal, 105,* 677–725.

Chesney-Lind, M. (1977). Judicial paternalism and the female status offender: Training women to know their place. *Crime and Delinquency, 23* (2), 121–30.

Flowers, R. B. (1990). *Minorities and criminality.* New York: Greenwood Press.

Free, M. D. (1996). *African Americans and the criminal justice system.* New York: Garland Publications, Inc.

Georges-Abeyie, D. (ed.). (1984). *The criminal justice system and blacks.* New York: Clark Boardman.

Goetting, A. (1988). When females kill one another. *Criminal Justice and Behavior, 15,* 179–89.

Mann, C. R. (1979a). Making jail the hard way: Law and the female offender. *Corrections Today, 41,* 35–41.

———. (1979b). The differential treatment between boys and girls in juvenile court. *Juvenile and Family Court Journal, 30,* 37–48.

———. (1980a). Legal and judicial battles affecting runaways. *Journal of Family Issues, 1,* 229–48.

———. (1980b). Court room observations of extra-legal factors in the juvenile court dispositions of runaway boys: A field study. *Juvenile and Family Court Journal, 30,* 43–52.

———. (1984a). *Female crime and delinquency.* Tuscaloosa, Alabama University Press.

———. (1984b). Race and sentencing of female felons: A field study. *International Journal of Women's Studies, 7,* 160–72.

———. (1987). Black women who kill. In R. L. Hampton (ed.), *Violence in the black family* (pp. 157–86). Lexington, MA: D.C. Heath.

———. (1988). Getting even: Women who kill in domestic violence encounters. *Justice Quarterly, 5,* 33–51.

———. (1989). Minority and female: A criminal justice double bind. *Social Justice, 16,* 95–114.

———. (1990a). Black female homicide in the United States. *Journal of Interpersonal Violence, 5,* 176–201.

———. (1990b). Random thoughts on the ongoing Wilbanks-Mann diiscourse. In B. D. MacLean & D. Milovanovic (eds.), *Racism, empiricism and criminal justice.* Vancouver: Collective Press.

———. (1991). Black women who kill their loved ones. In R. L. Hampton (ed.), *Black family violence: Current research and theory* (pp. 129–46). Lexington, MA: D.C. Heath.

———. (1992). Female murderers and their motives: A tale of two cities. In E. Viano (ed.), *Intimate violence* (pp. 73–81). Washington, DC: Hemisphere Publishing Corporation.

————. (1993a). Sister against sister: Female intrasexual homicide. In C. Culliver (ed.), *Female criminality: The state of the art* (pp. 195–223). New York: Garland Publishing Company.

————. (1993b). Maternal homicide of preschoolers. In A.V. Wilson (ed.), *Homicide: The victim/offender connection* (pp. 227–46). Cincinnati, OH: Anderson Publishing.

————. (1993c). *Unequal justice: A question of color.* Bloomington: Indiana University Press.

————. (1994). A minority view of juvenile justice. *Washington and Lee Law Review, 51,* 465–78.

————. (1995a). Seventeen white men and me. In A. Goetting & S. Fenstermaker (eds.), *Individual voices, collective visions: Fifty years of women in sociology* (pp. 273–83). Philadelphia: Temple University Press.

————. (1995b). Women of color and the criminal justice system. In B. Raffel Price & Natalie J. Sokoloff (Eds.), *The Criminal Justice System and Women.* New York: Clark Boardman.

————. (1995c). The contribution of institutionalized racism to minority crime. In D. F. Hawkins (ed.), *Ethnicity, race, and crime* (pp. 259–80). Albany: SUNY Press.

————. (1996). *When women kill.* Albany: SUNY Press.

————. (1997). We need no more wars. *Valparaiso University Law Review, 31,* 565–78.

Mann C. R. & Zatz, M. S. (1998). *Images of color, images of crime.* Los Angeles: Roxbury Publishing Company.

Mann, C. R. & McNeely, R. L. (1990) Domestic violence is a human issue. *Journal of Interpersonal Violence, 5* (1), 129–30.

Miller, J. (1996). *Search and destroy: African-American males in the criminal justice system.* Cambridge: Cambridge University Press.

Russell, K. (1996). The racial hoax as crime: The law as affirmation. *Indiana Law Journal, 71* (3), 594–621.

————. (1998). *The color of crime: Racial hoaxes, white fear, black protectionism, police harassment, and other macroaggressions.* New York: New York University Press.

Tonry, M. (1995). *Malign neglect: Race, crime, and punishment in America.* New York: Oxford University Press.

Walker, S., Spohn, C. & DeLone, M. (1996). *The color of justice: Race, ethnicity, and crime in America.* Belmont, CA: Wadsworth Publishing Company.

Wilbanks, W. (1987). *The myth of a racist criminal justice system.* Monterey, CA: Brooks/Cole Publishing Company.

————. (1990). The myth of a racist criminal justice system. In B. D. MacLean & D. Milovanovic (eds.), *Racism, empiricism and criminal justice* (pp. 5–11). Vancouver: Collective Press.

Wolfgang, M. & Cohen, B. (1970). *Race and crime: Conceptions and misconceptions.* New York: Institute of Human Relations Press.

William Julius Wilson

Six

WILLIAM JULIUS WILSON
(1935–   )

INTRODUCTION

A product of extremely humble beginnings, William Julius Wilson has risen to the apex of the academic establishment. Many consider Wilson, a sociologist, one of the preeminent scholars of the last quarter of the twentieth century. His most significant works focus on race, class, and specifically the underclass or the truly disadvantaged (those persons remaining in the depths of poverty within the inner cities). Increasingly, however, his work has become more criminologically oriented. This is probably a result of the increasing national concern about crime in the inner cities where Wilson specializes.

Only recently, however, have criminologists begun to take notice of Wilson's two recent tomes, *The Truly Disadvantaged* (1987) and *When Work Disappears* (1996). Bernard (1990), for example, has presented a criminological theory incorporating Wilson's research on the truly disadvantaged. And recent research has found substantial support for Wilson's work as it pertains to crime (see, for examples, Krivo & Peterson, 1996; Parker & McCall, 1999). Other recent publications by Wilson, in collaboration with influential criminologists (Elliott, Wilson, Huizinga, Sampson, Elliott & Rankin, 1996; Sampson & Wilson, 1995), have landed him squarely in the center of discussions on crime in urban areas. In fact, over the past few years, Wilson has consistently been called upon to offer his opinions and suggestions on issues related to the urban poor. He has willingly served in this role, which, at times, has brought him invitations to the White House (Remnick, 1996). Thus, while Wilson's work is not as widely discussed as it likely deserves to be in criminal justice and criminology circles, his influence in affecting policies that relate to inner-city problems such as crime cannot be overstated.

BIOGRAPHICAL INFORMATION

The first of six children born to Esco Wilson and Pauline Bracey Wilson, William Julius Wilson was born 20 December 1935 in the rural community of Derry Township located about forty miles East of Pittsburgh, Pennsylvania (Billingsley, 1989; Williams, 1993). His family lived in a two-bedroom home, where he and his five siblings shared one room. Wilson's father worked in the coalmines and steel mills of

Pittsburgh until his untimely death at the age of thirty-nine from lung disease (Flowers, 1989). Because of his sudden death, Wilson's family had to go onto public assistance for a brief period. Discussing this difficult period, Wilson commented:

> We used to go hungry a lot. It was real poverty . . . We were struggling all the time. We lived on an inadequate diet. For a family of seven, we had one quart of milk a week. Thank God, we had a garden and could grow string beans, carrots, corn, tomatoes, squash, and can them all for winter. (Wilson as quoted in Remnick, 1996, p. 99)

Wilson's mother eventually found part-time work in town as a domestic, which helped the family through these difficult times.

Wilson recalls his family being one of only a few African American families in town. As could be expected in this era, this caused Wilson, on occasion, to be called a "nigger." Additionally, Wilson acknowledged that he engaged in some fights instigated by racial slurs directed at him (Remnick, 1996, p. 99). He also remembers discrimination occurring in some stores in his hometown. Wilson specifically recalls an incident where a restaurant refused to serve his family.

Even with these impediments, Wilson never considered his situation abject poverty. That is, he never felt that he was destined to a life of poverty. As he put it:

> We were poor, but we *didn't* feel trapped in poverty . . . Even though my parents didn't go past the ninth and tenth grades, it never occurred to me that I wasn't going to college—that I wouldn't have a bright future. There was never that feeling of hopelessness, of despair. (Wilson as quoted in Remnick, 1996, p. 99)

In fact, despite their situation, all of Wilson's siblings were expected to go to college. According to Wilson, they all did (Remnick, 1996, p. 99).

Two early influences in Wilson's life were his teachers and his aunt Janice Wardlaw. Wilson recalls that his teachers never gave up on him or his siblings. One teacher recognized his potential (he had a high I.Q.) and told him to live up to it (Remnick 1996, p. 99). Janice Wardlaw, Wilson's father's sister, had a profound impact on him. Wardlaw was the first person in Wilson's family to get a college education. Since her education was partially funded with the help of Wilson's father, Wardlaw took extra care in ensuring that Wilson received the guidance and financial support he needed to attend college (Flowers, 1989, p. 79). Wilson spent summers with Wardlaw, who resided in New York and regularly took him on trips to various museums in New York. In addition to her constant encouragement, these trips gave Wilson the confidence he needed during his early schooling and professional appointments (Remnick, 1996, p. 99).

Following high school, Wilson enrolled at Wilberforce University in Ohio, where he was financed with money from his church and his aunt. While at Wilberforce, Wilson came under the influence of sociologist Maxwell Brooks, who sparked his interests in social problems and race (Remnick, 1996, p. 99). This interest was further instigated with Wilson's reading of the works of notable African American scholars W. E. B. Du Bois, Charles Johnson, E. Franklin Frazier, and the key figures of the golden age of the Chicago School of Sociology, Robert Park and Ernest Burgess. After his exposure to the writings of these scholars, Wilson became interested in an academic career. In 1958, Wilson graduated with a B.A. in sociology and history.

From 1958 to 1960, Wilson served in the U.S. Army, where his actions earned him a Meritorious Service Award in 1960. Immediately upon his return to civilian life, Wilson enrolled at Bowling Green State University in Ohio. In 1961, Wilson received a M.A. in sociology and history. Keeping with his career aim of academics, Wilson applied to graduate school. Although he was accepted in the highly respected doctoral program at Columbia University (where Robert K. Merton was on the faculty), Wilson chose instead to attend Washington State University (Remnick, 1996, p. 99).

Wilson was recruited to Washington State by a white liberal southerner named T. H. Kennedy, who had recruited other African American students to the Pullman, Washington campus. According to Billingsley (1989, p. 8), during this period "Washington State was one of the few major universities to welcome Black graduate students, and until recently it had produced more Black doctorates in sociology than any other." At Washington State, Wilson specialized in theory and the philosophy of the social sciences (Wilson, 1988). Reflecting on his experience at Washington State, Wilson commented: "I became a star out there and came into my own . . . It was a real ego boost" (Wilson as quoted in Remnick, 1996, p. 99).

In 1965, after four years in the program, Wilson left and accepted an appointment back East as an assistant professor of sociology at the University of Massachusetts, Amherst. A year later, in 1966, under the direction of Professor Richard H. Ogles, Wilson completed his dissertation, "Preference, Evaluation, and Norms: Empirical Exploration in Measurement," and received a doctorate in sociology and anthropology. Three years later, Wilson was promoted to associate professor of sociology. And, in 1970, he received the Distinguished Teacher of the Year Award.

In 1971, following his success at the University of Massachusetts, Amherst, Wilson accepted a visiting faculty appointment in the Department of Sociology at the University of Chicago. This appointment led to a permanent position at the University of Chicago the following academic year. Wilson's appointment at the University of Chicago began a long and productive tenure as a faculty member in the Department of Sociology. After being on the faculty for four years, Wilson was promoted to the rank of professor. In both of these academic appointments, Wilson received exceptional opportunities and support (Billingsley, 1989). In fact, Wilson has said that following his early graduate school period, he does not recall experiencing any overt racial discrimination in or outside of academe (ibid., 1989, p. 9).

The year 1978 was one of tremendous achievement and controversy for Wilson. Already widely respected as a scholar, the publication of *The Declining Significance of Race* made Wilson one of the most widely known figures in America. At the same time, however, two separate interpretations of the book's thesis (which is discussed later) cast Wilson in two different lights. On the one hand, conservatives embraced Wilson's book as a work in support of their belief that affirmative action was no longer needed. Conversely, liberals, and particularly African Americans (including the Association of Black Sociologists), denounced the book, stating that it was a "misrepresentation of the black experience" (Wilson, 1988, p. 79). The book essentially polarized Wilson from many persons with whom he had long professional associations.

Wilson became chairperson of the Department of Sociology in 1978. During the end of his first tenure as chairperson (he also served as chair from 1984 through 1987), Wilson was appointed the Lucy Flower professor of urban sociology (1980–1984). From 1984 through 1990, Wilson served as Lucy Flower distinguished service professor. And, from 1990 through 1996, he served as Lucy Flower university professor and as director of the Center for the Study of Urban Inequality.

Early in 1996, Henry Louis Gates Jr., chairperson of the Department of Afro-American Studies at Harvard University, threw a dinner for Wilson in Cambridge, Massachusetts. Present were Harvard's most notable African American intellectuals, including Anthony Appiah, Orlando Patterson, Leon and Evelyn Higginbotham, Charles Ogletree, and Cornel West. Wilson described this evening as "one of the most exciting . . . of my life" (Remnick, 1996, p. 105). The evening impressed Wilson not only because the dinner was in his honor, but because of the wide intellectual discussion: "Harvard has somehow collected this critical mass of black intellectuals, and I could no longer resist it. No matter what Chicago could still offer, I had to make the change. I had to come" (Remnick, 1996, p. 105). So after twenty-four years at the University of Chicago, Wilson headed to Cambridge as the Malcolm Wiener professor of social policy in the John F. Kennedy School of Government at Harvard University. He also has a joint appointment in the Department of Afro-American Studies.

Over the past twenty years, Wilson has been one of the most celebrated sociologists in the United States and overseas. His achievements have included many awards, honorary doctorate degrees (twenty-six as of 1997), and, from 1989 through 1990, Wilson became only the second African American to serve as president of the American Sociological Association. These many achievements have resulted in Wilson being a much sought after consultant on various local, state, and national social policy issues. Highlighted below are Wilson's most important contributions to criminology and criminal justice.

CONTRIBUTIONS TO CRIMINOLOGICAL THOUGHT

Interestingly, much of Wilson's early work focused on sociological theory construction (Wilson & Dumont, 1967; Wilson & Dumont, 1968; Wilson & Nye, 1966; Wilson, Sofias, & Ogles, 1964; Wilson, 1969a). Not until the fall of 1969, three years after he received the doctorate, did Wilson address any substantive topics related to race (Wilson, 1969b). Wilson has noted that although he did not have a specialty in race and ethnic relations, the civil rights movement and the urban riots of the 1960s sparked his "intellectual curiosity for the subject" (Wilson, 1988). Soon afterward, Wilson decided to develop a specialty in this area.

Wilson's development of a specialty in race and ethnic relations is central to his contributions to criminology/criminal justice because it is from his specialty in this area that his significant contributions emanate. This section includes a discussion of Wilson's early research in the area of race and class, which is followed by a discussion of his research on the truly disadvantaged and his recent theoretical perspective on race and crime with Robert Sampson.

Early Research

Wilson's early research on race and ethnic relations had very little to do with crime. Much of this early work attempted to investigate race relations and various African American issues overall (Wilson, 1969b, 1970, 1972a, 1972b; Wilson & Tausky, 1971 Rose, Rothman & Wilson, 1973). Wilson has suggested that his first book, *Power, Racism, and Privilege* (1973), was an outgrowth of his concern "about the lack of theoretical, historical, and cross-cultural studies in the field of race relations" (Wilson, 1988, p. 81). This publication was a comparison of race relations in the United States and South Africa. Of this book, Wilson has commented:

> By the time the book was in press and much too late to retrieve . . . my thinking about the field of race relations in America had already begun to change and I regretted that I not only paid so little attention to the role of class in understanding the issues of race, but also that I tended to treat blacks as a monolithic socioeconomic group. (Wilson, 1988, p. 82)

It was from this shortcoming that Wilson began to become more interested in the examination of "social structures and the differences in personal trajectories of professional blacks . . . from those mired in the ghetto" (Wilson, 1988, p. 82). In the fall of 1973, Wilson touched on this issue in an edited volume on race relations (see Rose, Rothman & Wilson, 1973); however, it was not until the publication of *The Declining Significance of Race* (1978) did Wilson's ideas on race and class, as he put it, "sufficiently crystallize" (Wilson, 1988, p. 82).

Wilson's ideas on race and class in *The Declining Significance of Race* are the hallmarks of his later significant contributions to criminal justice. Wilson has summarized his thesis in *The Declining Significance of Race* as follows:

> the basic argument in *The Declining Significance of Race* is that different systems of production in combination with different policies of the state impose different constraints on the structuration of racial group relations by producing dissimilar contexts not only for the manifestation of racial antagonisms but also for racial-group access to rewards and privileges. (1988, p. 83)

While Wilson had hoped to accentuate two equally important trends with this book, the more important message regarding the worsening conditions of the African American underclass got lost in his discussion of the improving conditions of the African American middle class (Wilson, 1988, p. 83). It was not until several years after the book's publication that observers began to take notice of Wilson's arguments on the increasing African American underclass. By then, however, Charles Murray's highly influential work *Losing Ground* (1984) was published and had become the conservative treatise on the underclass and social policy during the Reagan presidency.

Because of the controversy over *The Declining Significance of Race* and the preoccupation with his discussion of the improving conditions of the African American middle class, Wilson set the following objectives for his next research project: first, he wanted to highlight the plight of the urban underclass, and, second, he wanted to clearly present the policy implications of his work (this was another persistent criticism of *The Declining Significance of Race*). The result of his efforts to achieve these two objectives was *The Truly Disadvantaged: The Inner City, the Underclass, and Public Policy* (1987). While *The Truly Disadvantaged* is not a book about crime per se, its discussion about the urban underclass or "The Truly Disadvantaged" (the group of persons at the bottom of the underclass) remains an important work in the area of the etiology of urban crime. Besides *The Truly Disadvantaged,* more recent works by Wilson have brought more structure to his ideas on the underclass as they directly relate to crime in urban areas (Elliot et al., 1996; Sampson and Wilson, 1995; Wilson, 1996).

The Truly Disadvantaged and Urban Crime

It is fitting that much of Wilson's work on the truly disadvantaged was conducted while he was a faculty member in the Department of Sociology at the University of Chicago. This department has been the setting for some of the earliest pioneering sociological studies (Anderson, 1923; Frazier, 1932; Shaw, 1929; Shaw and McKay, 1942). While at Chicago, Wilson continued the legacy of pioneering sociological research on social issues concerning both Chicago and other urban cities throughout the United States. Speaking of the influence of the city on his research on the truly disadvantaged, Wilson (1987) has noted that "many of the central theoretical arguments of *The Truly Disadvantaged* were inspired . . . by my travels to inner-city neighborhoods in the city of Chicago in the past several years" (p. viii). Much like his famous predecessors at the University of Chicago, Wilson used the city of Chicago as a laboratory to examine the plight of the urban underclass. In general, Wilson believes that many of the inner-city social problems, including crime, are the result of racial inequality (Wilson, 1987, p. 20). However, he also believes that these problems "cannot be accounted for simply in terms of racial discrimination or in terms of a culture of poverty. Rather, they must be seen as having complex sociological antecedents that range from demographic changes to problems of economic organization" (Wilson, 1987, p. 22). In an effort to disentangle the cause of crime and other "social dislocations" (i.e., joblessness, out of wedlock births, female-headed families, and welfare dependency), Wilson presents several interrelated explanations for the conditions in urban areas, including societal considerations, demographic information, and neighborhood variables (ibid., p. 30).

Societal considerations include historic and contemporary discrimination. Historic discrimination represents discrimination occurring before the middle of the twentieth century. Contemporary discrimination includes discrimination occurring following the earlier period. Wilson believes you must separate the two periods of discrimination to determine one of the central causes of the plight of the current ghetto underclass. Wilson further believes that of the two, historic discrimination provides the better explanation. On this theme, Wilson cites the example of the large number of underclass African Americans residing in inner cities as a result of historic discrimination. Drawing on the work of Stanley Lieberson, *A Piece of the Pie: Black and White Immigrants since 1880* (1980), Wilson writes that

> blacks were discriminated against far more severely in the early twentieth century than were the new white immigrants from southern, central, and eastern Europe. The disadvantage of skin color . . . is one that blacks shared with the Japanese, Chinese, and other nonwhite groups. However, skin color per se "was not an insurmountable obstacle." Because changes in immigration policy cut off Asian migration to America in the late nineteenth century, the Chinese and Japanese populations did not reach large numbers and, therefore, did not pose as great a threat as did blacks. (1987, p. 33)

Therefore, Wilson believes that what we see today in the inner cities is a direct result of the discrimination encountered by blacks upon their arrival in northern cities during the late nineteenth and early twentieth centuries.

Besides the role of historic discrimination, Wilson also points to the relevance of the age structure in the inner city as another contributor to social dislocations. In this area, Wilson endorses the following thesis of James Q. Wilson: "[A]n abrupt rise in the number of young persons has an 'exponential effect on the rate of certain social problems." W. J. Wilson believes that this thesis is particularly relevant in inner city neighborhoods, and especially in public- housing projects. Public-housing projects, which often contain thousands of economically disadvantaged residents, do not lend themselves to neighborly interaction. Furthermore, the increasing number of teenage and young adults compounds the social disorganization in these areas (Wilson, 1987, p. 38).

Economic change is another variable included in Wilson's explanation of urban area social dislocations. Wilson stresses the impact of structural changes on minorities:

> Urban minorities have been particularly vulnerable to structural economic changes, such as the shift from goods-producing to service-

producing industries, the increasing polarization of the labor market into low-wage and high-wage sectors, technological innovations, and the relocation of manufacturing industries out of the central cities (1987, p. 39).

Wilson believes that because of these structural changes and the increasing educational and skill requirements for these new jobs, urban minorities have been subjected to acute jobless rates.

A final consideration discussed by Wilson to explain social dislocations is something he refers to as "concentration effects." This concept is based on the changes in the inner city as they pertain to the current income demographics of residents in the inner city. That is, Wilson suggests that another area of importance in explaining inner-city social dislocations is the increasing number of persons in poverty areas (census tracts with a poverty rate of at least 20 percent) within inner cities. This coupled with the exodus of nonpoor persons from the inner cities leaves a heavy concentration of poor persons in poverty areas that continue to grow. To highlight the magnitude of the problem, Wilson reviewed data on the five largest cities (New York, Chicago, Los Angeles, Philadelphia, and Detroit). Using data from 1970 to 1980, Wilson notes, "Whereas the total white population in the extreme-poverty areas [census tracts with a poverty rate of at least 40 percent] in the five largest cities increased by 45 percent and the white poor population by only 24 percent, the total black population in these areas increased by 148 percent and the poor black population by 164 percent" (1987, p. 46).

These changes resulted in a disturbing trend, which included the "movement of middle-class black professionals from the inner-city, followed in increasing numbers by working-class blacks, leaving behind a much higher concentration of the most disadvantaged segments of the black urban population" (Wilson, 1987, p. 49). According to Wilson,

> the exodus of middle-and working-class families from many ghetto neighborhoods removes an important "social buffer" that could deflect the full impact of the kind of prolonged and increasing joblessness . . . This argument is based on the assumption that even if the truly disadvantaged segments of an inner-city area experience a significant increase in long-term spells of joblessness, the basic institutions in that area (churches, schools, stores, recreational facilities, etc.) would remain viable if much of the base of their support comes from economically stable and secure families. (1987, p. 56)

To demonstrate the possible effects of these changes, Wilson uses ghetto youth as an example. In this example, Wilson postulates that when there are working and professional families in depressed areas, the youth get to see some families go to and from work. This gives the youth a sense that there is a connection between education and work. Additionally, although there may be a large number of single-parent households in these areas, the existing two-parent households provide some balance to the views of the youth. Finally, youths in the inner city are regularly exposed to criminal activity; however, with the presence of working and professional families, they also see that many residents do not engage in this activity (Wilson, 1987).

Wilson believes that this interaction is essential so that inner-city youth are not just exposed to a singular experience. As he notes: "Unlike poor urban whites or even inner city blacks of earlier years, the residents of highly concentrated poverty neighborhoods in the inner-city today only infrequently interact with those individuals or families who have had a stable work history and have had little involvement with welfare or public assistance" (Wilson, 1987, p. 60). This leaves these individuals in a form of what Wilson calls "social isolation," "the lack of contact or of sustained interaction with individuals and institutions that represent mainstream society" (ibid.).

As demonstrated above, Wilson's explanation for the causes of social dislocations points to a complex set of interrelated concepts. His remedies for solving inner-city social dislocations are equally as complex and, in some minds, controversial. Formulated from his research on the truly disadvantaged and a review of cross-cultural underclass strategies, Wilson's policy recommendations include reducing the use of race-specific policies (i.e., affirmative action), the enactment of universal (nonracial) policies, such as full employment; the maintenance of balanced economic growth; a child support assurance program; a child care strategy; a nationally oriented labor market strategy; and manpower training and education. Of these, we focus here on Wilson's most controversial recommendation, the reduction of affirmative action policies.

This recommendation, more so than any of his other arguments in *The Truly Disadvantaged,* has evoked significant debate. Of race-specific policies, Wilson believes "programs of preferential treatment applied merely according to racial and ethnic group membership tend to benefit the relatively advantaged segments of the designated groups" (Wilson, 1987, p. 115). He adds that "although affirmative action programs do in fact create opportunities for some less advantaged minority individuals, ghetto underclass individuals are severely underrepresented among those who actually benefit from such programs" (ibid.). Wilson is convinced that only universal or nonrace-specific programs will survive into the twenty-first century. That is, he believes that current affirmative action policies will not continue to receive the support and commitment from the majority required for them to continue. He further adds, "The situation is exacerbated by increased hostility to affirmative action by dominant-group workers who fear the loss of their own jobs to minority competition."

As Wilson sees it, the policies best suited to assist the truly disadvantaged in moving out of their situation must include "[c]omprehensive economic policies aimed at the general population but that would also enhance employment opportunities among the truly disadvantaged—both men and women" (1987, p. 150).

This would involve the creation of "a macroeconomic policy designed to promote both economic growth and a tight labor market" (ibid.,p. 151). On this point, Wilson also advocates an increased investment in on-the-job training programs and apprenticeships to enable the truly disadvantaged and other interested persons to attain the skill level required for the currently available employment opportunities. These suggestions constitute what Wilson refers to as the "hidden agenda." It is Wilson's belief that the hidden agenda refers to Wilson's belief that, in order to improve the life's prospects of the truly disadvantaged, policies must be appealing to the more advantaged groups of society to garner support (ibid., p. 155).

While initially considered controversial, Wilson's arguments regarding the dissolution of affirmative action, as with his arguments in *The Declining Significance of Race,* have proven prophetic. With the recent passing of Proposition 209 in California, several years after Wilson professed the above insights, the country has swayed against affirmative action programs. One begins to wonder how many of these programs, as Wilson predicted, will survive in the twenty-first century?

As previously noted, much like *The Declining Significance of Race, The Truly Disadvantaged* evoked both praise and criticism within the scholarly community (see, for examples, Bonacich, 1989; Dill, 1989; Gomes & Fishman, 1989; Marks, 1989). However, as has been his tradition, Wilson not only answers his critics with written rejoinders (see, for examples, Wilson, 1989, 1991a), but he also responds to them by embarking on more ambitious projects that usually further clarify his position. Leading up to his next major project, Wilson continued to regularly contribute to the inner-city dialogue (Wilson, 1989, 1991, 1992, 1994a, 1994b, 1995). While completing these works, he was simultaneously conducting his most ambitious project yet. Funded at the sum of more than $2.5 million, Wilson set out to continue his research on the impoverished communities of Chicago, using ethnographic (including participant observation and life history interviews) and survey methodologies to further explore the plight of the truly disadvantaged. Additionally, Wilson spent a year overseas observing, studying, and comparing the dynamics of race, poverty, and joblessness in the United States to several European countries. The result of this massive research project is Wilson's recent book, *When Work Disappears: The World of the New Urban Poor* (1996). As with *The Truly Disadvantaged,* while not about crime, *When Work Disappears* speaks to the conditions that Wilson believes are significant contributors to the etiology of urban crime. While a full review of *When Work Disappears* is beyond the scope of this chapter, we highlight some of Wilson's discussion that continues his arguments from *The Truly Disadvantaged.*

Early in *When Work Disappears,* Wilson states his thesis: "Many of today's problems in the inner-city ghetto neighborhoods—crime, family dissolution, welfare, low levels of social organization . . . are fundamentally a consequence of the disappearance of Work" (1996, p. xiii). In the chapters that follow, Wilson presents a plethora of statistics and ethnographic accounts that lend support to his thesis. Specifically, as in *The Truly Disadvantaged,* Wilson highlights the severity of inner-city problems and recommends both short-term and long-term initiatives to address them.

Notable additions to Wilson's earlier arguments briefly reviewed here include survey data on employer impressions of young African American males and Wilson's short- and long-term proposals. Based on a survey of 179 firms in the Chicago area, Wilson investigated employer perceptions of inner-city workers in the following areas: job skills, basic skills, work ethic, dependability, attitudes, and interpersonal skills. The results were striking. Wilson reports that many of the employers interviewed "consider inner-city workers—especially young black males—to be uneducated, unstable, uncooperative, and dishonest" (1996, p. 111).

Unfortunately, this finding confirms some of the worst fears of many African American males, who believe that they are often not employed because of the ongoing "assassination" of the African American male image (see Hutchinson, 1994). Furthermore, with employers expressing such negative feelings regarding African American male workers, the likelihood that young African American males will leave the underground economy (i.e., drug dealing) to pursue legitimate employment opportunities is obviously diminished.

To address the increasing employment needs of the truly disadvantaged, Wilson recommends the following long-term and short-term initiatives: the development of a system of national performance standards in public schools, family policies to reinforce the learning system in the schools, a national system of school-to-work transition, and ways to promote city-suburban integration and cooperation. Additionally, Wilson suggests the development of job information and placement centers and the creation of jobs like those of the Works Progress Administration (WPA),[1] which would include a number of employment opportunities in public works activities (i.e, highway construction, housing construction).

Based on the research from *The Truly Disadvantaged*, *When Work Disappears*, and that of his former colleague at the University of Chicago Robert J. Sampson (1987), the two formulated a perspective to explain race and violent crime (Sampson and Wilson, 1995). The perspective is discussed below.

A Theory of Race, Crime, and Urban Inequality

In response to the paucity of productive discussions on race and crime, Sampson and Wilson (1995) make a significant contribution to the race and crime literature. They combine the results of their earlier individual research efforts to examine race and violent crime. The result, as Hagan and Peterson (1995) suggest is "a powerful structural and cultural analysis." On race and crime, Sampson and Wilson offer the following explanation:

> [Our] basic thesis is that macro social patterns of residential inequality give rise to the social isolation and ecological concentration of the truly disadvantaged, which in turn leads to structural barriers and cultural adaptations that undermine social organization and hence the control of crime. This thesis is grounded in what is actually an old idea in criminol-

ogy that has been overlooked in the race and crime debate—the importance of communities. (1995, p. 38)

Sampson and Wilson stress the important role of communities in explaining race and crime in urban areas. Using a macro social or community-level approach, they draw upon the classic work of Shaw and McKay (1942) to examine inner-city crime. The community-level approach of Shaw and McKay found that irrespective of who resided in certain areas of the inner city, high rates of delinquency persisted. Noting the relevancy of Shaw and McKay's work today, Sampson and Wilson ask the following questions: (1) to what extent do black rates of crime vary by type of ecological area? and (2) is it possible to reproduce in white communities the structural circumstances in which blacks live?

To answer the first question, Sampson and Wilson consider whether, irrespective of where African Americans reside, they exhibit the same criminal behaviors. According to the earlier work of Shaw and McKay, the answer is no. Sampson and Wilson suggest that present-day research also supports this notion. For example, they use Sampson's earlier research to show that "joblessness and poverty appear to exert much of their influence [on violent crime (murder and robbery)] indirectly through family disruption [i.e., female-headed households]" (p. 40). Although the African American community has more family disruption than white families, the effects are the same in terms of a positive influence on juvenile and adult violence (Sampson and Wilson, 1995). This finding clearly supports Shaw and McKay's earlier findings.

As for the second question, Sampson and Wilson note that, while there may be similar causes of African American and white violent crime, the conditions in which whites and African Americans live are remarkably different "especially with regard to concentrated urban poverty" (p. 41). Therefore, the noticeable difference in black and white rates of violence is likely a product of their dramatically different communities. On this point, Sampson and Wilson reviewed the 1980 race-specific census data on the 171 largest cities and could not find one city in which blacks and whites lived in equality in regard to economic and family organization. This finding supports Wilson's (1987) previously reviewed ideas on "concentration effects" and shows that the answer to the second question is also no.

As for the role of culture in their perspective, Sampson and Wilson incorporate Wilson's (1987) previously discussed idea of social isolation. As noted earlier, Wilson believes that since the truly disadvantaged remain isolated from mainstream individuals and institutions, they are forced to adapt to the constraints and opportunities afforded them vis-à-vis the internalization of norms associated with culture-of-violence or culture-of-poverty theories.

With their perspective, Sampson and Wilson demonstrate the power of community-level research. The implications of their research are far-reaching, especially as they pertain to combating inner-city crime. They offer the following suggestion for policymakers contemplating potential remedies for inner-city crime: "[O]ur framework suggests the need to take a renewed look at social policies that focus on prevention. We do not need more after-the-fact (reactive) approaches that ignore the structural context of crime and the social organization of inner cities" (1995, p. 54).

CONCLUSION

This chapter reviewed William Julius Wilson's writings on the truly disadvantaged. The review showed that Wilson's work has serious implications for criminologists interested in explaining inner-city crime. While Wilson is not yet commonly cited as an authority in criminology/criminal justice, his works are becoming increasingly recognized for their relevancy to the discipline. Interestingly, Wilson is already recognized as a central figure in the social sciences, as evidenced by his being the most cited African American scholar for the fifth year in a row (*Journal of Blacks in Higher Education*, 1998). This is a far cry from Wilson's showing in the criminology or criminal justice literature, where he is rarely cited in the six major criminology and criminal justice journals (Cohn and Farrington, 1998). So even though Wilson has firmly etched his name in the annals of American sociology, we believe that, when all is said and done, the name *William Julius Wilson* will be similarly etched in the annals of American criminology.

Finally, as Wilson settles into his new home at Harvard, we can expect, within a few years, to see an extensive research project underway in the depressed areas of Boston. Wilson will once again respond to his critics with an impressive product on the truly disadvantaged.

References

Anderson, N. (1923). *The hobo*. Chicago: The University of Chicago Press.

Bernard, T. (1990) Angry aggression among the truly disadvantaged. *Criminology, 28* (1), 73–95.

Billingsley, A. (1989). The sociology of knowledge of William J. Wilson: Placing the truly disadvantaged in its socio-historical context. *Journal of Sociology and Social Welfare, 16* (4), 7–41.

Bonacich, E. (1989). Racism in advanced capitalist society: Comments on William J. Wilson's The Truly Disadvantaged. *Journal of Sociology and Social Welfare, 16* (4), 41–55.

Cohn, E. & Farrington, D. (1998). Changes in the most-cited scholars in major American criminology and criminal justice journals between 1986–1990 and 1991–1995. *Journal of Criminal Justice, 26* (2), 99–116.

Dill, B. (1989). Comments on William Wilson's *The Truly Disadvantaged:* A limited proposal for social reform. *Journal of Sociology and Social Welfare, 16* (4), 69–77.

Elliott, D., Wilson, W. J., Huizinga, D., Sampson, R. J., Elliott, A. & Rankin, B. (1996). The effects of neighborhood disadvantage on adolescent development. *Journal of Research in Crime and Delinquency, 33* (4), 389–426.

Flowers, B. (ed.). (1989). *Bill Moyers a world of ideas: Conversations with thoughtful men and women about American life today and the ideas shaping our future.* New York: Doubleday.

Frazier, E. F. (1932). *The negro in Chicago.* Chicago: The University of Chicago Press.

Gomes, R. & Fishman, W. K. (1989). A critique of *The Truly Disadvantaged:* A historical materialist (Marxist) perspective. *Journal of Sociology and Social Welfare, 16* (4), 77–99.

Hagan, J. & Peterson, R. (Eds.). (1995). *Crime and inequality.* Stanford: Stanford University Press.

Hutchinson, E. (1994). *The assassination of the black male image.* Los Angeles: Middle Passages Press.

The Journal of blacks in higher education. (1998). Ranking black scholars according to academic citations and mentions in the national presss. (Spring); 6–8.

Krivo, L. & Peterson, R. (1996). Extremely disadvantaged neighborhoods and urban crime. *Social Forces, 75* (2), 619–50.

Marks, C. (1989). Occasional labourers and chronic want: A review of *The Truly Disadvantaged. Journal of Sociology and Social Welfare, 16* (4), 57–68.

Murray, C. (1984). *Losing ground: American social policy, 1950–1980.* New York: Basic Books.

Parker, K. F. & McCall, P. L. (1999). Structural conditions and racial homicide patterns: A look at the multiple disadvantages in Urban areas. *Criminology, 37,* 447–478.

Remnick, D. (1996, 29 April & 6 May). Dr. Wilson's neighborhood. *The New Yorker,* 96–107.

Rose, P. I., Rothman, S. & Wilson, W. J. (Eds.). (1973). *Through different eyes: Black and white perspectives on American race relations.* New York: Oxford University Press.

Sampson, R. & Wilson, W. J. (1995). Toward a theory of race, crime, and urban inequality. In J. Hagan & R. Peterson (eds.), *Crime and inequality* (pp. 37–54). Stanford: Stanford University Press.

Sampson, R. J. (1987). Urban black violence: The effects of male joblessness and family disruption. *American Journal of Sociology, 93,* 348–82.

Shaw, C. (1929). *Delinquency areas.* Chicago: University of Chicago Press.

Shaw, C. & McKay, H. (1942). *Juvenile delinquency and urban areas: A study of rates of delinquents in relation to different characteristics of local communities in American cities.* Chicago: University of Chicago Press.

Wilson, W. J., Nicholas, S. & Ogles, R. (1964). Formalization and stages of theoretical development. *Pacific Sociological Review, 7,* 74–80.

Williams, M. (1993). *The African American encyclopedia.* New York: Marshall Cavendish.

Wilson, W. J. (1969a). An empirical explication of norm and value. *Indiana Sociological Bulletin, 7* (October): 39–56.

———. (1969b). The quest for a meaningful black experience on white campuses. *The Massachusetts Review, 10* (Autumn), 737–46.

———. (1970). Cultural nationalism "versus" revolutionary nationalism: Dimensions of the black power movement. *Sociological Focus, 3* (Spring), 43–51.

———. (1972a). Black demands and the American government's responses. *Journal of Black Studies, 3* (September): 7–28.

———. (1972b). Race relations models and ghetto behavior. In P. I. Rose (ed.), *Nation of nations: The ethnic experience and racial crisis* (pp. 259–75). New York: Random House.

———. (1973). *Power, racism, and privilege: Race relations in theoretical and socio-historical perspectives.* New York: The Macmillan Company.

———. (1978). *The declining significance of race: Blacks and changing American institutions.* Chicago: The University of Chicago Press.

———. (1987). *The truly disadvantaged: The inner city, the underclass, and public policy.* Chicago: The University of Chicago Press.

———. (1988). Academic controversy and intellectual growth. In M. W. Riley (ed.), *Sociological Lives* (pp. 79–90). Beverly Hills: Sage Publications.

———. (1989). A response to critics of the truly disadvantaged. *The Journal of Sociology and Social Welfare, 16* (December): 133–48.

———. (1991a). The truly disadvantaged revisited: A response to Hochschild and Boxill. *Ethics, 101,* 593–609.

———. (1991b). Public policy research and the truly disadvantaged. In P. E. Peterson & C. Jencks (eds.), *The urban underclass* (pp. 460–82). Washington, DC: Brookings Institution Press.

———. (1994a). Citizenship and the inner-city ghetto poor. In B. van Steenbergen (ed.), *The condition of citizenship.* London: Sage Publications.

———. (1994b). The new urban poverty and the problem of race. *Michigan Quarterly Review, 33* (3), 247–73.

———. (1996). *When work disappears: The world of the new urban poor.* New York: Alfred A. Knopf.

Wilson, W. J. & Dumont, R. (1967). Aspects of concept formation, explication and theory construction in sociology. *American Sociological Review, 32,* 985–90.

———. (1968). Rules of correspondence and sociological concepts. *Sociology and Social Science Research, 52,* 217–27.

Wilson, W. J. & Gavernas, L. L. (1992). Can local policy affect the flight of industry from American cities? A review of local strategies to combat deindustrialization. In *In the National Interest: The 1990 Urban Summit* (pp. 55–64). New York: The Twentieth Century Fund Press.

Wilson, W. J. & Nye, I. (1966). Some methodological problems in the empirical study of value. *Washington State University Bulletin* (July).

Wilson, W. J. & Tausky, C. (1971). Work attachment among black males. *Phylon: The Atlanta Journal of Race and Culture, 32* (Spring), 23–30.

Wilson, W. J. & Wacquant, L. (1989b). Living in the ghetto: The cost of racial and class exclusion. *Annals of the American Academy of Political and Social Sciences, 501,* 8–25.

Notes

1. This program was founded during Franklin D. Roosevelt's administration. The program lasted eight years and was responsible for several major housing, highway, and other construction projects (Wilson, 1996, p. 229).

Lee P. Brown
Photo by Alvin Gee

SEVEN

LEE PATRICK BROWN
(1937–   )

*[I]t is now time for blacks, particularly black criminal justice
practitioners, to develop our own strategies for addressing the problem of
crime . . . Who is in a better position to develop new techniques for
controlling crime in the black community than black police officials?
Black police deal with the problem of crime on a daily basis from the
vantage point of the black experience.*
—(Brown, 1977b, p. 40)

INTRODUCTION

In December 1997, the Honorable Lee P. Brown was elected mayor of Houston,
Texas. His election as Mayor is historic for many reasons. First, he is Houston's first
African American mayor. Second, this is the first time he has been elected to a public
office. Third, his educational background and experience are in law enforcement and
criminal justice. Prior to his election, Mayor Brown served as chief of the Houston
Police Department from 1982 through 1990. As chief, he transformed the agency in
several ways, most notably by implementing neighborhood-oriented policing. This
community policing strategy brought police and residents together to address both
crime and other community problems. As mayor, he continues his dedication to
empowering citizens to improve their safety, security, and quality of life (Office of the
Mayor, 1998).

For over thirty years, Mayor Brown has been at the forefront of the progressive
policing movement in America. He has a distinguished career, as well as a local,
national, and international reputation. His law enforcement experience began as a
patrolman, in San Jose, California, in 1960 and culminated in 1993 when he was
selected by President Clinton to serve as the director of the White House Office of
National Drug Control Policy, a cabinet-level position. In the interim, Mayor Brown
served as police commissioner in the New York City Police Department (1990–
1992), public safety commissioner in Atlanta, Georgia (1978–1982), director of
Justice Services (1976–1978), and sheriff in Multnomah County, Oregon (1975–
1976). In each position, he was an avid proponent of (1) community policing, (2)
affirmative action for both minorities and women, and (3) preserving the agency's
history. Throughout his career he has emphasized that to address crime, social and
economic problems must be solved (Brown, 1987a).

Dr. Brown's academic career parallels the development of criminology and criminal justice programs in America. He entered law enforcement during one of the most important decades of the twentieth century and witnessed firsthand historic developments, including the civil disturbances of the 1960s, passage of the 1968 Omnibus Crime Control and Safe Streets Act, creation of the Law Enforcement Assistance Administration (LEAA), and the Law Enforcement Education Program (LEEP). His experience has included both teaching and administrative positions at San Jose (CA) State, Portland (OR) State University, Howard University (Washington, DC), and Texas Southern University (Houston, TX). Most recently, he was the Radaslav A. Tsanoff professor of public affairs in the Department of Sociology and a scholar in the James A. Baker III Institute for Public Policy at Rice University in Houston.

Lee P. Brown's most important contributions to criminological thought are found in his groundbreaking research on police community relations and community policing. While some agencies are still discovering the community problem-solving approach, as early as 1966, the San Jose Police Department's Police Community Relations Unit, with Brown as director, was utilizing a proactive approach and acting as a catalyst for community action (Brown, 1968b). In the 1980s, as Chief of Police in Houston, Texas, Brown implemented several policing strategies to improve the quality of life in the city (Brown, 1984). Both fear reduction programs and neighborhood-oriented community policing were designed to improve the cooperation between Houston's police and citizens. As community policing became more widely utilized across the country in the 1990s, the Houston model became a key component of the national anticrime strategy (Office of the Mayor, 1998). Dr. Brown has also contributed to our understanding of the unique role of African American police administrators in how to address violent crime, the drug epidemic, and policing changing environments.

BIOGRAPHICAL INFORMATION

Lee P. Brown was one of six children born to Andrew and Zelma Edwards Brown in Wewoka, Oklahoma. Both of his parents were originally from Mississippi and had little formal education. Andrew Brown, a laborer, and Zelma Brown, a cook, moved the family to Fowler, California, when Lee was five. According to Brown, his mother was a strong influence in his life and inspired him to go on to college.

Brown attended Fowler High School and remembers an English teacher who took a special interest in him, insisting that he take college preparatory courses. She made sure that Brown was not "tracked" into vocational courses such as wood shop and automobile mechanics, common for black males at that time. In 1955 Brown graduated from high school. A few years later, he married the late Yvonne Streets Brown, who died in 1992. During their thirty-four years of marriage, they had four children and nine grandchildren. He is now married to Frances Young Brown, a mother and school teacher in the Houston, Texas, Independent School District. In 1991 Brown received the Father of the Year Award from the National Father's Day Committee (Office of the Mayor, 1998).

ACADEMIC BACKGROUND AND EXPERIENCE

Lee P. Brown belongs to the first wave of African Americans to pursue graduate studies in criminology and criminal justice. After the 1968 Omnibus Crime and Safe Streets Act and the creation of the LEAA, numerous criminal justice and law enforcement programs were established across the country to improve both the education and training of police in American society. At this time, there were very few African Americans in policing, and like the majority of police, even fewer with bachelor's degrees. Brown and several other African Americans (Julius Debro, George Napper, Gywnne Peirson) would be among the first to continue their education to the doctoral level.

Interestingly, Brown never intended to major in criminology. He aspired to be a high school football coach and intended to major in physical education. However, on the day he was able to catch a ride with a friend to register for classes at Fresno State, they were not registering physical education majors. Brown decided to sign up for criminology. He financed his undergraduate education by working full time in a restaurant as a dishwasher, floor mopper, and cook. As a result, Brown did not develop any special relationships with his college professors. He received his bachelor's in criminology from Fresno State University in 1961.

Although Brown's first desire was to become a juvenile probation officer, he became a police officer with the San Jose, California, Police Department in 1960. Four years later he received his master's degree in sociology from San Jose State University. In 1968, he completed a master's degree in criminology at the University of California at Berkeley. His thesis was entitled *The Development of a Police-Community Relations Program: An Assessment of the San Jose Project* (Brown, 1968a).

Brown credits Julian Roebuck with encouraging him to go on for a doctorate degree. Brown was one of the first police officers to receive a fellowship from the Office of Law Enforcement Administration (OLEA) to further his graduate studies. He was awarded the degree of doctor of criminology in 1970 from the University of California at Berkeley. At Berkely, Joseph Lohman was his first adviser, and Gordon Misner chaired his dissertation committee. His dissertation, entitled "Evaluation of Police-Community Relations Programs" provided one of the earliest and most comprehensive overviews of police-community relations (PCR) programs and criteria for their evaluation. Brown is also a graduate of the Michigan State University's National Institute on Police and Community Relations.

Brown undertook his graduate studies and taught at San Jose State College while serving as director of the San Jose Police Department's Police Community Relations Unit. Additionally, he was selected as the San Jose Police Officer of the Year twice while with the agency (LEAA Newsletter, 1972). He also became widely known as an expert on police-community relations, conducted training for numerous agencies, and later served as a consultant to the office of Community Relations Service in the United States Department of Justice. In 1968, Brown left the San Jose Police Department and joined the faculty at Portland State University where he developed the Adminstration of Justice Program and served as both professor and chair.

Four years later, in 1972, Brown left Portland State University to become associate director for the Institute for Urban Affairs and Research, professor of Public Administration, and director of Criminal Justice at Howard University. The institute, under the leadership of Brown and Lawrence Gary, was instrumental in developing an Administration of Justice program at Howard, sponsoring workshops to examine the administration of justice in the black community, and conducting research on crime (Brown, 1974). As associate director, Brown was also instrumental in focusing attention on the need for changing the administration of justice (Brown, 1974; Gary and Brown, 1976).

In 1975 Brown accepted the position of sheriff of Multnomah County, Oregon. A year later, he became the director of Justice Services for the county and was responsible for its criminal justice programs, including the office of the sheriff. During the same time, Brown also served as chairperson of the LEAA National Minority Advisory Council (NMAC), established by Richard Velde, LEAA's administrator, to advise the agency as well as federal, state, and local governments on minority concerns. The council and its research staff were responsible for holding public hearings, assessing LEAA staffing, minority participation in the Law Enforcement Education Program (LEEP), minority contractors and grantees, and developing a community crime prevention program to be implemented in minority communities. The commission also prepared several policy papers related to crime and criminal justice in minority communities.

In 1972 Atlanta elected its first black mayor, Maynard Jackson. Jackson was part of the first wave of African Americans who transformed the landscape of both urban politics and life. Jackson and other black mayors appointed other blacks to key positions in their administrations. In 1978, Brown left Oregon to become the first African American commissioner of public safety in Atlanta, Georgia. A decade after his initial implementation of police community relations (PCR) strategies in San Jose, California, Brown found an even greater need for PCR in Atlanta. In spite of political empowerment and improved race relations in Atlanta and other parts of the South, the police and their communities were still quite separated. Prior to his arrival, the Atlanta Police Department had been embroiled in one controversy after another. During his administration, the city experienced a wave of killings, known as the "Atlanta murders," which was one of the greatest challenges of Brown's police career. When offered the chief position in Houston, Texas, in 1982, he accepted.

His appointment as chief of the Houston, Texas, Police Department carries as much historical significance as his more recent election as mayor. During the early 1980s the city's police department had a notorious reputation for brutality and corruption, Brown was instrumental in reshaping the agency (discussed below) before relocating to New York City, where he assumed the position of police commissioner in 1990. Brown (and many others) considers an appointment as police commissioner in New York City to be the apex of a police officers' career and one of his greatest professional accomplishments (Brown, 1999).

In addition to his academic career and law enforcement experience, Brown is a member of several professional associations, including the International Association of Chiefs of Police (IACP), the National Organization of Black Law Enforcement Executives (NOBLE), and the Police Executive Research Forum (PERF). Recognizing the need for creating an organization that would provide support for black law enforcement officials, Brown was a key player in NOBLE's creation. He also has served in a leadership capacity in some of these organizations, most recently as past president of the IACP. Brown also serves on the boards of directors of several other local and national associations, including the Police Foundation, American Leadership Forum, Houston Area Urban League, and Sam Houston Council of the Boy Scouts of America. He is also the recipient of numerous honors and awards (Office of the Mayor, 1998).

CONTRIBUTIONS TO CRIMINOLOGICAL THOUGHT

As previously stated, Mayor Brown is best known for his progressive approaches to law enforcement. During the past thirty years, Brown has contributed to our understanding of black perspectives on crime and policing, community policing, establishing and evaluating police community relations programs, handling complaints against the police, neighborhood oriented policing, strategies for controlling drugs, reducing fear of crime, team policing, and violent crime. The remainder of this chapter focuses on his contributions to criminological thought found in his research on police community relations, black perspectives on crime, and community policing.

Police Community Relations

During the 1960s as a police officer in San Jose, California, Brown was actively involved in community relations. In response to the social unrest on San Jose's east side, Brown was asked by Chief Ray Blackmore to look at what could be done to prevent disorder. One of Brown's recommendations was to create a police community relations (PCR) unit. Shortly thereafter, the unit was created, and Brown was chosen by the chief to serve as its director. Brown's experience in San Jose would shape his beliefs about and contributions to PCR for years to come. His thesis (Brown, 1968a), dissertation (Brown, 1970), and several articles (Brown, 1968b, 1972) are classics in the study of PCR. In his dissertation, Brown (1970) provided a contextual framework for understanding the role of the police in a changing society and the emergence of

PCR. While the primary objective of the dissertation was to develop criteria for evaluating PCR, it also provided one of the first descriptions of PCR programs nationwide. In two articles, Brown (1968b, 1972) describes the history and components of the San Jose PCR model that served as a guide to other agencies considering PCR programs. Two other publications and the dissertation (Brown, 1970, 1972; Gordon, Misner, Brown, 1981) provided strategies for evaluating PCR programs. Brown's research on the San Jose PCR program, evaluating PCR programs, and what he refers to as the "death of police-community relations" are summarized below.

The San Jose PCR Program

The San Jose PCR program was implemented in October 1966. It was the latest in a series of efforts by the agency to serve the community, especially its youth. As early as 1949, the department had a Citizen's Advisory Committee (Brown, 1968a). In the late 1960s Brown was asked to develop a PCR program that would improve police-community relations and could be applied elsewhere in the city (Brown, 1972). Unlike many of his contemporaries, Chief Blackmore recognized the need for police to engage in social service work as well as law enforcement (Brown, 1968b).

Brown, and another officer immediately recognized the importance of community involvement in the planning stages for a PCR program. They interviewed residents, and based their ten recommendations to Chief Blackmore upon the residents opinions. The Community Relations Unit also received funding from the federal government to further plan and develop its program. The San Jose PCR model focused upon working with the community to solve problems and maintaining dialogue between the police and the public.

Brown (1968b, 1972) described the best strategies for establishing PCR and emphasized the importance of the total support of the chief and implementing a full-time program with full-time staffing. Brown (1972) also provided guidelines for selecting program directors and officers. He believed directors should be experienced officers, college graduates, capable of performing administrative tasks, and knowledgeable of both problem solving and program development. Interest and dedication were viewed as the most important characteristics propsective directors should possess.

Evaluation of PCR Programs

While many agencies were establishing PCR programs during the late 1960s and early 1970s, very little research was available on their effectiveness. In his dissertation, Brown (1970) noted that many police officials cited the accomplishments of their programs without any empirical proof. These accomplishments included reduced community tension, more citizen involvement in community activities, better communication between police and residents, reduction in police brutality, and increased public trust (ibid., p. 6–7). Furthermore, the success of PCR programs was often based on statistical compilations of meeting and participants (ibid., p. 200).

Brown identified several criteria to guide the evaluation of PCR programs (1970, p. 202–4):

1. Evaluations should be guided by the goals and objectives of the PCR program.
2. Evaluations should be externally done.
3. A variety of research techniques should be used.
4. An evaluation component should be built into the PCR program from its inception.

Brown also developed criteria for evaluating public relations programs, crime prevention programs, youth programs, and PCR training programs, often operated under the PCR title.

Acknowledging that PCR evaluations are complicated by numerous uncontrollable variables, Brown focused on assessing the effectiveness of specific PCR program components. Brown also identified three measures of performance as an alternative to the popular cost-benefit analysis. These measures included a description of the problem the program is designed to address, the establishment of quantifiable goals and objectives, and an assessment of program results based upon goal achievement (1970, p. 223). Brown also encouraged an assessment of public attitudes toward the police and police attitudes toward the public. Last, Brown encouraged the use of a systems model that required input and feedback to assess program components on an ongoing basis.

While Brown advocated PCR programs, he was also cognizant of the overall failure of police agencies to successfully integrate PCR into their operations. He believed the police establishment needed to reform itself before PCR programs could be effective. Many agencies became comfortable with the image-building role of PCR programs and ignored the overall effectiveness of their programs as determined by better police-community relations (Brown, 1973). Several years would pass before the importance of police-community interaction and reform of the police establishment would actually occur in agencies nationwide.

BLACK PERSPECTIVES ON CRIME AND LAW ENFORCEMENT

Interest in black perspectives on crime and the administration of justice heightened after the tumultuous decade of the 1960s, especially those of black police administrators. Although majority scholars focused on both unequal justice and police deviance, including the use of excessive force, corruption, and other abuses of power, African Americans were usually absent from discussions of these and other issues of concern in the black community. As educational opportunities increased for African Americans, and they pursued graduate studies, their research and perspectives on crime became more readily available, especially during and after the 1970s (Young and Taylor Greene, 1995). In one of the first edited volumes of black perspectives on crime (Woodson, 1977), Vernon Jordan, noted that "the record shows that black people have been relentlessly excluded from active participation and policy making in anti crime efforts. And in large part, that is why the much publicized anticrime drives have failed" (ibid., p. vi).

Brown was at the forefront of the movement to acknowledge the role of blacks in understanding crime and criminal justice. He wrote extensively on the topic and participated in numerous workshops, conferences, and symposiums. When the *Journal of Afro-American Issues* published a special issue devoted to blacks and the United States criminal justice system in 1974, Brown was a contributor. He explained the role of the Black criminologist utilizing the sociology of knowledge theory by Merton (1957). The impact of crime in black communities was explained according to the Social Reality of Crime Theory by Quinney (1970). Brown like Staples (1973) thought that black criminologists should examine crime in the context of both race and class. Like several other black scholars, Brown noted that both socioeconomic conditions and racism contributed to the problem of crime among blacks (Brown, 1974).

Brown and several other black criminologists and practitioners participated in two symposiums that specifically addressed crime in the black community (Bryce, 1977; Woodson, 1977). Brown (1977b) noted that the increasing population of blacks in urban areas, the problem of crime, and the race problem required the participation of black police administrators in formulating public policy. Echoing Jordan's sentiments, Brown (ibid., p. 40) believed that nonblacks would have difficulty conceptualizing the problem of crime in the black community.

Several policy issues were identified by Brown (1977a, 1977b) in his research and writings that specifically addressed policing in the black community and the causes of crime. At the federal level, he encouraged Congress to address unemployment, drug importation, drug addiction, inadequate health care, housing, gun control, urban revitalization, tax reform, and white collar crime. He also recommended making funds available to community groups for crime control.

Over two decades ago, Brown encouraged state and local governments to hire black police executives and officers, especially in urban areas, and to address the problems of brutality and attitudes of white officers toward blacks (ibid., p. 61). Brown also challenged the black community to take an active role in challenging crime through their organizations and by letting criminals know their detrimental effect. Perhaps most important, Brown called for the creation of an organization comprised primarily of black police administrators. During a symposium sponsored by the Joint Center for Political Studies, the Police Foundation, and LEAA, the National Organization of Black Law Enforcment Executives was created (Velde in Bryce, 1977).

Police practices in the black community was another important issue addressed by Brown (1977a). In a symposium sponsored by the National Urban League in the 1970s he stated,

In essence, the mission of the police was developed for white people and not black people. The police consider themselves as representatives of the white community and not the black community. Hence, within the black community, the police are indeed looked upon as an occupying army protecting the interests of the ruling class in a neo-colonial setting. Thus, within the black community, police harassment, police brutality, police corruption does exist. (ibid., p. 87)

To address these problems, he called for community control of police departments that would provide a mechanism for citizen input into decision making. Additionally, he identified the need for innovative police leaders, increased minority representation, and cultural sensitivity training.

COMMUNITY-ORIENTED POLICING

Policing has undergone a dramatic shift from traditional policing to community policing during the last decade. While more prevalent today than a decade ago, community policing is still quite new and different to many officers and agencies and continues to be controversial. In light of his interest in police-community relations (PCR), Brown's advocacy of community policing (often referred to as "neighborhood-oriented" policing) is not surprising. Interestingly, while many community policing proponents distanced themselves from the PCR movement, for Brown, both address similar problems in similar ways.

Brown (1987) identified crime as the most serious domestic problem confronting our country. The unequal distribution of crime is directly related to the country's social, economic, and political systems. To address this dilemma, Brown believed the police need a new mission, "That mission must be to do what is necessary, and what is possible given the resources available, to improve the quality of life in the community" (Brown, 1987a, p. 134). This new mission and new approach is commonly referred to as "community policing." It is defined as "an interactive process between the police and the community to mutually identify and resolve community problems" (Brown, 1989a, p. 78). Departments must adopt a set of values and a philosophy of community policing that require fundamental changes to the traditional policing approach. These changes are evolutionary and take several years to accomplish.

During the late 1980s, the National Institute of Justice funded the Executive Session on Policing at the John F. Kennedy School of Government, Harvard University. The meetings were designed to bring together police chiefs, scholars, and others to share and discuss information on policing. Brown participated in the sessions, while chief of police in Houston, Texas. He prepared an essay published by both the *Executive Session* and *Police Chief* that serves as a guide for implementing community policing (Brown, 1989a, 1989b). The article is a significant contribution to understanding community policing because it presented the characteristics of both traditional and community policing, the origins of community policing, and its benefits to police and citizens and described Houston's experience. Brown also emphasized that community policing is evolutionary and usually involves at least two phases. Community policing under Brown's leadership in Houston is described below.

Houston's Neighborhood-Oriented Policing Program

According to Brown (1989a, 1989b) Houston implemented phase 1 of its community policing program in 1982. At the time, the department had a few programs that provided the foundation for phase 2, described by Brown as a more comprehensive policing strategy. The Directed Area Responsibility Team (DART) was one of the first programs developed in phase 2. According to Skolnick and Bayley (1986), it began in 1983, emphasized community participation, and decentralized management in one area of Houston. A few years later, DART was implemented in other parts of the city (Brown, 1987a). Other programs developed in Houston included Project Oasis, the Community Organizing Response Team (CORT), Direct Citizen Contact program, Neighborhood Information Network, Victim Recontact program and beat redesign (Brown, 1987, 1989a, 1989b; Skolnick and Bayley, 1986). Finally, police community storefronts were opened in conjunction with Houston's fear reduction program in several areas.

After five years, the Houston Police Department began phase 2, which emphasized organizational commitment to the community policing philosophy. This meant the agency would utilize operational strategies that emphasized accountability, decentralization, citizen involvement, beat redesign, permanent assignment, and empowerment of beat officers. Phase 2 would have even greater benefits for both citizens and police that include customized police service; community organization; greater citizen support; shared responsibility; job satisfaction; better internal relationships; and support for organization changes in training, management, and performance evaluation (Brown, 1989a).

In Brown's model, the transition to community policing is evolutionary, often beginning with a program thrust and culminating in a revision of the agency's mission and philosophy. Equally as important, community policing was both cost effective and efficient (Brown, 1989b).

Brown believes the community policing era will continue in the twenty-first century. He views it as the most significant development in policing in spite of some misconceptions about what it is. While some still view COP as a program, it must evolve into a department-wide philosophy to be instrumental in addressing many challenging problems, including violent crime and drug-related crime. The neighborhood-oriented policing model provides a unique opportunity for police leaders to join together with educators, corporations, the media, and clergy to address such problems. In his opinion, community policing will alleviate one of the most serious policing problems today, poor police-race relations.

Conclusion

As a former drug czar, Brown is acutely aware of the national security threat posed by drug distribution and use in our country. He is a proponent of a national strategy that encompasses prevention, education, and treatment. He is also concerned about the problem of violent crime and the acceptance of violence in our culture.

Mayor Brown is considered to be one of the most influential police leaders of the twentieth century. He has had a profound impact on police and criminal justice policy and practices for more than thirty years. As early as 1971, he chaired the Advisory Task Force on Education, Training, and Manpower Development for the National Advisory Commission on Criminal Justice Standards and Goals (LEAS Newsletter, 1972). Heretofore, there have been few studies that specifically address his contributions. In the future researchers should continue to examine his contributions to police-community relations, black perspectives on crime, and community policing, as well as controlling police use force, the role of women in policing, capturing police departmental history, and drug prevention and control.

References

Brown, L. (1968a). *The development of a police-community relations program: An assessment of the San Jose project.* M.A. Thesis, University of California at Berkeley.

———. (1968b). Dynamic police-community relations at work. *Police Chief, 35,* 44–50.

———. (1970). *Evaluation of police-community relations programs.* Ph.D. Dissertation. Berkeley: University of California. Ann Arbor: University Microfilms.

———. (1972). Establishing a police-community relations program. *Police, 16,* 57–65.

———. (1973). *The death of police-community relations.* Washington, DC: Howard University Institute for Urban Affairs and Research.

———. (ed.). (1974). *The administration of criminal justice: A view from black America.* Washington, DC: Howard University Institute for Urban Affairs and Research.

———. (1976a). *Crime and its impact on the black community.* Washington, DC: Institute for Urban Affairs and Research.

———. (1976b). Neighborhood team policing and management by objectives. *Police Chief, 43,* 72–76.

———. (1977a). Bridges over troubled waters: A perspective on policing in the black community. In Robert L. Woodson (ed.), *Black perspectives on crime and the criminal justice system* (pp. 79–106). Boston: G. K. Hall & Co.

———. (1977b). Causes of crime. In Herrington Bryce (ed.), *Black crime: A police view* (pp. 37–65). Washington, DC: Joint Center for Political Studies.

———. (1978). The role of the sheriff in the future of policing. Alvin W. Cohn (ed.), *The future of policing.* Beverly Hills: Sage Publications.

———. (1984). Strategies to reduce the fear of crime. *Police Chief, 51* (6), 45–46.

————. (1987a). Innovative policing in Houston. *Annals of the American Academy of Political and Social Science, 494,* 129–44.

————. (1987b). Policing Houston: Reducing fear and improving services. *Crime and Delinquency, 33,* 71–89.

————. (1989a). Community policing: A practical guide for police officials. *The Police Chief 56,* 72–82.

————. (1989b). Community policing: A practical guide for police officials. *Perspectives on Policing* (Number 12). Washington, DC: US Department of Justice, National Institute of Justice.

————. (1992). Violent crime and community involvement. *FBI Law Enforcement Bulletin, 61,* 5:2–5.

Brown, L. & Wycoff, M. (1987). Policing Houston: Reducing fear and improving services. *Crime and Delinquency, 33,* 71–89.

Bryce, Harrington (Ed.). (1977). *Black crime: A police view.* Washington, DC: Joint Center for Political Studies.

Gary, L. & Brown, L. (eds.). (1976). *Crime and its impact on the black community.* Washington, DC: Howard University Institute for Urban Affairs and Research.

Johnson, T., Misner, G. & Brown, L. (1981). *The police and society.* Englewood Cliffs, NJ: Prentice-Hall, Inc.

Law Enforcement Assistance Administration (1978). *Newsletter.*

Merton, R. (1957). *Social theory and social structure.* Glencoe, IL: The Free Press.

Office of the Mayor. (1998). *Lee P. Brown biography.* Houston: Office of the Mayor.

Quinney, R. (1970). *The social reality of crime.* Boston: Little, Brown and Company.

Skolnick, J. & Bayley, D. (1986). *The new blue line.* New York: The Free Press.

Staples, R. (1973). What is black sociology? Toward a sociology of black liberation. In J. Ladner (ed.), *The death of white sociology.* New York: Vintage Books.

Woodson, R. (ed.). (1977). *Black perspectives on crime and the criminal justice system* Boston: G. K. Hall & Co.

Young, V. & Taylor Greene, H. (1995). Pedagogical reconstruction: Incorporating African-American perspectives into the curriculum. *Journal of Criminal Justice Education, 6,* 85–104.

Lee P. Brown
Selected References

Brown, L. (1968). *The development of a police-community relations program: An assessment of the San Jose project.* M.A. Thesis, University of California at Berkeley.

————. (1968). Dynamic police-community relations at work. *Police Chief, 35,* 44–50.

————. (1970). *Evaluation of police-community relations programs.* Ph.D. Dissertation. Berkeley: University of California. Ann Arbor: University Microfilms.

————. (1972). Establishing a police-community relations program. *Police, 16,* 57–65.

———. (1973). *The death of police-community relations.* Washington, DC: Howard University Institute for Urban Affairs and Research.

———. (ed.). (1974). *The administration of criminal justice: A view from black America.* Washington, DC: Howard University Institute for Urban Affairs and Research.

———. (1976a). *Crime and its impact on the Black community.* Washington, DC: Institute for Urban Affairs and Research.

———. (1976). Neighborhood team policing and management by objectives. *Police Chief, 43,* 72–76.

———. (1977). Bridges over troubled waters: A perspective on policing in the black community. In Robert L. Woodson (ed.), *Black perspectives on crime and the criminal justice system* (pp. 79–106). Boston: G. K. Hall & Co.

———. (1977). Causes of crime. In Herrington Bryce (ed.), *Black crime: A police view* (pp. 37–65). Washington, DC: Joint Center for Political Studies.

———. (1978). The role of the sheriff in the future of policing. In Alvin W. Cohn (ed.), *The future of policing.* Beverly Hills: Sage Publications.

———. (1984). Strategies to reduce the fear of crime. *Police Chief, 51* (6), 45–46.

———. (1987). Innovative policing in Houston. *Annals of the American Academy of Political and Social Science, 494,* 129–44.

———. (1987). Policing Houston: Reducing fear and improving services. *Crime and Delinquency, 33,* 71–89.

———. (1989). Community policing: A practical guide for police officials. *The Police Chief 56,* 72–82.

———. (1989). Community policing: A practical guide for police officials. *Perspectives on Policing* (Number 12). Washington, DC: US Department of Justice, National Institute of Justice.

———. (1992). Violent crime and community involvement. *FBI Law Enforcement Bulletin, 61,* 5:2–5.

Darnell F. Hawkins

DARNELL FELIX HAWKINS
(1946–   )

INTRODUCTION

Darnell Felix Hawkins represents an individual whose scholarship, like that of others in this volume, has been devoted to the study of African Americans and the criminal justice system. Much of his work has specifically focused on analyses of issues such as violence (particularly black-on-black homicide), theoretical criminology, the over-representation of African Americans in the criminal justice system, and ethnicity and crime. Hawkins has also sought to assist in the creation of appropriate solutions to criminal justice–related problems facing the African American community. He is one of the most productive and respected African American criminologists of the contemporary era.

BIOGRAPHICAL INFORMATION

Darnell Felix Hawkins was born on 24 November 1946 in Sherrill, Arkansas. He is the last of eleven children born to Busby H. Hawkins and Mary E. Johnson Hawkins. At the age of four, Hawkins moved to Pine Bluff, Arkansas, the fourth largest city in the state, which also maintained the second largest African American population in the state. Hawkins has fond memories of Pine Bluff, where many black students came to attend the University of Arkansas at Pine Bluff. Of this early period, Hawkins recalls: "The presence of the college in the town, as well as the sizeable African American population, provided for an environment that was very protective, encouraging, and supportive" (Hawkins, 1997).

In 1952 Hawkins attended the recently built Townsend Park Elementary School. He remembers the school being built due to legal and political pressures put on the school board to provide better educational facilities for African Americans. For grades eight through 12, Hawkins attended Townsend Park High School, which was one of four junior/high schools in the area for African Americans. Hawkins graduated from Towsend Park High School in 1964.

In the fall of 1964, Hawkins began his higher educational experience at Kansas State University in Manhattan, Kansas. Although he could have easily attended a college in his home state, he chose instead to venture to Kansas in an attempt to "explore the world." Hawkins was also unwilling to follow the prevailing policy that mandated blacks who were accepted to Arkansas schools to live off campus.

At Kansas State University, Hawkins majored in French. He selected this major because during his years at Towsend Park High School, he developed a close intellectual and personal relationship with his French teacher, Lois Faucette. In addition to his major in French, Hawkins began to develop an interest in the social sciences and minored in general social sciences. According to Hawkins, he, like many other persons living in the sixties and early seventies, was influenced by the social activities of this period. The civil rights movement and the Vietnam War in particular changed Hawkins's perspective on American society and life in general.

This change in perspective also swayed his intellectual interests from the humanities to the social sciences. Even though he had secured several appealing postgraduation opportunities, including: graduate school in French, a position in the Peace Corps, and teaching French in a high school in France, because of his change in interest, he declined them all. Instead, following his graduation from Kansas State University in 1968, Hawkins joined the Teachers Corps, a federally funded program to train teachers to work in schools with economically disadvantaged students. He participated in the program primarily for two reasons. First, like many other African Americans of the period, he became more politically and socially conscious. This increased consciousness led many African Americans and persons of other races to participate in various programs aimed at improving the general welfare of African American youth principally in inner-city areas. Second, like many other individuals of the period who became politically and socially conscious, he was not enthusiastic about being drafted into the armed forces to fight in the Vietnam War. Participation in the Teacher Corps program made Hawkins ineligible for the draft.

The program, which was associated with Wayne State University, allowed Hawkins to have a primary school teaching experience while also working toward a master's of arts in teaching (M.A.T.) degree. From 1970 through 1972, after completing both the teacher training and the degree requirements, Hawkins taught third- and fourth-grade students in the Detroit Public School System.

After teaching two years in the Detroit Public School System, Hawkins became disillusioned with public school teaching due to several factors, including the lack of administrative flexibility, unresponsiveness of schools to innovative teaching methods, and other frustrations. Subsequently, Hawkins changed his career path by applying for graduate school in the social sciences. Although he was accepted in the graduate school of Columbia University to study anthropology, Hawkins instead applied to the graduate program in sociology at the University of Michigan, where he was also accepted and began studies in 1972.

After four years in the program, Hawkins completed both an A.M. and a Ph.D. in sociology. His dissertation, "Nonresponse in Detroit Area Study Surveys: A Ten Year Analysis," directed by Professor Elmwood M. Beck, focused on the impact of nonresponses in social surveys conducted by the University of Michigan's Detroit Area Study (DAS). This review included analyses of the nonresponses in ten surveys conducted from 1956 to 1974. The key finding of this study suggested that researchers who experience extensive nonresponses should be cautious in the inferences made based on only those who responded. As researchers now commonly know, as the nonresponse rates in surveys increase the ability of researchers to make sound inferences on social phenomena decreases. Hawkins's dissertation was later published as the *Working Paper in Methodology No. 8* by the Institute for Research in Social Science at the University of North Carolina, Chapel Hill (see Hawkins, 1977). While at Michigan, Hawkins developed his interest in crime and justice. Hawkins suggests that his interest in crime and justice was part of his larger concern for matters pertaining to social and racial justice, which evolved from his life experiences (Hawkins, 1997).

In the fall of 1976, Hawkins returned South to begin his academic career as an assistant professor of sociology at the University of North Carolina (UNC) at Chapel Hill. During his tenure at Chapel Hill, Hawkins decided to broaden his knowledge of the legal system by enrolling in the UNC, Chapel Hill, Law School. He received the juris doctorate in 1981. These diverse educational experiences would shape Hawkins's focus and approach in his future research.

While enrolled at the UNC, Chapel Hill, Law School, Hawkins remained active, publishing several articles between 1978 and 1981 (see Hawkins, 1978a, 1978b, 1980, 1981). This productivity was rewarded with his promotion to associate professor of sociology in 1981. Even though his early publications were notable, he would later embark upon his most important contributions to criminology/criminal justice.

In 1987, Hawkins moved back to the Midwest to accept a position as associate professor of black studies and sociology at the University of Illinois at Chicago. Presently, Hawkins is professor of African American studies and sociology at the University of Illinois at Chicago. He is also a faculty affiliate with the Department of Criminal Justice.

CONTRIBUTIONS TO CRIMINOLOGICAL THOUGHT

Since the early 1980s Hawkins has addressed an array of criminal justice/criminology topics, including imprisonment rates among African Americans and whites (Hawkins, 1985b, 1986; Hawkins and Hardy, 1989), conflict theory (Hawkins, 1987), crime and ethnicity (Hawkins, 1993, 1994, 1995a, 1995b), African American homicide (Hawkins, 1983, 1985a, 1986a, 1990; Hawkins and Davis, 1986), and homicide news coverage in Chicago (Hawkins, Johnstone, Michener, 1994, 1995). These publications followed a number of early articles that established him as an up and coming race and crime specialist.

Early Research

Hawkins's early scholarship focused on methodological (Hawkins, 1977) and theoretical (Hawkins, 1978) issues. Of particular importance to this review is the latter article on applied research and social theory. In this article, Hawkins highlights the benefits of using applied research (or policy-oriented research) to enhance social theory. He also stresses that policy changes directed at social change must be guided by sound social theory. Hawkins concludes this early paper by pointing to the complex but complementary nature of applied research to social theory. Furthermore, he states, "Applied research also enriches social theory by allowing the theory to be constantly tested and reformulated. This is needed to produce theory that is more adequate for describing and predicting social phenomena" (Hawkins, 1978, p. 149). This early statement by Hawkins anticipates some of his later critiques of criminological theory and research.

Two other early articles, "Perceptions of Punishment for Crime" (1980), and "Causal Attribution and Punishment for Crime" (1981) show a natural progression into Hawkins's later scholarship. Both articles were based on data obtained from a self-administered questionnaire given to 662 students at the University of North Carolina, Chapel Hill (UNCCH), and North Carolina Central University (NCCU) in Durham, North Carolina. Hawkins used both a traditionally white institution, UNCCH, and a historically black institution, NCCU, to allow for comparisons between the races.

In the article "Perceptions of Punishment for Crime," Hawkins attempted to "build on and expand past studies of crime seriousness." To accomplish this he employed both a questionnaire (to elicit demographic information) and a listing of "25 criminal offense scenarios that depicted a variety of criminal acts and actors" (Hawkins, 1980, p. 197). As in previous research on crime perception (see Sellin and Wolfgang, 1964), the respondents were then asked to rate each scenario using a graphic numerical scale ranging from 0, no punishment, to 10, maximum punishment (death penalty).

Hawkins's analysis of the survey results found significant differences in the assignment of punishment between African Americans and whites in fifteen out of the twenty-five crime scenarios (Hawkins, 1980, p. 201). He reported that while the major differences in punishment assignment were found in criminal offense scenarios involving crimes against the property (especially white-collar crime), the greatest difference in punishment assignment was noted for crime 6 of his criminal offense scenarios (patrolman kills young man who has surrendered). African Americans probably assigned more punishment to this offense than whites because of the historical role police brutality has played in their community (see, for example, Taylor Greene, 1994). Naturally then, any crime scenario involving the police will evoke differential responses from African Americans and whites.

Since African Americans generally perceive whites as being heavily involved in white-collar offenses, which they also believe do not receive severe enough punishments, the significant difference between African American and white punishment assignment for these offenses could be expected. Hawkins addressed this phenomena, stating: "[B]lack and low-income [participants] in general . . . appear to be more punitive towards white-collar criminals than do middle- and upper-income [participants]. This may stem from a desire to see affluent people receive more punishment in the criminal justice system" (Hawkins, 1980, p. 208). Although Hawkins did caution readers regarding his findings because of his convenience sample, he did note the potential implications of his study as they apply to jury selection and jury decisions.

Using the same data set, Hawkins (1981) published "Causal Attribution and Punishment for Crime," which explored the relationships among perceived causes of crime, the assignment of punishment, and the perceived characteristics of the perpetrator of a crime. Again, Hawkins found race to be of significance when determining perceived cause (either personal or environmental factors). These early publications began Hawkins's consistent contribution to the criminological theory and race and crime literature. Of Hawkins's expansive research, we focus here on some of his notable contributions in the areas of African American homicide, conflict theory, ethnicity and crime, and African American and white imprisonment comparisons.

AFRICAN AMERICAN HOMICIDE

From 1983 through 1990, Hawkins produced what may be considered his seminal works. Within this period, his publications on African American homicide established him as a leading scholar in the area. His research included both theoretical critiques (Hawkins, 1983, 1986, 1990) and reviews of current policies created to prevent and or reduce African American homicide (Hawkins, 1985). We begin with a review of Hawkins's theoretical critiques.

Subculture of Violence Theory

In 1983, Hawkins critiqued the subculture of violence theory, which is commonly used to explain homicide differentials between African Americans and whites. Formulated by Marvin Wolfgang and Italian criminologist Franco Ferracuti (see Wolfgang and Ferracuti, 1967), the theory is based primarily on data from an earlier Wolfgang study (see Wolfgang, 1958) and homicide research conducted in Italy by Ferracuti (Wolfgang and Ferracuti, 1967, p. xix).

Drawing on the results of past studies and their own research findings, Wolfgang and Ferracuti formulated the "subculture of violence" theory. As for the focus of their theory, Wolfgang and Ferracuti state, "Our major concern is with the bulk of homicides—the passion crimes, the violent slayings—that are not premeditated and are not psychotic manifestations" (1967, p. 141). The theory includes the following seven propositions:

1. No subculture can be totally different from or totally in conflict with the society of which it is a part.

2. To establish the existence of a subculture of violence does not require that the actors sharing in this basic value element express violence in all situations.

3. The potential to resort or willingness to resort to violence in a variety of situations emphasizes the penetrating and diffusive nature of this culture.

4. The subcultural ethos of violence may be shared by all ages in a subsociety, but this ethos is most prominent in a limited age group ranging from late adolescence to middle age.

5. The counter-norm is nonviolence.

6. The development of favorable attitudes toward, and the use of, violence in this subculture involves learned behavior and a process of differential learning, association, or identification.

7. The use of violence in a subculture is not necessarily viewed as illicit conduct, and the users therefore do not have to deal with feelings of guilt about their aggression.

These propositions translate into the belief that for those persons in the subculture violence is considered normative. Vold and Bernard (1986) state that persons in this subculture "tend to value honor more highly than people in the dominant culture." Subsequently, the theory postulates that when a member of the subculture's honor is challenged, he or she may respond violently.

Hawkins (1983) offered both a critique and an alternative model for this theoretical approach as it applies to African Americans and violence. Based upon a summary of prior reviews of the subculture of violence theory, he proposes five major weaknesses of the theory:

1. There is an extreme emphasis on mentalistic value orientations of individuals—orientations which in the aggregate are said to produce a subculture;

2. the theory lacks empirical grounding and indeed is put in question by some empirical findings;

3. Much of the theory has tended to underemphasize a variety of structural, situational and institutional variables which affect interpersonal violence. For blacks, these variables range from historical patterns developed during slavery to the immediate social context of an individual homicidal offense to the operation of the criminal justice system, past and present;

4. Subcultural theory underemphasizes the effects of the law on patterns of criminal homicide;

5. There are other plausible ways apart from the inculcation of values by which the economic, political and social disadvantages of American blacks may produce high rates of homicide. (Hawkins, 1983, p. 113)

Following these criticisms, Hawkins proposed a causal model of black homicide. His model includes the following three propositions. Each proposition is listed below with a summary of Hawkins's views.

Proposition 1. American Criminal Law: Black life is cheap but white life is valuable. Borrowing from suggestions from earlier studies, Hawkins evokes history as an important link to understanding homicide patterns among African Americans. He aptly notes that during the early American slave era, masters who killed their slaves were not charged with a criminal offense (Hawkins, 1983, p. 114). Furthermore, all whites were free to injure slaves without fear of prosecution. Conversely, Hawkins suggests that the killing of a white person by an African American slave was considered the worst type of offense.

Drawing upon this history, Hawkins expanded Guy B. Johnson's hierarchy of homicide seriousness (see Johnson, 1941). Based on Johnson's study of racial differences in three southern states, this hierarchy categorizes the seriousness that attaches to homicides based on the race of the offender and victim. Below are the hierarchies developed by Johnson and, more recently, Hawkins (see figures 1 and 2). Each hierarchy moves from the most serious offense to least serious.

Hawkins believes that this hierarchy may be important in explaining African American homicide rates because "blacks kill each other at higher rates because the legal system is seen as administering punishment unfairly. Based on the past behavior of the law, blacks may have come to believe that aggressive behavior of all types directed by blacks against each other will be tolerated and seldom severely punished" (Hawkins, 1983, p. 119).

Proposition 2. Past and present racial and social class differences in the administration of justice affect black criminal violence. Hawkins's second proposition centered on two sections: "Post-Homicide Punishment as a Deterrent" and "Pre-Homicide Behaviors and the Lack of Deterrence." The first section addressed the commonly asked question "given the extent of racial oppression, why is there not more on white oppression?" Hawkins responds to this question by suggesting that the "swift and cruel (lynching) punishment for blacks who have murdered whites have served to deter such behavior" (p. 120). Hawkins also believes that even though African Americans have progressed, America remains a segregated society. Because of this segregation, whites seldom come in contact with African Americans. Whites therefore seldom murder African Americans because of their few interactions (Hawkins, 1983, p. 121).

An additional concern expressed by Hawkins under proposition 2 is the handling of prehomicide behaviors. One prehomicide behavior is assault. It is commonly believed that since homicides usually occur in a social context, they can be anticipated (Hawkins, 1983, p. 121). If assaults are appropriately handled by the police and other

Figure 1   Johnson's Hierarchy of Homicide Seriousness

Negro versus White

White versus White

Negro versus Negro

(Source: Johnson, 1941)

Figure 2 ~~Hawkins's Hierarchy of Homicide Seriousness~~

RATING	OFFENSE
Most Serious	Black kills White, in authority
	Black kills White, stranger
	White kills White, in authority
	Black kills White, friend, acquaintance
	Black kills White, stranger
	White kills White, friend, acquaintance
	White kills White, intimate, family
	Black kills Black, stranger
	Black kills Black, friend, acquaintance
	Black kills Black, intimate, family
	White kills Black, stranger
	White kills Black, friend, acquaintance
Least Serious	White kills Black, intimate, family

(Source: Hawkins, 1983, p. 118)

justice system officials, then a homicide, in many cases, may be prevented. However, since there is often a strained relationship between the police and minority communities, prehomicide behaviors, such as assault, may be neglected because minorities lose faith in the police and do not report these behaviors.

On a similar note, the police may have a differential response to minority complaints because of this strained relationship. Subsequently, the response times may be slower in African American communities than white ones. Besides the police, prosecutors may also adapt negative stereotypes that may affect their actions in cases involving African Americans. Since African Americans and individuals from lower socioeconomic status are viewed as "normal primitives," they are subsequently treated more harshly. However, black-on-black homicides may be treated with leniency because the result (a dead undesirable) is not seen as a problem.

Proposition 3. Economic deprivation creates a climate of powerlessness in which individual acts of violence are likely to take place. Hawkins's final proposition in his causal model addresses the role economics plays in violence among African Americans. Here Hawkins focuses on the socioeconomic background of offenders who engage in violent crime. Specifically, Hawkins recommends that "an adequate theory [of black violence] must explore the direct link between present-day African American disadvantage and violent crime" (1983, p. 125).

Rejecting the subcultural theory notion that the pathway between African American socioeconomic disadvantage and crime is mediated by the intervening variable cultural values, Hawkins suggests an alternate view:

[S]uch disadvantage generates sociopathological conditions in which violent crime among lower class blacks represents a socially disapproved, but predictable, effort to achieve some measure of control in an environment characterized by social, political and economic powerlessness. (Hawkins, 1983, p. 125)

Hawkins adapted this thought from Fanon's colonial theory (see Fanon 1952, 1963), which has been notably resurrected by Staples (1974) and more recently by Tatum (1994). This paper established Hawkins as a leading critic and scholar in the area of African American homicide.

Homicide Prevention Strategies

Inherent in Hawkins's criticism of the subcultural approach is his concern with the usage of "flawed" theories to devise strategies to address African American homicide. Ultimately, as he stated in his early article on the role of social theory (Hawkins, 1978), these theories should translate into policies and/or programs that will address concerns such as African American homicide. The development of appropriate intervention and prevention strategies represents another area of focus for Hawkins.

In 1985, he surveyed the literature to determine its adequacy for devising prevention strategies for African American homicide (Hawkins, 1985). Hawkins subsequently suggested two areas of attacking the African American homicide problem. First, he pointed to structural considerations, such as the improved living conditions of the "black underclass," which would also need to address both the high underemployment and unemployment among African American youths and young adults who have the highest rates of homicide in the African American community (ibid.). However, since he understood that these macrolevel considerations would be relegated to long-term goals, especially during the conservative Ronald Reagan era (1980–1988), Hawkins focused on more realistic considerations, which could be addressed in the short term. These include:

1. The identification of high risk groups (both offenders and victims).
2. More effective and rapid police and medical personnel prehomicide behavior, e.g., assaults, verbal threats, and murder attempts.
3. Gun Control.
4. Educational programs, especially those targeted at the youth.
5. Community organization and education, including the physical rehabilitation of blighted neighborhoods.
6. Mental health centers for counseling and other forms of intervention for offenders, victims, and their families.
7. Social scientific studies to help identify the social interactional clues to homicide, e.g., verbal and nonverbal behaviors, threats, and social histories of hostilities.

8. More effective control and rehabilitation of potential and actual offenders by the various agencies of the criminal justice system. (Hawkins, 1985a, p. 96)

Hawkins remains cautionary with the above interventions until additional studies were conducted that address sociodemographic characteristics of homicide victims and offenders, individual and situational correlates of homicide; and evaluations of similar intervention efforts (Hawkins, 1985a, p. 99). Besides the subculture of violence theory, Hawkins also devoted scholarly attention to conflict theory (Hawkins, 1987), which is also commonly used to explain African American criminality.

THE CONFLICT PERSPECTIVE

Hawkins's article "Beyond Anomalies: Rethinking the Conflict Perspective on Race and Criminal Punishment" represents a critique of an established model, conflict theory, which is regularly used to explain the overrepresentation of poor persons and minorities in the justice system. According to Hawkins, however, in its original form, it requires significant revision to more accurately explain race and punishment patterns, especially as they relate to African Americans.

After reviewing the abundant literature on racial bias and the administration of criminal justice, Hawkins notes that "a large number of these studies . . . report significantly greater rates and level of punishment for blacks than for whites. Others report no significant differences between the races. Still others find that in certain instances, whites receive significantly more punishment for crime than do blacks" (1987, p. 719). Additionally, he suggests that when this type of research reveals that whites receive significantly more punishment than African Americans, it is considered an anomaly or inconsistency (ibid.). It is so defined because the conflict model used to explain the differences in punishment between African Americans and whites does not account for this finding.

Previous studies that reported anomalies, such as whites being punished more harshly than African-Americans, were usually subjected to methodological criticisms. That is, methodological flaws were attributed to the anomalous findings. To some extent, Hawkins supports this conclusion, but he also believes that "there are major problems of conceptualization and theory that underlie the inconsistencies observed across studies of racial discrimination in the administration of justice" (Hawkins, 1987, p. 720). Because of his concern with what he perceived as shortcomings of the present conflict model, Hawkins set out to make suggestions to strengthen the model. He approaches this task in a twofold manner. First, he examined the anomalous findings reported in previous research. Second, based upon his examination, Hawkins anticipates making suggestions on how to possibly strengthen the model through proposed revisions.

From his review of the available studies, Hawkins concludes that many of the perceived anomalies in the racial bias research are the result of an oversimplification of the conflict model (Hawkins, 1987, p. 721). Referring to the classic works on conflict theorists, Quinney (1970) and Chambliss and Seidman (1982), Hawkins suggests that the oversimplification of the model based upon the writings of these conflict theorists has occurred because their models are actually perspectives not theories. While Hawkins acknowledges that these models meet some criteria for classification as a theory (i.e., testable hypotheses), he believes, however, that they fall short (Hawkins, 1987, p. 722). Another concern expressed by Hawkins regarding the two conflict models is their focus on social class instead of race when discussing the administration of justice (Hawkins, 1987, p. 722).

Although conflict theorists Quinney, Chambliss, and Siedman generally acknowledge the existence of racial discrimination in the criminal justice system, they tend to favor class to explain this discrimination. Considering the long and troubled history of American race relations, Hawkins expresses concern over the scant discussion by conflict criminologists regarding the role race discrimination plays in criminal justice administration (Hawkins, 1987, p. 723). He suggests that since the theory only minimally addresses race, researchers who conduct research in this area are left without theoretical referents for their research designs and findings (ibid., p. 732). Besides social class concerns, Hawkins also points to the importance of certain mediating factors that may explain some of the anomalous findings in the race and punishment literature. Victim racial characteristics and the region where the offense occurred are areas that Hawkins felt deserved additional attention. Using the available literature, Hawkins concluded that along with homicide, research has shown support for the significant role that the race of the victim plays in criminal punishment for other offenses, including rape and robbery (ibid., pp. 724–25).

After considering the role the race of the victim plays in racial discrimination in the administration of justice, Hawkins pointed to three related factors that may also account for anomalies in the race and punishment literature including: the type of crime committed, the race of the offender, and the appropriateness of the offense. Attempting to illuminate this connection, Hawkins proposed the following: "Certain types of crime in multiracial societies are perceived by the public at large and by agencies of social control as race-specific or race-appropriate. A member of a given racial group will receive the harshest punishment for committing those crimes perceived to be racially inappropriate" (1987, p. 728).

This proposition relays the notion that certain crimes are considered "appropriate" or are expected of certain groups in society. Therefore, if, for example, an African American person commits an offense traditionally viewed as a white offense, he or she is likely to be punished more severely than a white person would be for committing a similar offense. Essentially, African Americans would be punished more severely because they committed an offense that is perceived as "inappropriate" for their race. Conversely, since street crimes, including rape, are generally perceived as offenses committed by African Americans, if a white person commits these offenses he or she too will be severely punished (Hawkins, 1987, pp. 728–30). Hawkins also suggests that the victim-offender characteristics is applicable here.

Race and region are considerations that Hawkins believes deserved additional attention by conflict theorists. Specifically, he suggests that while conflict theorists acknowledge that race and regional differences affect African American–white punishment patterns, in the theory's present state, this does not account for the differences in punishment. Hawkins also proposes that regional differences in African American–white punishment are related to group threat concerns, which also are not addressed by conflict theorists. According to Hawkins, conflict theorists generally focus on group status as opposed to group threat. Conflict theorists rely on group status to explain differential punishment for crime because they believe that group subordination and powerlessness have more explanatory power than group threat. Therefore, since lower-class persons generally have little to no resources, conflict theorists postulate that they are unable to "resist the imposition of criminal sanctions" (Hawkins, 1987, p. 734).

Drawing primarily on the work of Hubert Blalock (1967), Hawkins believes that the notion of a "power threat" is potentially applicable to conflict theory. Describing the power-threat hypothesis, Hawkins writes:

> Power threat is generally described as the actual or perceived potential of a minority group to pose a realistic challenge to white political or economic control. [There are] three types of discrimination or prejudice in which the power-threat factor should predominate . . . (1) restriction of minority's political rights, (2) symbolic forms of segregation, and (3) a threat-oriented ideological system. (1987, p. 735)

Following his discussion of the power-threat hypothesis, Hawkins suggests that some criminological research supports his contention that the above areas of discrimination are possibly linked to the overrepresentation of African Americans within the criminal justice system (Hawkins, 1987, pp. 735–36).

While Hawkins appears to agree with some of the foundations of conflict theory, he appears hesitant to endorse it completely as adequate to explain the overrepresentation of African Americans in the criminal justice system. Implicitly, however, Hawkins does appear willing to endorse the perspective with his proposed revisions. These revisions speak to considerations that generally have been overlooked by mainstream theorists. Notably, his critical analyses of prevailing criminological theories provide examples of how minority theorists can provide additional insights into theoretical discussions that, at some point, may have larger implications for changes in the administration of criminal justice.

AFRICAN AMERICAN AND WHITE IMPRISONMENT RATES

Not long after the publication of several landmark articles on the disproportionality of African Americans in the criminal justice system (see Blumstein, 1982; Christianson, 1981; Petersilia, 1983), Hawkins published three articles that focused on the imprisonment rates of African Americans and whites (Hawkins, 1983, 1986; Hawkins and Hardy, 1989). Hawkins's first article on the topic examined trends in the imprisonment of African Americans and whites in North Carolina over a one hundred-year period (Hawkins, 1983). The latter two articles are essentially replications of the aforementioned landmark research on disproportionality (Hawkins, 1986; Hawkins and Hardy, 1989).

Realizing the importance of examining long-term trends in imprisonment to explain present disproportionality among African Americans, Hawkins investigated long-term imprisonment trends in North Carolina. To this end, he reviewed "imprisonment data from annual or biannual state prison reports published by state authorities and other historical materials" (Hawkins, 1985b, p. 191). From this review, he found varying levels of disproportion over time for both African Americans and whites. According to Hawkins, these fluctuations could be traced to state labor needs and convict work assignments. That is, labor needs often dictated the justice distributed to African Americans (a finding noted by Du Bois and Work in earlier chapters).

Hawkins's analysis revealed that since whites viewed certain work as "black work" (i.e., railroad construction), as the need arose for more workers, so did the disproportion of African Americans in prisons. With the decline of railroad construction, Hawkins shows how African Americans were then moved to other work assignments, such as road work, rock quarries, mining, canal construction, and chain gang labor (Hawkins, 1985b, p. 199). Interestingly, since farm work was considered "white work" in the postslavery era, Hawkins saw a gradual increase in the number of white prisoners (ibid., 1985b, p. 199). In general, Hawkins believes that the fluctuations in African American and white imprisonment rates "are likely the results of a variety of structural forces" (ibid., p. 204). He also asserts that the key to understanding the present disproportionality of African Americans in the criminal justice system lies in a careful review of historical trends (Hawkins, 1985b, p. 204).

As previously noted, Hawkins's two other articles in this area are replications of earlier landmark publications. Both articles compare African American and white imprisonment rates. Our focus here is on the first article (Hawkins, 1986), which reviews disproportionality in North Carolina. As in Blumstein's (1982) earlier study, Hawkins's aim was to explore the disproportion between arrest and imprisonment rates between African Americans and whites. For example, if whites make up 40 percent of arrests for assault, they should also be expected to make up 40 percent of the prisoners incarcerated for this offense. Any deviation from the 40 percent is considered unexplained disproportionality. Hawkins (1986) replicated Blumstein's study, which found that nationally the total unexplained disproportionality was about 20 percent, by reviewing arrest data from the Uniform Crime Reports (UCR) for North Carolina (1978–1982) and imprisonment data obtained from the State Department of Corrections (Hawkins, 1986, p. 254). From these data, Hawkins reported some interesting findings, including "the population-adjusted rate of imprisonment for blacks in North Carolina exceeds that of whites by four to one" (ibid., 1986, p. 255). He also found that in North Carolina, from 1978 through 1982, the unexplained disproportionality ranged from 30 percent to 42 percent (ibid., p. 257). Similar to Blumstein's results, Hawkins found that drug offenses showed the most disproportionality, 49% in Blumstein's study and 45% in Hawkins's research (p. 257). Other offenses that Hawkins found to have high levels of disproportion include forgery and drunk driving.

To further investigate these results, Hawkins considered the interaction between race and the type of offense committed. Looking at the period 1981 through 1982, he examined the postconviction dispositions by race and offenses, reporting the percentage of African Americans and whites who did or did not receive prison sentences for a variety of offenses. The results, some of which are presented below, speak to the importance of these two variables in explaining disproportionality. Some highlights of Hawkins's findings include:

   a. African Americans were more likely than whites to be sentenced to a prison term for involuntary manslaughter;
   b. Fewer African American than white assault offenders received prison sentences;
   c. African Americans and whites convicted of selling large quantities of drugs are both likely to receive prison terms;
   d. African Americans are more likely to go to prison for minor drug sales and for major and minor drug possession (1986, pp. 260–61)

As for the latter finding, Hawkins aptly suggests that the reason African Americans are overrepresented in prison for drug offenses has a lot to do with both pre- and postconviction decision making (1986, p. 261). Since Hawkins's explanations for his findings in this study are similar to his arguments in his previously reviewed work on conflict theory (Hawkins, 1987), we move now to another area of his scholarship, crime and ethnicity.

CRIME AND ETHNICITY

A final area of Hawkins's scholarship that we review is his recent work in the area of crime and ethnicity (Hawkins, 1993, 1994, 1995a, 1995b).[1] Over the years, Hawkins believes that ethnicity has become a forgotten area of inquiry in the search for explanations for the current disproportionality among African Americans and other minorities. An apparent outgrowth of his interest in the subculture of violence theory and conflict theory (see specifically Hawkins, 1993, 1994), Hawkins's examination of crime and ethnicity reviews these theories as they have been used to explain the high criminality among both white and nonwhite ethnics. Specifically, Hawkins reminds us of the earlier disproportionate involvement of white ethnics in the criminal justice system. He believes that we can learn much from a careful analysis of this earlier period. For example, during the late nineteenth and early twentieth centuries, Irish, Italian, and Jewish immigrants exhibited higher rates of crime than other ethnic groups (i.e., English, Scottish, and German) (Hawkins, 1994). According to Hawkins (1994, p. 103), "the study of [these] differences in crime among white ethnics can contribute much to our knowledge of American social control." Hawkins then proposes the following research questions and propositions for future study. First, to what extent were disproportionate rates of reported crime among pretwentieth-century Irish, Italians, and other white ethnic groups in the United States a result of bias in the administration of justice? From this question, Hawkins proposes the following two-part proposition derived partly from the earlier work of Sellin (1938) and Blalock (1967).

Proposition 1a: The nature and extent of the social control of an ethnic or racial group is partly a function of its relative insularity vis-à-vis dominant groups or their agents.

Proposition 1b: Given similar levels of insularity, those ethnic/racial groups that are characterized as the greatest "social distance" from the dominant group will be subject to the greatest social control (Hawkins, 1994, p. 109). These propositions point to Hawkins's belief that:

> [t]he reportedly high rates of social control found among nineteenth-century Irish and Italians may reflect in part their concentration in occupations and geographic sites that afforded them minimal protection from the social control of [the] dominant group. Urban areas, in contrast to smaller towns and rural sites, have historically displayed higher levels of social control. Cities, due to their greater economic resources, can afford to support the mechanisms (jails, prisons, and the like) and agents (police, courts) of social control. Both population density and the structuring of urban life may reduce the degree of insularity that potentially conflicting groups can achieve. (1994, p. 110)

The second proposition formulated by Hawkins was created to explore the following questions: what explains the gradual reduction over time in the rate of reported crime and punishment among various white ethnic groups in the United States? Does this change have relevance for our understanding of crime patterns currently found among African Americans, Latinos, and other nonwhite populations?

Proposition 2: Because they are recruited from among economically marginal groups, including those populations characterized by high rates of social control, the police and other lower-level agents of social control play a pivotal role in determining the extent of ethnic/racial differences. As marginal ethnic/racial groups become represented as lower-level agents of social control, the disproportionate representation of members of their group will gradually be reduced (Hawkins, 1994, p. 113).

Hawkins believes that if we track the changes in white ethnic patterns of crime, we will see that as they became more involved in law enforcement agencies, fewer of them became enmeshed in the criminal justice system. Thus, he surmises that as the number of nonwhite ethnic law enforcement agents increases, it is likely that their numbers in the criminal justice system will decrease (Hawkins, 1994, p. 114). While we are uncertain of the validity of Hawkins's propositions on ethnicity, his critical perspective provides yet another example of a minority view on crime and justice.

CONCLUSION

In the past fifteen years, Darnell Hawkins has remained a consistent voice in the area of race and crime. Many of his publications have included much-needed critiques, which have not only helped advance theory but have also provided guidance in the creation of intervention and prevention strategies particularly for African American homicide. During the twenty-first century, we anticipate that he will remain a significant contributor to the advancement of the discipline.

References

Blalock, H. M. (1967). *Towards a theory of minority group relations.* NY: John Wiley.
Blumstein, A. (1982). On the racial disproportionality of the United States prison populations. *The Journal of Criminal Law and Criminology, 73* (Fall), 1259–81.
Chambliss, W. J. & Seidman, R. B. (1971/1982). *Law, order, and power.* Reading: Addison-Wesley.
Christianson, S. (1981). Our black prisons. *Crime and Delinquency, 27* (July), 364–375.
Fanon, F. (1952/1967). *Black skin, white masks.* New York: Grove Weidenfeld.
————. (1963). *The wretched of the earth.* New York: Grove Weidenfeld.
Hawkins, D. F. (1977). *Nonresponse in Detroit area study surveys: A ten year analysis.* Chapel Hill: University of North Carolina Institute for Research in Social Science.
————. (1978a). Applied research and social theory. *Evaluation Quarterly, 2* (1), 141–52.
————. (1978b). The theory of cultural deprivation: A sociology of knowledge critique. *Quarterly Journal of Ideology, 2* (Summer).
————. (1980). Perceptions of punishment for crime. *Deviant Behavior, 1,* 193–215.
————. (1981). Causal attribution and punishment for crime. *Deviant Behavior, 2,* 207–30.
————. (1983/1986). Black and white homicide differentials: Alternatives to an inadequate theory. *Criminal Justice and Behavior, 10, 407–40.* Reprinted in D. F. Hawkins (Ed.), *Homicide among black Americans* (pp. 109–35). Lanham, MD: University Press of America.

————. (1985a). Black homicide: The adequacy of existing research for devising prevention strategies. *Crime and Delinquency, 31* (January), 83–103.

————. (1985b). Trends in black-white imprisonment: Changing conceptions of race or changing patterns of social control? *Crime and Social Justice, 24* (December), 187–209.

————. (1986). Race, crime type and imprisonment. *Justice Quarterly, 3,* 251–69.

————. (1987). Beyond anomalies: Rethinking the conflict perspective on race and criminal punishment. *Social Forces, 65,* 719–45.

————. (1990). Explaining the black homicide rate. *Journal of Interpersonal Violence, 5,* 151–63.

————. (1993). Inequality, culture and interpersonal violence. *Health Affairs, 12,* 80–95.

————. (1994). Ethnicity: The forgotten dimension of American social control. In G. S. Bridges & M. A. Myers (eds.), *Inequality crime and social control* (pp. 99–116). Boulder: Westview Press.

————. (ed.). (1995). *Ethnicity, race, and crime: Perspectives across time and place.* Albany: State University of New York Press.

————. (1997). Biographical data furnished to the authors.

Hawkins, D. & Davis, R. (1986). Homicide prevention within the black community: Public health and criminal justice concerns. In D. F. Hawkins (ed.), *Homicide among black Americans* (pp. 231–37). Lanham, MD: The University Press of America.

Hawkins, D. F. & Hardy, K. (1989). Black-white imprisonment rates: A state-by-state analysis. *Social Justice, 16,* 75–94.

Hawkins, D. F., Johnstone, J. & Michener, A. (1994). Homicide reporting in Chicago dailies. *Journalism Quarterly, 71,* 860–72.

————. (1995). Race, social class, and newspaper coverage of homicide. *National Journal of Sociology, 9,* 113–40.

Johnson, G. B. (1941). The Negro and crime. *Annals of the American Academy of Political and Social Sciences, 217,* 93–104.

Marshall, I. H. (1997). Minorities, migrants, and crime: Diversity and similarity across Europe and the United States. Thousand Oaks: Sage Publications.

Petersilia, J. (1983). *Racial disparities in the criminal justice system.* Santa Monica: The Rand Corporation.

Quinney, R. (1970). *The social reality of crime.* Boston: Little, Brown and Company.

Sellin, T. & Wolfgang, M. (1964). *The measurement of delinquency.* New York: Wiley.

Staples, R. (1974). Internal colonialism and black violence. *Black World, (23),* 16–34.

Tatum, B. (1994). The colonial model as a theoretical explanation of crime and delinquency. In A. T. Sulton (ed.), *African-American perspectives on: Crime causation, criminal justice administration, and crime prevention* (pp. 33–52). Englewood, CO: Sulton Books.

Taylor Greene, H. (1994). Black perspectives on police brutality. In A. T. Sulton (ed.), *African-American perspectives on: Crime causation, criminal justice administration, and crime prevention* (pp. 139–48). Englewood, CO: Sulton Books.

Wolfgang, M. (1958). *Patterns in criminal homicide.* Philadelphia: University of Pennsylvania Press.

Wolfgang, M. & Ferracuti, F. (1967). *The subculture of violence: Towards an integrated theory in criminology.* London: Tavistock.

Vold, G. & Bernard, T. (1986). *Theoretical criminology,* 3rd Edition. Oxford: Oxford University Press.

Darnell F. Hawkins
Selected References

Hawkins, D. F. (1975). Estimation of nonresponse bias. *Sociological Methods and Research, 3,* 461–85.

———. (1977). *Nonresponse in Detroit area study surveys: A ten year analysis.* Working paper No. 8 of the working papers in methodology series of the Institute for Research in Social Science, University of North Carolina, Chapel Hill.

———. (1978a). Applied research and social theory. *Evaluation Quarterly, 2,* 141–52. (Now *Evaluation Review*).

———. (1978b). The theory of cultural deprivation: A sociology of knowledge critique. *Quarterly Journal of Ideology, 2* (Summer).

———. (1980a). Social structure as metatheory: Implications for race relations theory and research. In *Research in Race and Ethnic Relations, 2,* JAI Press, Inc.

———. (1980b). Perceptions of punishment for crime. *Deviant Behavior, 1,* 193–215.

———. (1981). Causal attribution and punishment for crime. *Deviant Behavior, 2,* 207–30.

———. (1983). Black and white homicide differentials: Alternatives to an inadequate theory. *Criminal Justice and Behavior, 10,* 407–40.

———. (1984). State versus county: Prison policy and conflicts of interest in North Carolina. In *Criminal Justice History: An International Annual, 5,* Meckler.

———. (1985a). Black homicide: The adequacy of existing research for devising prevention strategies. *Crime and Delinquency, 31,* 83–103.

———. (1985b). Trends in black-white imprisonment: Changing conceptions of race or changing patterns of social control? *Crime and Social Justice, 24* (December), 187–209.

———. (1986a). Race, crime type and imprisonment. *Justice Quarterly, 3,* 251–69.

———. (Ed.). (1986b). *Homicide among black Americans.* Lanham, MD: University Press of America.

———. (1987a). Devalued lives and racial stereotypes: Ideological barriers to the prevention of family violence among blacks. In R. Hampton (ed.), *Violence in the black family: Correlates and consequences* (pp. 189–205). Lexington, MA: DC Heath.

———. (1987b). Beyond anomalies: Rethinking the conflict perspective on race and criminal punishment. *Social Forces, 65,* 719–45.

———. (1989). Intentional injury: Are there no solutions? *Law, Medicine and Health Care, 17,* 32–41.

———. (1990). Explaining the black homicide rate. *Journal of Interpersonal Violence, 5,* 151–63.

———. (1991). The discovery of institutional racism: An example of the interaction between law and social science. In *Research in race and ethnic relations* (pp. 167–82) 6, JAI Press, Inc.

———. (1993a). Crime and ethnicity. In B. Frost (ed.), *The socio economics of crime and justice* (pp. 89–120). Armonk, NY: M. E. Sharp.

———. (1993b). Inequality, culture and interpersonal violence. *Health Affairs, 12,* 80–95.

———. (1994). Ethnicity: The forgotten dimension of American social control. In G. S. Bridges & M. A. Myers (eds.), *Inequality crime and social control* (pp. 99–116). Boulder: Westview Press.

———. (1994). Afterword. *Law and Human Behavior, 18,* 351–60.

———. (1995a). Comments on a comprehensive approach to violence prevention: Public health and criminal justice partnership. In L. B. Joseph (ed.), *Crime, communities and public policy* (pp. 259–63). Chicago: The University of Chicago Press.

———. (Ed.). (1995b). *Ethnicity, race, and crime: Perspectives across time and place.* Albany: State University of New York Press.

———. (1997). Which way toward equality? Dilemmas and paradoxes in public policies affecting crime and punishment. In C. Herring (ed.), *African-Americans, the public agenda, and the paradoxes of public policy* (pp. 238–52). Thousand Oaks: Sage Publications.

———. (1998). The nations within: Race, class, region, and American lethal violence. *University of Colorado Law Review, 69,* 905–26.

Hawkins, D. F. & Davis, R. (1986). Homicide prevention within the black community: Public health and criminal justice concerns. In D. F. Hawkins (ed.), *Homicide among black Americans* (pp. 231–37). Lanham, MD: The University Press of America.

Hawkins, D. F. & Hardy, K. (1989). Black-white imprisonment rates: A state-by-state analysis. *Social Justice, 16,* 75–94.

Hawkins, D. F. & Jones, N. (1989). Black adolescents and the criminal justice system. In R. Jones (ed.), *Black adolescents* (pp. 403–25). Richmond, CA: Cobb, and Henry Publishers.

Hawkins, D. F. & Onwauci-Saunders, C. (1993). Black-white differences in injury: Race or social class? *Annals of Epidemiology, 3* (March).

Hawkins, D. F. Johnstone, J. & Michener, A. (1994). Homicide reporting in Chicago dailies. *Journalism Quarterly, 71,* 860–72.

Hawkins, D. F., Crosby, A. & Hammett, M. (1994). Homicide, suicide, and assaultive violence: The impact of intentional injury on the health of African-Americans. In I. Livingston (ed.), *Handbook of black American health: The mosaic of conditions, issues, policies, and prospects.* Westport, CT: Greenwood Press.

Hawkins, D. F. Johnstone, J. & Michener, A. (1995). Race, social class, and newspaper coverage of homicide. *National Journal of Sociology, 9,* 113–40.

Hawkins, D. F. & Ross, L. E. (1995). Legal and historical views on racial biases in prison. *Corrections Today,* 192–95.

Notes

1. Marshall (1997) has recently credited Hawkins with reintroducing the concept of ethnicity in the study of minorities & crime.

Daniel Georges-Abeyie

NINE

DANIEL E. GEORGES-ABEYIE
(1948–   )

The complexity that surrounds the definitional issues of crime and criminality [is] further complicated by the issues of race and ethnicity, poverty, urbanization, urbanism, and ghettoization . . . Thus, the prime issue for some criminologists concerned with minority criminality and criminal victimization is not simply whether or not nonwhites are disproportionately represented among the ranks of the criminal and the victimized, but rather what role race, ethnicity, and poverty play in this complex relationship.
—Daniel Georges-Abeyie (1984c, p.7)

INTRODUCTION

Daniel E. Georges-Abeyie is a professor in the Administration of Justice Department and associate dean for international studies at Arizona State University West in Phoenix, Arizona. He has made outstanding contributions to both criminological thought and the administration of justice during the past two decades. As a result of his interdisciplinary research on a wide range of topics, including arson, bombings, the geography of crime, ghetto formation and maintenance, minorities and crime, political violence, racial and ethnic violence, social ecology, terrorism, victimization, and violence and justice, he is widely known in several disciplines.

In addition to his scholarly research, Georges-Abeyie has held numerous administrative positions at several universities and served as a consultant to criminal justice agencies in California and Florida. During the past several years, he has been active in Amnesty International and currently serves as the chair of the Amnesty International U.S.A. Western Regional Planning Group (WRPG) and as the Amnesty International U.S.A., Arizona Death Penalty Abolition coordinator (SDPAC). He has received numerous awards for his efforts on behalf of Amnesty International, including the first Bruce Collmar Award, October 1997, the Outstanding Amnesty Volunteer Award for the Western Region, 1996, and the Alaska Volunteer Award, 1996.

BIOGRAPHICAL BACKGROUND

Born in New York City in 1948, Daniel Georges-Abeyie is of West Indian and African American descent. He traces his ancestry to Lumbee Indians and escaped slaves in the Gullah-Geechee community of the South Carolina Sea Islands (George-town, Johns Island, and James Island), Tortola (British Virgin Islands), Panama, and Puerto Rico. His father, Luther Ernest Georges, was a New York City Transit Authority police officer, and his mother, Edith Isolene Beachum was a caretaker and housewife. The family resided in the Afro-Caribbean Fort Apachee district of the South Bronx for the first twenty-three years of his life.

Georges-Abeyie's mother was his greatest inspiration as a child. She was the most brilliant and intellectually curious individual he has ever known. He has fond memories of stories she read daily or would have her children read to her. As a Gullah-Geechee female child growing up in the Sea Islands of South Carolina, she was not allowed to go beyond the sixth grade in school, yet her intellectual curiosity and honesty were insatiable. Thus, in spite of her limited formal education, she had a great deal of knowledge and wisdom that she passed on to her children along with the Gullah-Geechee stories, mores, and legends communicated in the oral tradition of West, Central, and South Africa.

Georges-Abeyie attended PS 118, Clark Junior High, and Dewitt Clinton High School. Throughout his formative years, there were several individuals who served as mentors. In elementary school, his fifth-grade teacher, Ms. Sayers, an African American woman, constantly reminded her students that their destiny had to be taken into their own hands and that the United States of America was not a land of milk and honey for its Negro citizens. In junior high school, two Jewish teachers, Mr. Tannebaum and Mr. Abolofia, acted as mentors, along with Dr. Blackman, an African American science teacher. Each had a strong influence on him and, along with his mother, were instrumental in guiding him to attend college (Georges-Abeyie, 1998).

ACADEMIC BACKGROUND

Dr. Georges-Abeyie has a distinguished career as an academician that began during the early 1970s. Unlike many African Americans educated during this time, he had several persons that both guided his development and mentored him during his undergraduate and graduate studies. Each recognized his intelligence and drive and believed it should be rewarded. Individuals he identifies as his mentors/guides include Dr. Donald Clelland and Mr. James Hall, sociologists; Dr. James L. Newman, a geographer; and Dr. Hans Toch, a social psychologist and criminologist. Interestingly, many of his mentors also had a poverty background and a history of persecution, although none of these men were African American.

For his undergraduate degree, Georges-Abeyie attended Hope College in Holland, Michigan. He graduated cum laude, majoring in sociology in 1969. At Hope College he was influenced by Dr. Donald Clelland, a Marxist sociologist and New Order Mennonite. After graduation, he returned to New York City to serve as supervisor of the New York City Neighborhood Youth Corps, South Bronx Division.

Two years later (1971), he completed an M.A. in sociology at the University of Connecticut.

Georges-Abeyie began his teaching career as an instructor at the University of Connecticut at Stamford, the summer after he graduated. From 1972 through 1973 he taught in the Department of Geology and Geography at Herbert H. Lehman College of the City University of New York. In the summer of 1972, he served as the research coordinator and assistant director of the Community Progress Corporation, South Bronx Division.

Dr. Georges-Abeyie completed his Ph.D. in the geography of crime and justice, urban social, cultural and political geography at Syracuse (NY) University in 1974, becoming one of the first persons of Negro ancestry to receive a Ph.D. in geography from a predominantly white university. His dissertation is entitled "Arson: The Ecology of Urban Unrest in an American City—Newark, New Jersey, A Case Study in Collective Violence." Dr. James L. Newman, an Africanist, demographer, and geographer, was an inspiration to him during his doctoral studies and continues to be both a friend and his closest mentor. He inspired Georges-Abeyie to write "The Geography of Crime and Violence," a resource paper in the official Association of American Geographers monograph series for college geography, and *Crime: A Spatial Perspective*, with Dr. Keith Harries, recognized as a classic in contemporary geography.

Since completing his doctoral studies, he has taught at Florida State University (tenured), the California State University at Bakersfield (tenured), the Pennsylvania State University (tenured), Southern Illinois University at Carbondale (tenured), the State University of New York at Albany, the University of Oklahoma, the University of Texas at Arlington, the John Hopkins University, and the City University of New York. Throughout his academic career he has also held several administrative positions, including that of associate dean for international studies (Florida State); associate dean and de facto acting dean, School of Criminology and Criminal Justice (Florida State); chair of the Afro-American/black studies program at the Pennsylvania State University; and chair of the criminal justice programs at the California State University and Arizona State University West. As a professor, his first and greatest mentor was Hans Toch (Georges-Abeyie, 1998).

CONTRIBUTIONS TO CRIMINOLOGICAL THOUGHT

Georges-Abeyie's research includes several issues and themes, although he specializes in the study of blacks and criminal justice and collective violence (Georges-Abeyie, 1984a). Since completion of his doctoral studies, he has been one of very few American geographers who revived interest in both the social ecological approach and spatially based crime analysis. He has written extensively on blacks, crime, and the criminal justice system (1981b, 1984a, 1984b, 1984c, 1984d, 1989, 1990a, 1992). An important theme in these studies has been the need for a more realistic approach to understanding Blacks and the criminal justice system that includes the spatial dynamic. His geography of crime studies also includes spatial analyses of arson (1975) bombings and bomb threats (Georges-Abeyie & Zandi, 1978–1979a, 1978–1979b, 1983a), crimes against the elderly (Georges-Abeyie & Kirsey, 1977–1978), criminal victimization (1989), and terrorism (1980, 1981a, 1983b, 1991). His most recent research focuses upon death penalty abolition (forthcoming). An overview of his research is presented below.

Blacks, Crime, and Justice

In 1984, Georges-Abeyie published *The Criminal Justice System and Blacks,* an edited volume that provided an in-depth examination of theory, practice, and research on crime, race, and justice. It included contemporary research by both black and white scholars, described by Georges-Abeyie as new criminologists. He provided an overview of several important issues in chapter 9, including the contributions of black criminologists and jurists (Georges-Abeyie, 1984b).

One of Georges-Abeyie's most significant contributions in the study of blacks and criminal justice is sensitizing criminologists to the limitations of the black ethnic monolith paradigm (discussed below) and the omission of the spatial reality of (blacks) crime and criminal justice in the research literature. He also introduced the concepts of ethclass, social distance, and petit apartheid (discussed below) in his research.

Georges-Abeyie has also been involved in an ongoing debate within the discipline of criminology concerning bias and racism in the criminal justice system. Wilbanks (1987) argued that the view of the criminal justice system as racist was a myth. Georges-Abeyie (1984a, 1989) and several other black criminologists refuted Wilbanks's position. Georges-Abeyie specifically challenged Wilbanks's omission of death penalty statistics on sentence commutation, a spatial analysis, his reliance on official data, and use of a black ethnic monolith paradigm.

Collective Violence and the Geography of Crime

Georges-Abeyie's first geographical study of crime and dissertation topic examined arson and urban unrest in Newark, New Jersey, during 1967. Newark was one of 164 cities that experienced collective violence and one of eight cities that experienced a major disorder during 1967 (Georges-Abeyie, 1975). The study provides a historical context of arson during the World War I riots; an overview of Newark's socioeconomic characteristics, including its revenues, housing conditions, unemployment rates, and education levels; critical events in Newark that preceded the riot of 1967; and characteristics of arsons during the 1967 riot. The study concluded that most arsons occurred at night and targeted property and that arson, proportion of blacks in a given area, and economic deprivation were correlated.

According to Georges-Abeyie (1983a, 1983b), criminal bombings and bomb threats have been overlooked by social scientists. Thus, he is one of the first geographers to utilize spatially based crime analysis to explore bombings and bomb threats. In his study of bombings in Dallas, Texas, he provides a summary of bombing incidents reported to the Dallas Police Department during 1975 that included the object of attack, motive, method, and zonal analyses of bomb threats by age and gender (1978–1979a, 1983a) and race or ethnicity of suspects (1978–1979a, 1983a). In another study (Georges-Abeyie & Zandi, 1978–1979b), bomb data collected by the Federal Bureau of Investigation (FBI) National Bomb Data Center was analyzed within a spatial and criminological perspective to better understand regional variations in targets, methods, motives, and bomb types (ibid., p. 299). The authors concluded that during 1975, "psychic terror" (ibid., p. 333) was the most common result of bombings. Most bombing incidents occurred in industrialized states in the Pacific, East North Central and South Atlantic regions.

Georges-Abeyie's collective violence research also includes terrorists and their involvement in political terrorism. Interestingly, he is the only black scholar who has studied terrorism in a social-cultural-historical context. The primary focus of his research has been the use of criminal violence by terrorists to change governments and their policies. He has developed a terrorism severity index, a theory of women as terrorists that takes into consideration feminist principles and the changing role of women in many societies, as well as analyses of terrorism in neocolonial settler states (Georges-Abeyie, 1983a, 1983b, 1991).

Criminal Victimization

During the 1970s, Georges-Abeyie conducted research exploring the geography of criminal victimization. As an urban social geographer, he examines the spatial manifestation of violence. In "Violent Crime Perpetrated against the Elderly in the City of Dallas, October 1974–September 1975," Georges-Abeyie and Kirksey (1977–1978, p. 150) analyzed police records to examine the spatial and social interactional aspects of elderly victimization. The research included characteristics of the victim and suspect (age, race/ethnicity), victimization locations (micro-level), and temporal variables (day, dates, time). The study included reported murders, assaults, rapes, and robberies.

The majority of elderly victims in Dallas were white (69.5 percent). Residents age fifty and older were most likely to be victims of either robbery or assault. While most robberies and murders took place on the street, most assaults and rapes took place in single-family dwelling units. Overall, most elderly victimizations occurred on the street (Georges-Abeyie & Kirksey, p. 161). With the exception of murder and robbery, most suspects were known by the victim prior to the crime (ibid., p. 188).

Explaining Black Criminality

As previously stated, Georges-Abeyie, a social urban geographer, has contributed to the reconceptualization of (1) blacks and their involvement in crime and (2) patterns of crime and victimization. He challenges the ability of traditional criminological theories to explain either crime causation in general or "black criminality" (Georges-Abeyie, 1981b, p. 100). His crime and victimization research also challenges traditional approaches to studying crime. Throughout his research, Georges-Abeyie emphasizes the importance of studying the spatial distribution of crime and challenges traditional assumptions about the administration of justice.

As a social ecologist and environmental criminologist, Georges-Abeyie has contributed to the synthesis of spatial theories of crime and traditional criminological theories. In his reconceptualization of social ecology theory, he offers a spatial ecology theoretical model to explain "black ghetto crime" (Brantingham and Brantingham, 1981). He introduces several themes in his research, including refutation of the black ethnic monolith paradigm, ethclass, ghetto morphology, social distance, and petit apartheid. In addition to these themes, his use of a spatial ecological approach, perspectives on female terrorists, and terrorism in geopolitical colonial settler-states are also important in the study of criminology. His contributions to criminological thought are described below.

Unlike other scholars, Georges-Abeyie does not challenge the reality of black criminality. He believes the real issue is, "whether blacks manifest unique biological, psychological, sociological, and cultural attributes which result in their above average criminality, or whether they reside in 'natural areas' of crime" (Georges-Abeyie, 1981b, p. 100). He posits that most if not all traditional criminological theories totally ignore black ethnic heterogeneity, extralegal social control, and black ghetto racial/ethnic and economic heterogeneity (ibid.). Thus, they cannot adequately explain black criminality. He also points out that the contributions of anthropologists, geographers, and social ecologists who study crime, perhaps more realistically than traditional criminologists, are limited as well. While researchers do consider at least some racial and economic factors, overall, they have not studied the relationship, if any, of crime and black ghetto morphology (explained below). Georges-Abeyie provides a theoretical framework for understanding black criminality that he refers to as a "spatial ecological" model.

The Spatial Ecology of Crime

The social ecological approach developed at the Chicago School of Sociology emphasized the social and spacial reality of crime. According to this perspective, "the above average rate of black criminality is in large part due to the fact that blacks reside in 'natural areas' of crime, that is, blacks reside in the ecological complex demarcated by . . . social, economic, psychological, cultural, and spatial factors" (Georges-Abeyie, 1981b, p. 99).

The social ecology approach also considers site and situational characteristics of the criminal event. Place, organization, environs, and time (POET) comprise a social-spatial complex that allows researchers to better understand criminal events. POET requires the analysis of the place or site of the criminal event, offender's and victim's residence, place/site of apprehension/arrest, situational characteristics of the criminal event (victim/offender relationship, weapon involved), and time and temporal factors.

The social ecological approach provides a more descriptive approach to understanding patterns of crime. However, researchers studying black criminality have overlooked the heterogeneity of blacks and the black ghetto. Since black ghettoes contain residents of varying racial and ethnic identities, economic wealth, and power, as well as "diverse and complicated patterns of residential racial dominance," these factors must be considered when studying crime (Georges-Abegie 1981b, p. 101–102). Georges-Abeyie offers the spatial ecological approach as a tool for studying and explaining black criminality. Two key concepts used in his approach, black ethnic heterogeneity and ghetto morphology are explained below.

Black Ethnic Heterogeneity

The most significant contribution of Georges-Abeyie to understanding blacks, crime, and justice is his challenge to the black ethnic monolith paradigm. This theme appears in several of his publications (Georges-Abeyie, 1981b, 1989) but is elaborated upon extensively in "Race, Ethnicity, and the Spatial Dynamic: Toward a Realistic Study of Black Crime, Crime Victimization, and Criminal Justice Processing of Blacks," (Georges-Abeyie, 1989). This article was included in a special issue of *Social Justice* entitled *Racism, Powerlessness, and Justice,* edited by Bernard Headley. In this article he criticizes traditional criminology and criminal justice theories for failing to increase our understanding of black criminality, victimization, and criminal justice processing (ibid., p. 37).

According to Georges-Abeyie contemporary criminological approaches lack a social-ecological sensitivity that results in overreliance on the black ethnic monolith paradigm and overlook differences in site and situational realities of both crime and the criminal justice system (1989, p. 37). He also emphasizes the interrelatedness of black ethnic diversity, social distance, and spatial factors.

In earlier research, Georges-Abeyie (1981b, 1984c) comments on the difficulty of defining both race and ethnicity and the differences between the two concepts. In his refutation of the black ethnic monolith paradigm, he requires criminologists to be more cognizant of the heterogeneity within black ethnic groups and the effect it might have on criminality and criminal victimization. He argues that we must take into consideration differences in identities among blacks of Puerto Rican, Cuban, Jamaican, African, American, and other national origins. In doing this, color/hue, cultural, religious, and class differences must also be considered.

Recognition of Black ethnic diversity requires that we rethink the involvement of blacks in crime and criminal justice processing. Georges-Abeyie asks,

[T]hen is it not also conceivable that different Black ethnic groups are more involved in extralegal and illegal activity than are others, and that certain Black ethnics dominate certain criminal activities (or are believed to) and are thus viewed as more threatening than are other Black ethnics? (Georges-Abeyie, 1989, p. 40)

Georges-Abeyie also points out that some black ethnic groups may be the victims of labeling and unfair criminal justice processing.

In addition to these factors, social distance between black ethnic groups as well as between blacks and whites must also be considered. Georges-Abeyie uses Parrillo's definition of social distance, which is "the degree of closeness or remoteness one desires in interaction with members of a particular group" (1989, p. 38).

Ghetto Morphology

Georges-Abeyie combines the geographical and sociological contexts of crime to increase our understanding of the behavioral characteristics of both offenders and victims. The concept ghetto morphology is used by Georges-Abeyie to refer to characteristics of residential zones (1989). It provides a framework for understanding the microspatial distribution of crime in areas of varying minority group residential dominance. Black ghetto and slum-ghetto morphologies include:

> A Zone of Transition where 30% to 49% of the residents are Black.
> A ghetto/slum-ghetto fringe where the population is 50% to 75% Black.
> A ghetto/slum-ghetto core where 75% to 100% of the resident population is Black. (Ibid.)

Zones of transition are in the process of becoming part of the ghetto. Ghettos and slum ghettos are distinguished from one another not only by the black percentage of occupation of spatial units but also by the extent of adequate (ghetto) or inadequate housing and other patterns of social disorganization (slum-ghettoes).

Ghetto morphologies provide an analytical framework for understanding both site and situational factors of crime. When the site of the crime and of the offenders', victim's, and jurors' residence are considered, both criminal events and criminal justice outcomes are better understood.

Petit Apartheid

In a discussion of the spatial factors in criminal justice, Georges-Abeyie (1989, p. 46) presents the concept of petit apartheid, which he uses to refer to "the informal practices of criminal justice agents and agencies, which include selectively inhumane and demeaning behavior by law enforcement, court, and corrections officials directed at nonwhite suspects and arrestees." According to Georges-Abeyie, blacks, especially those in the lower class, are subjected to insults, stopping and questioning, and various other forms of rude and indifferent behavior on a daily basis. Although

Georges-Abeyie does not elaborate on petit apartheid or present it in any other article, he provides a useful framework for understanding criminal justice practices that are reminiscent of an earlier era in U.S. history. The concept also may contribute to our understanding of the controversial practice of racial profiling by police.[1]

Understanding Terrorists and Terrorism

As previously stated, Georges-Abeyie has made a unique contribution to understanding terrorism. Specifically, his research on female terrorists, terrorism in colonial settler states, and development of the terrorism severity index are important. His theories for understanding female terrorists and perspectives on geopolitical violence in colonial settler states are presented below.

The limited research that is available on female terrorists documents their historical low level of participation in terrorist groups. In "Women as Terrorists" (Georges-Abeyie, 1983c, 1987), female involvement in terrorist organizations during the late 1970s and the nature of their involvement are described. Some females committed terrorist acts independent of group involvement. Others served as leaders and comprised a sizeable number of the memberships (although less than one-fifth) in terrorist groups, including Armed Forces of National Liberation (FALN), Weather Underground, Fuerzas Armed Revolutionaries (FAR), Irish Republican Army (IRA), Red Brigades, and the Red Army Faction in West Germany. A review of earlier explanations of (1) female criminality and (2) their memberships in terrorist organizations precedes Georges-Abeyie's formulation of a theory of women as terrorists. He notes the shortcomings of these theories, as well as the rudimentary formulation he develops. His theory consists of five propositions that include variables associated with female terrorist behavior (Georges-Abeyie, 1983c, p. 81). Georges-Abeyie summarizes the propositions, and the theory as follows:

> [O]ne may expect a considerable amount of female terrorists in organizations that exhibit and preach feminist or socialistic principles. These organizations, and, thus, sizable number of female cadres may exist in societies undergoing dramatic challenge to, or change in, their present economic system. Trained female terrorists can be expected to function in a manner similar to their male counterparts. And female terrorists most likely will serve as integrated cadres in both socialistic and nationalistic struggles, and not as autonomous legions of Amazon-oriented warriors. (Ibid., p. 83)

Interestingly, Georges-Abeyie notes the effect that emancipation of females from household and domestic functions might have on their future involvement in revolutionary and terrorist activities. He encourages future research on female terrorists to examine the role of feminism, socialism, and changing modes of female criminality.

Georges-Abeyie (1991) examined political terrorism in South Africa, the Fiji Islands, and New Caledonia. These three countries are representative of Third World colonial settler states, where urban violence (terrorism) exists. In these political entities, the indigenous population was subjected to the creation of an exploitative nation-state that utilized violence or the threat of violence for political reasons. In these geopolitical areas, guerilla warfare is a reaction to and result of colonization.

Another contribution by Georges-Abeyie to understanding terrorism was his proposal to develop a terrorism severity index. He believed that an index would "enable us to appraise more realistically the illegal actions of terrorists and terrorist groups as well as what often appears to be an inappropriate societal and governmental response to such activities" (Georges-Abegie, 1983b, p. 23). People damage, property damage, political significance, political beliefs, mehtods of operation, weapons, victims, location, perpetrators, media interpretation, and length of the terrorist incident were identified as important factors to be included in a terrorism severity index.

Conclusion

Georges-Abeyie has made unique contributions to our understanding of blacks, crime, and justice, arson, bombings, criminal victimization, terrorism, and the geography of crime. It is important to note that rarely does his research focus on the individual and that the nature and scope of his research have changed over the years. In spite of the significance of his research, there have been few replications of his research and/or tests of his theoretical contributions. This is unfortunate because the continued lack of empirical research in many of these areas, including arson, female terrorism, and terrorism severity affects the body of knowledge.

Georges-Abeyie strongly believes that academicians must not solely involve themselves in research and theory but should also contribute to the practice of criminal justice. Two examples of his contributions are his involvement in the Florida Supreme Court Racial and Ethnic Bias Study Commission (Shaw, 1992) and Amnesty International. The Study Commission was a historical examination of the status, experiences, and treatment of minorities by the court system, juvenile justice system, law enforcement agencies, and adult criminal justice system (ibid.). Amnesty International is a leader in the death penalty abolition and human rights movements. Georges-Abeyie also continues to produce scholarly research.

References

Brantingham, P. & Brantingham, P. (Eds.). (1981). *Environmental criminology.* Beverly Hills: Sage Publications, Inc.

Georges-Abeyie, D. (1974). *Arson: The ecology of urban unrest in an American city—Newark New Jersey, A case study in collective violence.* Ph.D. Dissertation, Syracuse University.

——. (1975). The ecology of urban unrest: The case of arson in Newark, New Jersey *Journal of Environmental Systems, 5,* 203–28.

——. (1980). Political crime and terrorism. In G. Newman (Ed.), *Deviance and crime: A comparative perspective* (pp. 313–32). Beverly Hills: Sage Publications.

——. (1981a). Terrorism and the liberal state: A reasonable response. *Journal of Police Studies, 4,* (3), 34–53.

——. (1981b). Toward the development of a realistic approach to the study of black crime. In P. Brantingham & P. Brantingham (eds.), *Environmental criminology* (pp. 97–109). Beverly Hills: Sage Publications, Inc.

——. (1983a). The social ecology of bomb threats: Dallas, Texas. *The Journal of Black Studies, 13,* 305–20.

——. (1983b). Toward the development of a terrorism severity index. *Journal of Police Studies, 6* (4), 22–29.

——. (1983c). Women as terrorists. In L. Freedman and Y. Alexander (Eds.), *Perspectives on terrorism* (pp. 71–84). Wilmington, DE: Scholarly Resources, Inc.

——. (1984a). *The criminal justice system and blacks.* New York: Clark Boardman.

——. (1984b). The criminal justice system and minorities—a review of the literature. In D. Georges-Abeyie (Ed.), *The criminal justice system and blacks* (pp. 125–156. New York: Clark Boardman.

——. (1984c). Definitional issues: Race, ethnicity, and official crime victimization statistics. In D. Georges-Abeyie (Ed.), *The criminal justice system and blacks* (pp. 5–19). New York: Clark Boardman.

——. (1984d). An uncertain future. In D. Georges-Abeyie (Ed.), *The criminal justice system and blacks* (pp. 337–43). New York: Clark Boardman.

——. (1989). Race, ethnicity, and the spatial dynamic: Toward a realistic study of black crime, crime victimization, and criminal justice processing of blacks. *Social Justice, 16,* (4), 35–54.

——. (1990a). Criminal justice processing of non-white minorities. In B. MacLean and D. Milovanovic (Eds.), *Racism, empiricism, and criminal justice* (pp. 25–34). Vancouver: Collective Press.

——. (1990b). The myth of a racist criminal justice system? In B. MacLean and D. Milovanovic (Eds.), *Racism, empiricism, and criminal justice* (pp. 11–14). Vancouver: Collective Press.

——. (1991). Political criminogenesis of democracy in the colonial settler-state: terror, terrorism and guerilla warfare. *Terrorism: An International Journal, 14,* 1–18.

——. (1992). Law enforcement and racial and ethnic bias. *Florida State University Law Review, 19,* 717–26.

——. (1998). Telephone Interview.

Georges-Abeyie, D. & K. Harries (1980). *Crime: A spatial perspective.* New York: Columbia University Press.

Georges-Abeyie, D. & K. Kirksey. (1977–1978). Violent crime perpetrated against the elderly in the city of Dallas for the year 1975. *Journal of Environmental Systems, 7,* 149–98.

Georges-Abeyie, D. & M. Zandi. (1978–1979a). The study of bombings, incendiaries, and bomb threats in the city of Dallas for the year 1975. *Journal of Environmental Systems, 8,* 57–97.

———. (1978–1979b). Terrorism by the bomb: A national perspective. *Journal of Environmental Systems, 8,* 297–336.

Shaw, Leander J., Jr. (1992). Introduction to the report and recommendations of the Florida Supreme Court bias study commission. *Florida State University Law Review, 19,* 89–590.

Wilbanks, W. (1987). *The myth of a racist criminal justice system.* Monterey, CA: Brooks/Cole Publishing Company.

Daniel Georges-Abeyie
Selected References

Georges-Abeyie, D. (1974). *Arson: The ecology of urban unrest in an American city—Newark New Jersey, A case study in collective violence.* Ph.D. Dissertation, Syracuse University.

———. (1975). The ecology of urban unrest: The case of arson in Newark, New Jersey. *Journal of Environmental Systems,* 203–28.

———. (1979). The geography of crime and justice: An evaluation of the1978 and 1979 AAGCJ session-new directions. *Transition,* 9–11.

———. (1979). The geography of crime and criminal victimization: A time to start theory building. *American Association of Geographers Proceedings 13,* 18–21.

———. (1980). The political and psychological potential of hostage taking: A potent weapon of the few against the many. *Contemporary Psychology, 25,* 729–30.

———. (1980). Professional schools: Their obligations to minority development. *Social Science Journal Symposium, 17,* (2), 27–32.

———. (1980). Political crime and terrorism. In G. Newman (Ed.) *Deviance and crime: A comparative perspective* (pp. 313–32). Beverly Hills: Sage Publications.

———. (1981). Terrorism and the liberal state: A reasonable response. *Journal of Police Studies, 4,* (3), 34–53.

———. (1981). Toward the development of a realistic approach to the study of black crime. In P. Brantingham & P. Brantingham (Eds.), *Environmental criminology* (pp. 97–109). Beverly Hills: Sage Publications, Inc.

———. (1983). The social ecology of bomb threats: Dallas, Texas. *The Journal of Black Studies, 13,* 305–20.

———. (1983). Toward the development of a terrorism severity index. *Journal of Police Studies, 6,* (4), 22–29.

———. (1983). Women as terrorists. In L. Freedman and Y. Alexander (Eds.), *Perspectives on terrorism* (pp. 71–84). Wilmington, DE: Scholarly Resources, Inc.

———. (1984). *The criminal justice system and Blacks.* New York: Clark Boardman.

———. (1984). The criminal justice system and minorities—a review of the literature. In D. Georges-Abeyie (Ed.), *The criminal justice system and blacks* (pp. 125–56. New York: Clark Boardman.

———. (1984). Definitional issues. Race, ethnicity, and official crime victimization statistics. In D. Georges-Abeyie (Ed.), *The criminal justice system and Blacks* (pp. 5–19). New York: Clark Boardman.

———. (1984). An uncertain future. In D. Georges-Abeyie (Ed.), *The criminal justice system and Blacks* (pp. 337–43). New York: Clark Boardman.

———. (1989). Race, ethnicity, and the spatial dynamic: Toward a realistic study of black crime, crime victimization, and criminal justice processing of blacks. *Social Justice, 16,* (4), 35–54.

———. (1990). Criminal justice processing of non-white minorities. In B. MacLean and D. Milovanovic (Eds.), *Racism, empiricism, and criminal justice* (pp. 25–34). Vancouver: Collective Press.

———. (1990). The myth of a racist criminal justice system? In B. MacLean and D. Milovanovic (Eds.), *Racism, empiricism, and criminal justice* (pp. 11–14). Vancouver: Collective Press.

———. (1991). Political criminogenesis of democracy in the colonial settler-state: Terror, terrorism and guerilla warfare. *Terrorism: An International Journal, 14,* (1), 1–18.

———. (1992). Law enforcement and racial and ethnic bias. *Florida State University Law Review, 19,* 717–26.

Notes

1. At the 1999 American Society of Criminology annual meeting in Toronto, Canada, two panels, organized by Drs. Katheryn Russell and Dragan Milovanovic, were devoted to the application of the "petit apartheid" concept to the interactions between American minorities and agents of the criminal justice system.

Vernetta D. Young

Vernetta Denise Young

Introduction

One of the first African American women to receive a doctorate in criminology or criminal justice, Vernetta Young has produced several important publications in the areas of black female criminality, the historical development of juvenile institutions, and African American contributions to criminology and criminal justice. Her 1980 publication, "Women, Race, and Crime," is a classic response to the liberation hypothesis, which has been one of the most controversial theories of the last thirty years. Young's recent historical research on the development of juvenile institutions has contributed to the increasing body of literature that views the development of these institutions as devices of social control to secure cheap (and mostly African American) labor. And her research on African American contributions to the study of crime and justice has served as a forerunner to the present volume.

Biographical Information

One of six children born to Mary R. Young Haigler, Vernetta Denise Young was born in Washington, DC, just before the landmark *Brown v. Board of Education* decision that outlawed the "separate but equal" principle. Young's grandparents, William P. Young and Agnes M. Young, played a large role in Young's upbringing. Young attended St. Joseph Colored Elementary School, Banneker Junior High School, and Chopticon High School in St. Mary's County, Maryland, where, as a youth, she resided during the school year. When school was not in session, she returned to Washington, D.C.

She remembers being a mischievous child who could have easily become a juvenile delinquent. Young described a few incidents that confirmed this possibility. First, when a cousin took her bike without permission, she remembers running after him, grabbing him, and choking him without consideration for the potential harm she might have caused with her actions. Fortunately, her aunt stepped in and told her to stop. Second, she confronted a male who used to "torment" her with a knife and stabbed him to the point where she drew blood. Young suggests that had the boy not moved back, he would likely have been seriously injured. She also suggests that there were other "incidents" that could have landed her in the juvenile justice system.

Young remembers that the only thing that saved her from this fate was that she was a good student who participated in several extracurricular activities. Normally, the principal would have expelled students for the same behavior for which Young received detention. Looking back, Young recalls being frightened about the harm she could inflict upon people. These incidents may have steered Young toward the discipline of criminology/criminal justice to understand her own behavior.

Following her graduation from high school, she enrolled at the University of Maryland, College Park, as a mathematics major. She later changed her major to psychology, but after realizing that it would take her an extended period to finish the psychology degree requirements, she looked to another area. At this point, she enrolled in a criminology class in the Sociology Department. She found the class interesting because "they were talking about all these theories, and I thought they were talking about black folks, but they would never say they were talking about black folks" (Young, 1998). Intrigued by this, Young decided to major in sociology with a concentration in criminology. During her junior year, she was encouraged to pursue graduate studies. Following this advice, Young applied to the graduate program in criminal justice at Florida State University, where she was accepted.

After graduating from the University of Maryland in May 1972, Young enrolled in the master's degree program in criminal justice at Florida State University. After a year and a half of some frustrations at Florida State, Young withdrew from the program. She returned to Washington, D.C, and accepted a job at a local bank. During this period, she had also applied to the University of California at Berkeley criminology program and the Department of Criminal Justice at the State University of New York (SUNY) at Albany.

While at work one day, she received a call from the late Dr. Michael J. Hindelang regarding her application to SUNY Albany. He was inquisitive about why Young had not accepted a fellowship offer to attend SUNY Albany. Young, thinking that Albany was New York City, expressed concerns about the limited financial package she was offered. To her approval, Hindelang also offered her employment at the Criminal Justice Research Center that he directed. She accepted the offer, quit her job, and, in the fall of 1974, headed to upstate New York.

While at Albany, she does not remember any specific persons influencing her thinking, but she does remember being impressed with Hindelang. However, she recalls them having a strange relationship because she felt "he did not know what to do with a black female" (Young, 1998). By the fall of 1978, she decided it was time to leave Albany. After making contact with a former dean from Albany, who was now at American University in Washington, D.C, she accepted an appointment as an instructor in the School of Justice. Three years later, Young completed her dissertation, "Patterns of Female Criminality," under the direction of Michael Gottfredson.

According to Young, teaching at American turned out to be a good experience. However, one course assignment, social justice, was initially a problem. It was one of several introductory courses that required instructors to use a common syllabus and book. The assigned text was heavy on Marxist criticisms of capitalism. The criticisms of the capitalist system in the text were not well received coming from Young, considering her then Angela Davis persona. So, the next time she taught the course, she changed the book and experienced minimal problems. Although she had a good experience at American, in 1982, Young returned to her alma mater, the University of Maryland, to join the faculty of the Institute of Criminal Justice and Criminology.

Young recalls having an amicable relationship with the faculty at Maryland. During her tenure at Maryland, however, Young also recalls most of the African American and white female students clinging to her. They apparently felt more comfortable with her than the white male faculty members who were predominant in the department. In 1988, Young accepted a position at Howard University in Washington, D.C., where she is currently an associate professor of sociology in the Department of Sociology and Anthropology, specializing in criminal justice and criminology.

CONTRIBUTIONS TO CRIMINOLOGICAL THOUGHT

As with the other scholars profiled in this volume, Young's early research was based on her dissertation. Using victimization data, Young wrote on female offender victimization patterns (Young, 1979) and challenged Freda Adler's thesis of black female crime trends (Young, 1980). Young's most recent research includes historical research on juvenile institutions and African American scholarship. We begin with a review of some of her studies on women and crime, which include scholarship on African American female criminality and gender expectations and African American female criminality.

WOMEN AND CRIME

Black Female Criminality

Young's earliest contributions to criminology and criminal justice began in the late seventies and early eighties. Toward the end of her doctoral program, Young sought to address the prevailing women and crime theory (or liberation hypothesis) of the era. The two leading theorists of the era were Freda Adler (1975) and Rita Simon (1975). Both women believed that the women's movement of the 1960s and early 1970s had allowed women to advance within society in areas such as education, occupation, politics, and so on. According to Simon, based on this advancement, the following hypotheses regarding women and crime could be expected:

> The major hypotheses are that increased participation in the labor force
> provides women with more opportunities for committing certain types
> of crimes. As those opportunities increase, women's participation in

larceny, fraud, embezzlement, and other financial and white-collar crimes should increase. (1975, p. 19)

Adler, while echoing many of the same sentiments as Simon, devoted a chapter in her classic publication, *Sisters in Crime* (1975), to African American females. In this chapter, Adler considered the patterns of African American criminality and made several propositions (see ibid., pp. 134–39). Since Young believed that Adler's theory was based on "misconceptions and myths about the African American community derived from untenable assumptions about the historical impact of slavery on the African-American family" (Young and Sulton, 1991), she decided to test Adler's propositions. These propositions included

1. The patterns of criminal involvement for females differ by race with black female offenders concentrated in crimes against persons and property and white female offenders involved in both "blue collar" crimes (vice, assault, robbery, and so on) and white collar crime.
2. The pattern of criminal behavior of black females is closer to the pattern of white males than it is to that of white females.
3. Black female criminality parallels the criminality of black males more closely than the criminality of white females does that of white males.
4. The ratio of black to white female criminal involvement is much larger than the black to white male ratio. (Young, 1980, p. 27)

To test these propositions, Young made use of the National Crime Survey (now called the "National Crime Victimization Survey") data. The National Crime Survey had recently been initiated, and the results were based on surveys sent to households where respondents twelve and over reported victimizations during a twelve-month period. She focused primarily on single offender personal victimizations such as rape, robbery, and assault. However, on occasion, she does refer to multiple offender data. Her results found minimal support for Adler's propositions. For example, Young's test of Adler's first proposition found that:

Contrary to Adler's hypothesis, overall the patterns of criminal involve-ment in personal victimizations reported for lone female offenders by race were very similar across offense categories. Assault, simple and aggravated, comprised the bulk of offenses reported for both white and black female offenders. (Young, 1980, p. 30)

As for multiple offender patterns, white females were more than twice as likely as African Americans to be involved in assaultive offenses, as opposed to theft of-fenses. On the other hand, African American female offender groups were as likely to be involved in assault and theft-related offenses (Young, 1980, p. 30).

A test of Adler's second proposition, which predicted that African-American female crime patterns would parallel white male criminality vis-à-vis white female criminality, found some support. The NCS data showed similar patterns for lone African American females and lone white males and females. Adler's third proposition postulated that the patterns of crime for African-American males and females will be more alike than for white males and female was also not supported by the NCS data. The NCS data showed that "[s]imple and aggravated assault account for 75% of victimizations by lone white females and 71% of those by lone white males but 66% of victimizations by lone black females and only 40% of those by lone black males" (Young, 1980, p. 30). This finding was similar for theft offenses where Young reported "[t]heft offenses (robbery and larceny with contact) accounted for 25% of all victimizations committed by lone white females, 24% of those by lone white males, 34% of those by lone black females, and 55% of those by lone black males" (ibid.). This trend also held true in multiple offender victimizations.

The final hypothesis, which suggests that the ratio of black to white female criminality will be higher than the ratio of black to white male criminality, was not supported. Young (1980, p. 29) showed that, according to the National Crime Survey data, the ratio for both groups was about 2 to 1. Following her publication of this now classic challenge to Adler's work, Young continued her scholarship on women and crime (1986, 1992).

Black Female Characterizations and the Criminal Justice System

In 1986, Young published the article "Gender Expectations and Their Impact on Black Female Offenders and Victims." This article addressed the possible implications of negative characterizations of African American women. Specifically, the article shows how these characterizations have the potential to bias agents of the criminal justice system against African American women. Young begins by reviewing the prevailing negative characterizations of African American women, which she believes are rooted in the myth of the African American matriarchy. According to Young, "The matriarchal theory of black society characterizes the black family as either a female headed household or an intact family in which the wife is dominant" (1986, p.307). This characterization has resulted in two images of black females, the black Amazon and the "sinister sapphire."

The black Amazon characterization "focuses on the strong role of women in black families" (Young, 1986, p. 307). The "sinister sapphire" characterization is based on the premise that "as a result of her strong role in the family the black female has undermined the 'natural' leadership role of the black male" (ibid., p. 308). This characterization has led to the depiction of African American women as "nagging, shrewish, castrating, dangerous and 'treacherous toward and contemptuous of black men" (ibid.).

Young also addresses two other prevalent characterizations that are the result of the mythology of African American female sexuality. The two characterizations include the mammy and the seductress. Those African American women characterized as the mammies are seen as "longsuffering, a patient, nurturing and asexual—

therefore capable of adapting to any situation without any special consideration and whose abuse is either unlikely or unimportant" (Young, 1986, p. 310). The seductress characterization views the African American woman as "loose, immoral, and sexually depraved—therefore a willing participant in the violence perpetrated on her by males" (ibid.). In an attempt to determine if these characterizations have any influence on the participation of African American women in the criminal justice system, Young surveyed the literature in three areas: police arrest decisions, criminal court dispositions, and sentencing decisions (ibid., p. 312). From this review, Young deduced that

> studies that do find differential treatment of white and African-American females attribute it to gender role expectations; race of the victim was found to be an important variable in the decision to process rape cases, and this has also been attributed to gender role expectations; while the literature on battering was limited, there was some indication that race may also play a role in the handling of these situations as well. (ibid., p. 323)

Based on her findings, Young expressed concern that if these negative characterizations persisted, the impact would be seen in future social policies that would likely have a detrimental impact on African American females. She was obviously concerned about the impact these characterizations may have had on the increase of African American female involvement in the criminal justice system. Unfortunately, Young's work, like that of several scholars profiled in this volume, was prophetic. African American women currently represent a significant portion of the women incarcerated in the United States. Young had again touched on an important area that, until then, had not received the scholarly attention it deserved. Ten years after Young's examination of this topic, it has again become the focus of serious scholarly attention (see Huey and Lynch, 1996).

AFRICAN AMERICAN SCHOLARSHIP ON CRIME AND CRIMINAL JUSTICE

In 1991, Young wrote on another timely subject, the exclusion of African American scholarship to the study of criminology and criminal justice (Young and Sulton, 1991). This groundbreaking article was the first of two on the subject (see also Young and Taylor Greene, 1995). The first article primarily stressed the importance of including African-American perspectives in criminology. The second article specifically discusses which African-Americans past and present should be included in the criminal justice/criminology curriculum (Young and Taylor Greene, 1995). Since the latter article is essentially a forerunner to the present volume, we devote most of our focus to Young's 1991 article.

In the article, "Excluded: The Current Status of African American Scholars in the field of Criminology and Criminal Justice," Young and her coauthor, Anne Thomas Sulton, an African American criminologist and attorney, indict the discipline for excluding African American perspectives. As evidenced by the following passage, they believe the exclusion is far reaching:

> When reading supposedly comprehensive reviews of major theoretical paradigms, the unsuspecting observer would conclude that African-American criminologists have no ideas about crime and delinquency. When examining lists naming scholars awarded substantial sums of money to conduct large-scale research projects, one might assume that African-American criminologists have no interest in conducting empirical investigations. Lists naming scholars to serve as members of groups recommending public policies rarely include the names of African-American criminologists. And seldom are African-American criminologists included on the editorial boards of criminology journals, on the policymaking boards of criminology organizations, or on the criminology faculties of colleges and universities. Even the news media disregard the perspectives advanced by African American criminologists. (Young and Sulton, 1991, pp. 101–2)

They also believe that, while the perspectives of African American criminologists have been ignored, the perspectives of white criminologists "have assumed prominent positions in the field of criminology" (Young and Sulton, 1991, p. 102). This has resulted in tremendous financial support for white scholars, who according to Young and Sulton have accomplished little in comparison to the money spent to fund their research.

While Young and Sulton acknowledge that there is not a distinct African American perspective on African American crime, they do note that there are several recurring themes in the work of African American criminologists. These themes include racism, discrimination, and segregation. These themes point to a social structural approach that views crime as a symptom of larger societal problems (Young and Sulton, 1991, p. 103). Another important discussion includes their focus on the concept of disproportionality.

Young and Sulton note that many African American criminologists believe that this concept, which is based on official data, can be very misleading. Of this they write:

> African American criminologists generally are frustrated by their White counterparts' insistence on using available crime data to show that African Americans are disproportionately involved in crime, arguing that it is unprofessional to make such an allegation because the concept of "disproportionality," as employed by many White criminologists, is

based on the groundless assumption that the contribution of African Americans to the total population should somehow influence their contribution in other areas. Completely ignored by these White criminologists is the qualifier: "all things being equal." Totally disregarded is the fact that all things are not equal. And masterfully understated is the fact that the vast majority of African Americans are not involved in any type of crime. (1991, pp. 104–105)

In a later publication on the topic, Young clearly states the dangers of the repeated use of this concept. She writes that

disproportionality has been used to "criminalize" Black people, especially Black males. Over-reliance on this concept in our discussions of race and crime intimate that the crimes of Blacks are the crimes we should be most concerned with and that Black criminals are the criminals to be feared. The fact that most or just as many whites are arrested for offenses of criminal homicide and assault is ignored. (Young, 1994a, p. 79)

Young and Sulton close their discussion on African American perspectives by presenting the most frequently proposed remedies by African American criminologists. These include:

1. Equal and just administration of criminal laws
2. Equal access to educational opportunities
3. Economic revitalization of African-American neighborhoods
4. Community control of institutions and agencies providing services to African-American neighborhoods
5. Improvement in African-Americans' quality of life
6. Teaching African-Americans conflict resolution skills
7. Providing productive activities for African-American youngsters
8. Enacting legislation aimed at curbing handgun sales
9. Improving African-Americans' racial identity. (Young and Sulton, 1991, p. 105)

The second half of the article highlights specific findings regarding the extent of African American exclusion. Some of these findings include the following

African-Americans are rarely published in the 30 refereed journals that criminologists typically publish in;
only 2 out of 157 editorial board members of the top ten criminology journals were African-Americans;
seldom are African-Americans invited by criminal justice agencies to provide technical assistance, develop training programs, or conduct studies;

African American criminologists are rarely consulted or commissioned by policymakers;
from 1975 to 1980 the Office of Juvenile Justice and Delinquency Prevention awarded $55 million dollars to conduct research. Not one of these grants went to African-Americans; and the press rarely seek out opinions of African-American criminologists. (Young and Sulton, 1991, pp. 106–111)

Finally, Young and Sulton propose the following four strategies to include African American perspectives. First, they propose that white scholars include African American perspectives wherever relevant. Second, white scholars and funding agencies should include African American scholars on large research grants. Third, African-American scholars should be included on editorial boards and policy-making committees of national criminal justice organizations. Last, African American criminologists should be included on policymaking committees at the local, state, and national levels (Young and Sulton, 1991, pp. 113).

Undoubtedly, since the publication of their article, the status of African American scholars in criminology and criminal justice has improved. However, we believe, as did Young and Sulton in 1991, that even more progress is needed if the discipline is truly serious about solving crime, particularly in the African American community. The second stage of Young's research in this area resulted in the publication "Pedagogical Reconstruction: Incorporating African-American Perspectives into the Curriculum" (Young and Taylor Greene, 1995). This article provides a host of past and present African American scholars who should be included in the discipline of criminology and criminal justice (ibid., pp. 89–101). According to Young and Taylor Greene (ibid., pp. 86), only through the inclusion of these African-American scholars can the "reconstruction" of the discipline take place to attain a multicultural curriculum. Since this book is partially an outgrowth of that publication, we now move to a review of Young's most recent research on the historical development of juvenile institutions.

Race, Gender, and the Development of Juvenile Institutions

In recent years, Young has undertaken an ambitious historical analysis of the development of juvenile institutions in the South (see Young, 1993, 1994b). Unlike previous research, she incorporates the variables of race and gender into this history. Since her research is centered on the state of Maryland, we review her findings from that state. Young's thesis on the development of a house of refuge for African Americans in Maryland is that

the refuge for black juveniles was prompted by changes in race relations (e.g., the growth of the free black population, the abolition of slavery) and in the political economy (e.g., the need for agricultural workers, the shifting industrial base of the Maryland economy), while the refuge

movement for white juveniles was prompted by a concern for the detrimental effects of confining juvenile offenders with adult criminals.
(1993, p. 558)

She investigated this thesis using the Laws of Maryland from 1793 through 1880,
General Assembly Reports from 1842 through 1881, and Prisoner Records of the
Maryland Penitentiary from 1812 to 1830 (Young, 1993, p. 559).

During the pre–Civil War period, Young shows how Maryland followed the
national trend by establishing a house of refuge for juveniles in 1830. She notes that
the legislature's establishment of the house clearly stressed that educational and
corrective practices were to take place (Young, 1993, p. 560). Additionally, House of
Refuge managers could employ and bind juveniles into their care until they reached
the age of twenty-one for males and eighteen for females (ibid., p. 560). During this
time youths were apprenticed in one of several trades. This system, however, was not
for African American youth (ibid., p. 561).

Young, like McIntyre (1992), argues that with the free African American
population increasing steadily in the late 1700s and early 1800s, the state had to
create a way to "control" and "preserve" this labor. This was accomplished through
legislation that resulted in the differential punishment of whites, free African Americans, and slaves. Young observed also that as the free African American population
increased, so did legislation aimed at them. Since no juvenile institutions existed for
African American youth during this era, those not subject to "plantation justice" were
usually handled like adults. Eventually African American youth did become the focus
of legislation, which repeatedly changed to ensure that they remained under the
control of the state.

Apprenticeship programs, for example, were put in place to "help" the children
of free African Americans. However, this legislation was also created to control this
much-desired labor pool. Young describes how the General Assembly enacted legislation requiring law enforcement officials to monitor free African American families
and notify judges if they were not adequately providing for the children. If this was
the case, judges were ready to bring the children to court and bind them out as
apprentices (Young, 1993, p. 564). Often these youths ended up in situations similar
to that of slaves. Because of the state's actions, from 1812 to 1830, African Americans
predominated those confined in the Maryland Penitentiary. And as the free African
American population grew, the repressive legislation continued also.

In 1873, a House of Refuge was finally opened for African American youth. Of
this opening, Young asserts that

the establishment of a correctional institution for black juvenile delinquents in Maryland followed quickly on the heels of the emancipation of
blacks. The push to provide a place of "punishment" for black children
was motivated by the repeal of past mechanisms of control, namely the
apprenticeship programs. The managers of the House of Reformation

and Instruction for Colored Children clearly recognized the state need for agricultural, domestic and industrial labor and sought to train young black workers to supply the need. The managers also attempted to neutralize the political and social impact of the abolition of slavery by socializing free black children into continued subordination. (1993, p. 570)

Therefore, in both the pre–Civil War and post Civil War periods, states strategically used legislative enactments to ensure that the labor of African American youths remained under their control.

This area of Young's research is a notable contribution to the existing body of literature that argues that both the juvenile and adult penal systems have historically been used as social control devices to secure the labor of African American and other ethnic groups (see generally Mann, 1993).

Conclusion

Vernetta Young's contribution to criminology and criminal justice rests not in the multitude of her publications, but in the timeliness of her research. Since the late 1970s she has repeatedly addressed issues concerning African Americans that were in need of scholarly attention. Her test of Freda Adler's propositions on African American female criminality is considered a classic response to Adler's work, while her publication on the impact of gender expectations of African American women represents scholarship that we believe anticipated the impending crisis of African American women involvement in the criminal justice system. Last, her poignant indictment of criminology and criminal justice openly exposed the discipline for excluding African American perspectives. As the youngest of our contemporary scholars, we anticipate that Young will continue to take the lead on timely issues related to gender, race, and crime.

References

Adler, F. (1975). *Sisters in crime: The rise of the new female criminal.* New York: McGraw-Hill.

Huey, J. & Lynch, M. J. (1996). The image of black women in criminology: Historical stereotypes as theoretical foundation. In M. J. Lynch and E. B. Patterson (Eds.), *Justice with prejudice: Race and criminal justice in America* (pp. 72–88). Guilderland, NY: Harrow and Heston Publishers.

Mann Richey, C. (1993). *Unequal justice: A question of color.* Bloomington: Indiana University Press.

McIntyre, C. C. L. (1992). *Criminalizing a race: Free blacks during slavery.* Queens, NY: Kayode Publications

Simon, R. (1975). *Women and crime.* Lexington, MA: D. C. Heath and Company.

Young, V. (1979). Victims of female offenders. In W. Parsonage (Ed.), *Perspectives on victimology* (pp. 72–87). Beverly Hills: Sage Publications.

———. (1980). Women, race, and crime. *Criminology, 18,* 26–34.

———. (1986). Gender expectations and their impact on black female offenders and victims. *Justice Quarterly, 3,* 305–27.

———. (1992). Fear of victimization and victimization rates among women: A paradox? *Justice Quarterly, 9,* 419–41.

———. (1993). Punishment and social conditions: The control of black juveniles in the 1800s in Maryland. In A. Hess & P. Clement (Eds.), *History of juvenile delinquency: A collection of essays* (pp. 557–75). Aalen (West Germany): Scientia Publishers.

———. (1994a). The politics of disproportionality. In A. T. Sulton (Ed.), *African-American perspectives on: Crime causation, criminal justice administration, and crime prevention* (pp. 69–81). Englewood, CO: Sulton Books.

———. (1994b). Race and gender in the establishment of juvenile institutions: The case of the South. *The Prison Journal, 73,* 244–65.

———. (1998). Interview with the authors.

Young, V. & Taylor Greene, H. (1995). Pedagogical reconstruction: Incorporating African-American perspectives into the curriculum. *Journal of Criminal Justice Education, 6,* 85–101.

Young, V. & Sulton, A. T. (1991). Excluded: The current status of African-American scholars in the field of criminology and criminal justice. *Journal of Research in Crime and Delinquency, 28,* 101–16.

CONCLUSION

Throughout this book we have presented the contributions of each scholar to criminological thought. Here we will focus more specifically on their influence within criminology and criminal justice. While the individuals included in this book and their works are known to some, their influence on the discipline has never been studied and is very difficult to assess without additional research. We do know they have influenced each other as well as others studying crime and the administration of justice. We also know that they have been excluded within the discipline (Young and Sulton, 1991) and that efforts are underway to incorporate their research into the curricula (Young and Taylor Greene, 1995).

The question of influence is one that resonates when one thinks of pioneers and important scholars in any discipline, particularly a discipline that is emerging and seeking to lay down its founders and their important disciples. Moreover, some scholars measure the importance of an individual by either their impact on the discipline or their influence on a central figure who later becomes an influential scholar. Consequently, we focus our conclusion on three areas. First, we examine who may have been influenced by the scholars profiled here. Second, we examine the significant contributions of these scholars to an emerging discipline. And finally, we review directions for future research in this area.

Although this work began by profiling African American scholars such as Ida B. Wells-Barnett and W. E. B. Du Bois, earlier African American writers were also interested in achieving "Justice." While it was justice in a broader sense, which included the activities of African American abolitionists and other "activist/scholars" (see, for example, Douglass, 1845, 1855, 1881; Walker, 1830; Delaney, 1852), these issues were forerunners to the post–Civil War practice of using the criminal justice system to criminalize African Americans. The treatises of these early scholars centered on the "Negro question," which was largely concerned with attaining full citizenship and equality. Our scholars were no doubt influenced by these early writers.

In seeking to determine influences during the historical era, it is almost impossible to say definitively that someone was influenced by the work of the profiled scholars. Because, while we can find a scholar who may have cited the profiled scholars, one cannot presume that this shows influence. However, this does suggest that, at the very least, the citing scholar was familiar with the work of the cited African American. Additionally, during the historical era, very few white scholars would have openly admitted being influenced by the work of an African American or, for that matter, the scholarship of a woman.

As with earlier African American scholars, the early writers focused on issues concerning race. They were essentially race men or women. According to Anderson:

> A race man (or woman) was a particular kind of black leader who lived in a segregated society and felt strongly responsible to the black race, especially in front of whites or outsiders to the community. Often, he felt as though he carried the whole weight of the race on his shoulders, and in public had the need to put matters of race first. Such a person was intent on "advancing the race" by working as a role model, both to uplift the ghetto community and to disabuse the wider society of its often negative view of blacks. (1997, p. 116)

This commitment resulted in their focus on similar issues, which in turn probably resulted in mutual influence. For example, Ida B. Wells-Barnett's work more than likely had an impact on Du Bois, who later became an activist/scholar against lynching. As for Monroe Work and E. Franklin Frazier, Work was influenced by Du Bois having collaborated with him on a few Atlanta University studies, while Frazier openly acknowledged his intellectual heritage, dedicating his 1949 publication, *The Negro in the United States,* to both Du Bois and Robert E. Park.

The influence of the historical period scholars on white scholars is less clear. We can only speculate who may have been influenced by their work. While her radical and aggressive manner may have bothered some observers, Ida B. Wells-Barnett's antilynching work was successful in drawing support from liberal whites. Many of those same liberal whites became involved in organizations such as the NAACP. Along with these liberal white activists, white scholars likely took notice of Wells-Barnett's pamphlets as a source of reliable data on lynching in the South.

Two notable white scholars who may have been influenced by Du Bois are Robert E. Park and Thorsten Sellin. As Booker T. Washington's secretary during Du Bois's years at Atlanta University, Park undoubtedly kept a close eye on Washington's chief philosophical rival. Several years after Du Bois left Atlanta and Park Tuskegee, we see a school of social scientific research similar to that of Du Bois's surfacing at the University of Chicago, under the direction of Park (Gabbidon, 1999). Our research also revealed that the late Thorsten Sellin was "an admirer of Du Bois" (Myers & Simms, 1988, p. 7), but Sellin never openly credited Du Bois with influencing his early work on race and crime (see Sellin, 1928, 1930, 1935). Again, these examples suggest that prominent white scholars were aware of Du Bois's work, but, to our knowledge, no documents survive that suggest the importance of Du Bois's influence on their subsequent work.

Work's influence on white scholars is even less clear than that of Wells-Barnett and Du Bois. For most of his career, Work conducted research at Tuskegee Institute. It is plausible that much of the credit for his work went to Booker T. Washington. However, Work was very active in the sociological associations and the interracial movement and was published in national journals available at the time. Frazier, on the other hand, was quite influential and respected within the sociology profession, as evidenced by his ascent to the presidency of the American Sociological Association in 1948. As the first African American to achieve this honor, Frazier likely influenced some white scholars in the areas of race relations, family disorganization, and the black middle class.

It is important to recognize that, while some of the profiled scholars are not regularly discussed in the literature (this is less the case with contemporary scholars), their scholastic contributions to criminology/criminal justice are still noteworthy for inclusion in the historical record of the discipline. Undoubtedly, the early scholars had their greatest influence on each other as well as on other African Americans. As previously mentioned, Du Bois and Work collaborated on several early studies of the Negro and crime. Frazier credited Du Bois with establishing the tradition of research in the black community. Since most of the early scholars spent their careers at historically black colleges and universities, they influenced a cadre of future re-searchers and practitioners.

When we examine the research of contemporary scholars, we can see a con-tinuation of many themes first presented by the early writers. For example, Du Bois and Work provided a foundation for studies of historical discrimination and eth-nicity. Wilson was more than likely influenced by the research of early sociologists such as Frazier and Du Bois. At the same time, many of the contemporary scholars were not only influenced by the earlier scholars but also by each other's research. Table 3 presents an overview of the research topics of each scholar presented in the book.

Turning our attention to the influence of the contemporary scholars, it is important to note that each had a different influence within the discipline. When considered together, their greatest contributions to criminological research are their studies of specific and often neglected topics on African Americans, crime and justice, challenges to the race myths about African Americans and crime, and the develop-ment of theoretical explanations that include sociohistorical factors.

Clearly, the most important influence within the discipline has been challenges to the race myths about African Americans and crime. One race myth is the belief in the innate criminality of African Americans, especially males. Due in large part to biological determinism and racist ideologies, the earliest studies of race and crime accepted the inferiority of blacks. The early scholars (Du Bois, Work, Frazier) were among the first to challenge these myths and recognize the importance of slavery, emancipation, and segregation to understanding crime, especially among African Americans. Not surprisingly, there was very little recognition of these factors in early studies of crime by white scholars. Thus, many contemporary scholars included here (Mann, Young, Hawkins) have continued to present these themes in their research, due in part to the fact that within the discipline these sociohistorical factors are still overlooked.

Another myth revolves around the issue of disproportionality. Both African American and white scholars have alluded to the disproportionate representation of African Americans in the criminal justice system. Some seem to accept this as proof of

Table 3   The Historical and Contemporary Scholars' Contributions to
              Criminological Thought

SCHOLAR	TOPIC
Ida B. Wells-Barnett	Lynching
W. E. B. Du Bois	Convict-Lease System
	Negro Crime
	Criminal Class
	Slavery, Emancipation, Segregation
	Lynching
Monroe N. Work	Negro Crime
	The Administration of Justice
	Lynching
	Social Control
E. Franklin Frazier	Juvenile Delinquency
	Literature Review
	Social Disorganization
Coramae R. Mann	Female Crime and Delinquency
	Female Homicide
	Violence
	Minorities and Crime
Lee P. Brown	Police Community Relations
	Community Policing
	Black Perspectives on Crime
William J. Wilson	Race and Ethnic Relations
	Crime and Urban Areas
	The Underclass
	Race and Class
	Race and Crime
Darnell Hawkins	Violence
	Black-on-Black Homicide
	Theoretical Criminology
	Ethnicity and Crime
	Hierarchy of Homicide Seriousness
Daniel Georges-Abeyie	Black Ethnic Heterogeneity
	Blacks and Criminal Justice
	Collective Violence
	Spatial Dynamic
	Petit Apartheid
	Victimization
	Terrorism
Vernetta Young	Black Female Criminality
	History of Juvenile Institutions
	African American Contributions to Criminology and Criminal Justice
	Female Offender Victimization

their criminality. Others attribute disproportionality to discrimination at various stages of the administration of justice. A major contribution of African American scholars concerning this issue is their recognition of social, economic, and political conditions that contribute to disproportionality. That is, all things are not equal, and therefore comparisons of African Americans to whites in the criminal justice system are unfair (Young, 1994).

The issue of disproportionality has contributed to considerable research on discrimination in the administration of justice. The early scholars pointed to the convict lease system, the exclusion of blacks from the administration of justice as police, jurors, judges, and so on; the discriminatory application of the death penalty, sentencing disparities, and other factors that contributed to the over representation of blacks in the justice system. The contemporary scholars continued to focus on these themes. The issue came to the fore in the 1980s with Wilbanks's (1987) publication entitled *The Myth of the Racist Criminal Justice System*. Two of the contemporary scholars (Mann and Georges-Abeyie) challenged Wilbanks's nondiscrimination thesis (NDT). This debate was the first time in the study of criminology that the discrimination thesis (DT) and NDT were openly discussed. These heated discussions and subsequent publications have influenced the discipline in several ways.

The first influence of the DT/NDT debate has been greater recognition of African American perspectives within the discipline. Although numerous publications by black scholars appeared before the debate, afterward, many journals focused specifically on African American research (see, for example, *Social Justice*, 1989; *Justice Quarterly*, 1992). Another important influence is Mann's (1993) seminal publication *Unequal Justice*, which documents discrimination and racism experienced by African American and other minority groups in America. Evidence of the book's profound influence on the discipline is its wide adoption in both undergraduate and graduate courses. Last, the debate forced the discipline to recognize the effect of discrimination on understanding not only the administration of justice but also the study of crime more generally as well. As one colleague noted, few texts and/or researchers mention crime as a consequence of racism.[1]

Until very recently, most theoretical explanations in criminology have systematically ignored the influence of discrimination, racism, slavery, emancipation, and segregation. Although E. Franklin Frazier was the first to challenge sociological theories of crime and delinquency, many of the contemporary scholars have made notable contributions to theoretical criminology. Hawkins's work on the conflict perspective caused theorists to rethink their use of the theory to explain race and punishment. His critical dissection and suggested revisions of the perspective have made the theory more specific for future researchers. This will allow for future researchers to take into account key shortcomings of the theory and revise it accordingly to explain race and punishment.

Georges-Abeyie's most lasting influence on theoretical criminology should be his challenge to the black ethnic monolith paradigm. As discussed previously, Georges-Abeyie points out that as long as criminologists (and others) continue to view African Americans as one and the same, theories, research, and policies will be misguided. He argues for recognition of black ethnic heterogeneity as the starting point for understanding crime in the black community. Unfortunately, his thesis has not been incorporated into the study of crime; most contemporary research continues to focus on blacks as a monolithic group. Last, Young has influenced theories of gender and crime, while Wilson, along with Robert J. Sampson, offers a theory of race, crime, and urban inequality.

The influence of these African American scholars on policy is even more difficult to assess. Notable exceptions are Lee P. Brown, Darnell F. Hawkins, and William Julius Wilson. As a seasoned law enforcement administrator at the local and federal level, Brown has likely had the largest impact on criminal justice policy. Hawkins has been at the forefront of the development of policies to prevent African American homicide. Wilson has garnered the attention of the president, elected officials, and practitioners nationwide. Yet his influence on criminal justice policy is less well known.

It is our belief that with few exceptions the discipline has overlooked the policy recommendations of African Americans. Thus, an equally important issue to consider is to what extent research and policy on crime and the administration of justice might be different had the discipline acknowledged these scholars. While this may be a difficult question to answer definitively, some would suggest that considering the continuing crime problems within the African American community, following the policy suggestions of African Americans is a step in the right direction. Mann (1997) alludes to this dilemma when she points to the biased, inaccurate picture of minority crime produced by Caucasians over the last two decades.

In closing, we believe that future research on African American criminological thought could go in several directions. First, there needs to be an exhaustive review of African American and white scholarship in the historical era to delve further into the issue of influence. Several methodological approaches might be useful. These include identifying the extent of citations by others, the use of their materials in undergraduate and graduate courses, and their role in professional associations. Though such an undertaking was beyond the scope of the present volume, we see value in future scholars pursuing this endeavor. Second, we foresee the need to expand the present volume as the number of African American criminologists increases.

Finally, in a future volume, it may be feasible to look more closely at the policy impact of African American criminologists. While this volume has presented their scholastic contributions, to date, their influence on policy remains unknown. We hope that, in this century, unlike the last, the contributions of African American criminologists to both research and policy will be better recognized.

References

Anderson, E. (1997). The precarious balance: Race man or sellout? In E. Close (Ed.), *The Darden Dilemma* (pp. 114–32). NY: HarperPerennial.

Delaney, M. (1852/1968). *The condition, elevation, emigration and destiny of the colored people of the United States.* New York: Arno Press.

Douglass, F. (1845). *Narrative of the life of Frederick Douglass.* Boston: Anti-Slavery Office.

———. (1855). *My bondage and my freedom.* New York: Miller, Orton and Mulligan.

———. (1881). *The life and times of Frederick Douglass.* Hartford: Park Publishing.

Gabbidon, S. L. (1999). W.E.B. Du Bois and the Atlanta school of social scientific research: 1897–1913. *Journal of Criminal Justice Education, 10,* 21–38.

Justice Quarterly. (1992) 9(4) Academy of Criminal Justice Sciences.

Mann Richey, C. (1997). We don't need more wars. *Valparaiso Law Review, 31,* 565–78.

———. (1993). *Unequal justice: A question of color.* Bloomington, IN: Indiana University Press.

Myers, S. & Simms, M. (1988). *The economics of race and crime.* New Brunswick: Transaction Books.

Sellin, T. (1928). The Negro criminal: A statistical note. *The American Academy of Political and Social Sciences, 130,* 52–64.

Sellin, T. (1930). "The Negro and the problem of law observance and administration in light of social research. In C. S. Johnson (Ed.), *The Negro in American civilization* (chapter 28). NY: Henry Hott and Company.

———. (1935). Race prejudice in the administration of justice. *The American Journal of Sociology, 61,* 212–17.

Social Justice (1989) 16(4).

Walker, D. (1830). *Walker's appeal in four articles, together with a preamble, to the colored citizens of the world, but in particular, and very expressly to those of the United States of America.* Boston.

Wilbanks, W. (1987). *The myth of a racist criminal justice system.* Monterey, CA: Brooks Cole Publishing Company.

Young, V. (1994). The politics of disproportionality. In A. T. Sulton (Ed.), *African-American perspectives on: Crime causation, criminal justice administration, and crime prevention* (pp. 69–81). Englewood, CO: Sulton Books.

Young V. & Sulton, A. T. (1991). Excluded: The current status of African-American scholars in the field of criminology and criminal justice. *Journal of Research in Crime and Delinquency, 28,* 101–16.

Young V. & Taylor Greene, H. (1995). Pedagogical reconstruction: Incorporating African-American perspectives into the curriculum. *Journal of Criminal Justice Education, 6,* 85–101.

Notes

1. This comment was made by an anonymous manuscript reviewer.

About the Authors

Helen Taylor Greene is an associate professor and graduate program co-director in the Department of Sociology and Criminal Justice at Old Dominion University in Norfolk, Virginia. She completed her Ph.D. at the Department of Criminology and Criminal Justice, the University of Maryland, College Park. Her research interests include black perspectives on crime and justice, policing, and delinquency.

Shaun L. Gabbidon is an assistant professor of criminal justice in the School of Public Affairs at Pennsylvania State University, Capital College. He is a graduate of the Ph.D. program in criminology at Indiana University of Pennsylvania. He has also served as a Fellow at Harvard University's W. E. B. Du Bois Institute for Afro-American Research. His research interests are minorities and crime, inner-city crime, criminal justice education, and private security.

Name Index

SUBJECT INDEX